International Series in Operations Research & Management Science

Volume 218

Series Editor

Camille C. Price
Stephen F. Austin State University, TX, USA

Associate Series Editor

Joe Zhu
Worcester Polytechnic Institute, MA, USA

Founding Series Editor

Frederick S. Hillier
Stanford University, CA, USA

More information about this series at http://www.springer.com/series/6161

Tarja Joro • Pekka J. Korhonen

Extension of Data Envelopment Analysis with Preference Information

Value Efficiency

 Springer

Tarja Joro
Department of Accounting, Operations
  and Information Systems
Alberta School of Business
University of Alberta
Edmonton, Alberta, Canada

Pekka J. Korhonen
Department of Information and
  Service Economy
School of Business
Aalto University
Helsinki, Finland

ISSN 0884-8289   ISSN 2214-7934 (electronic)
ISBN 978-1-4899-7889-9   ISBN 978-1-4899-7528-7 (eBook)
DOI 10.1007/978-1-4899-7528-7
Springer New York Heidelberg Dordrecht London

Printed on acid-free paper

Springer is part of Springer Science+Business Media (www.springer.com)

To Paul, Elizabeth, and William
and
To Kaiju, Minna, Minni, Hannu, Janne,
Sasu, Merri, and Sissi

Preface

To improve performance is one of the key issues for managers in organizations. Demands to make operations more profitable and compatible as well as to cut public expenditure have been repeatedly present in headlines. The "goodness" of operations or performance is often simply measured in money; the firm making most money or the public sector unit having the least expenditure is considered to be the best one. However, the monetary measures do not always capture all aspects of the performance. Especially in the public sector it may be practically—or politically—impossible to attach prices to some goods or services produced: what is the price of a university degree, or of a medical operation saving a human life? We may be able to figure out the short-term costs of some operations, but what is— for instance—the price of the lost opportunity? How expensive it is not to educate, or to lose a life? Thus performance is clearly multidimensional in its nature, and several indicators (outputs) are required to characterize all essential aspects of performance. The factors (inputs) affecting performance are multidimensional as well. In practice, the relationships between outputs and inputs are often complex or unknown making direct performance evaluation a complicated task.

An alternative way to approach the performance evaluation problem is data envelopment analysis (DEA) developed by Charnes, Cooper, and Rhodes (1978 and 1979). Performance evaluation is carried out relatively by comparing decision-making units (DMUs) essentially performing the same task. The purpose is to study whether it is possible to find another comparable unit that produces more outputs with similar usage of inputs or achieves the same level of output production with less inputs. If such unit exists, it is quite clear that—other things being equal—the evaluated unit is not operating as well as it could be. In DEA, there is no need to explicitly know relationships between inputs and outputs. The values of inputs and outputs of the units are the only requisite information for the analysis.

DEA reveals the units which are supposed to be able to improve their performance and the units which cannot be recognized as poor performers. Because we use multidimensional factors to measure performance, "goodness" is not fully defined. For instance, we cannot name the best performer without preference information of somebody. DEA identifies technically efficient units, but it is value-free in the sense that it does not take into account importance of various factors. Whereas there are numerous books about DEA, none of them concentrates on incorporating preference or value information into the analysis. In many practical applications, the use of such information is a necessity.

The aim of this book is to provide an introduction to the methods currently available in the field of DEA to incorporate preference information. The book serves as a reference volume for the readers interested in those methods. In addition to theoretical considerations, numerous illustrative examples are included. Hence, the book can be used as a teaching text as well. Only a modest mathematical background is needed to understand the main principles. The only prerequisites are (a) familiarity with linear algebra, especially matrix calculus, (b) knowledge of the simplex method, and (c) familiarity with the use of computer software.

This book is organized as follows. Chapter 1 provides motivation and introduces the basic concepts. Chapter 2 provides the basic ideas and models of the DEA. The efficient frontier and production possibility set concepts play an important role in all considerations. That's why these concepts are considered closer in Chap. 3. Since the approaches introduced in this study are inspired by multiple objective linear programming, the basic concepts of this field are reviewed in Chap. 4. Chapter 5 also compares and contrasts DEA and multiple objective linear programming providing some cornerstones for approaches presented later in this book. Chapter 6 discusses the traditional approaches to take into account preference information in DEA. In Chap. 7 value efficiency is introduced, and Chap. 8 discusses practical aspects. Some extensions are presented in Chap. 9 and in Chap. 10 value efficiency is extended to cover the case, when a production possibility set is not convex. Three implemented applications are reviewed in Chap. 11.

The readers familiar with DEA may skip Chaps. 1 through 3, and the readers familiar with MOLP may skip Chap. 4. The readers interested in practical aspects may start to read Chap. 10 first and then "dig" necessary theory from the previous chapters into the extent needed.

Edmonton, Alberta, Canada   Tarja Joro
Helsinki, Finland   Pekka J. Korhonen

Contents

Chapter 1
Introduction

Basic Concepts

1.1 Motivation

Scarcity is one of the key concepts in economics. The fact that there are not enough resources to produce everything needed and wanted emphasizes the importance to utilize and allocate the existing ones in the best possible way. The demand for efficiency of operations both in private and public sectors has also been currently emphasized due to severe economic conditions and increased competition.

Most people inevitably associate efficiency with layoffs in the private sector and budget cuts in the public sector. The concept of efficiency itself is rather innocent: it just points out whether there is possibility to develop the firm or public organization—decision-making unit (DMU)—such that it performs better with the current resources or to keep the current performance with less resources. The methods which are used to evaluate efficiency aim at looking deeper than mere monetary figures: they examine the production process itself, how resources—inputs—are turned into products and services—outputs. This is a key factor contributing to their success: especially in the public sector it is often practically or politically difficult to put a price tag on some outputs, for example, when evaluating the performance of, say, the health care system.

With the absence of price information, we turn our attention to the production process itself and analyze *technical efficiency*. The DMUs are basically converting inputs into outputs. Schools use instructors, educational material, computer, and other facilities to provide education. Production uses plants, machinery, and man hours to produce physical products. In this framework it is possible to evaluate the technical efficiency of operations. In evaluating technical efficiency, we are primarily interested that the resources are efficiently used to produce outputs. Are we producing right things is a secondary question.

Because it is very hard to evaluate the absolute performance of the DMUs without any benchmarking unit, a more popular way is to evaluate relative

© Springer Science+Business Media New York 2015
T. Joro, P.J. Korhonen, *Extension of Data Envelopment Analysis with Preference
Information*, International Series in Operations Research & Management
Science 218, DOI 10.1007/978-1-4899-7528-7_1

performance. As a performance measure, a *relative technical efficiency* concept is used. The problem is: Is it possible to find another comparable unit that can produce more outputs with similar usage of inputs, or achieves the same level of output production with less inputs? If such a unit exists, it is quite clear that the unit under evaluation is not operating as well as it could be. Hence forward, we use the term technical efficiency to refer to relative technical efficiency.

To measure technical efficiency of homogeneous units operating in similar conditions, Charnes et al. (1978, 1979) developed a method called data envelopment analysis (DEA). Currently, DEA has become one of the most widely used methods in operations research/management science (OR/MS) (see Bragge et al. 2012). It has gained popularity in performance evaluation both in public and private sectors (see Seiford 1996 for a bibliography on DEA). See also a Fortune magazine article by Norton (1994) and an OR Newsletter article by Simons (1996). Being a linear programming-based performance evaluation tool, DEA has strong connections to both OR/MS and production economics fields.

Based on information about the performance of those units, the purpose of DEA is to empirically characterize the *efficient frontier*. If a DMU lies on that frontier, it is referred to as an *efficient unit*, otherwise *inefficient*. When a unit is inefficient, a *target (reference) unit* is sought for each inefficient unit by projecting it *radially* onto the efficient frontier. In *radial projection* the values of controllable (input or output) variables are proportionally improved until the boundary of the efficient frontier is achieved. The input/output values of the target unit are considered *target values* for the inefficient unit. DEA calculates for the inefficient units a measure—called *efficiency score*—that illustrates its degree of efficiency. Occasionally, we measure inefficiency, then we call the score *inefficiency score*. The appealing feature in DEA is inevitably its capability to compress information on the usage of several inputs and the production of several outputs into a single figure: the (in)efficiency score.

The underlying assumption in the radial projection technique is that the "most suitable" target values for each inefficient unit are found without any additional information merely by proportionally improving controllable variables. Radial projection is a value-free technique in the sense that it does not require the intervention of a decision maker (DM). It also enables a straightforward technique to specify an efficiency score. Radial projection does not allow any flexibility for a DM to choose a target unit for an inefficient unit. This can undermine the significance of a target unit in practice. Consequently, the standard use of radial projection has encountered occasional critique and suggestions of other methods. For example, see Thanassoulis and Dyson (1992) and Färe and Grosskopf (2000). Nevertheless, the actual behavior of DM searching for a target unit in practice has rarely been studied. An exception is the paper by Korhonen et al. (2003).

Figuratively speaking DEA makes it possible to add apples and oranges together without pricing them. However, as promising as it sounds, also this is a double-edged sword: the caveat lies very much in the recognition of the relevant inputs and outputs. This may sound rather straightforward, but this is not usually the case in practice. In most of the cases the importance of different outputs, and also inputs, is very different. A university can list Ph.D. and master's degrees and journal articles as outputs, but also, e.g., working papers, conference presentations, and so forth. Consulting done by faculty members may be considered as one of the outputs of a university department. The way technical efficiency is defined makes it possible for a particular department to become efficient solely by concentrating on consulting at the expense of academic research and teaching. If indeed it would be acceptable to specialize in any input or output, the analysis of technical efficiency would work well and the results would be relevant.

Rarely all the outputs produced are of equal value to the DM. Resulting from the way efficiency is defined, units have different possible strategies to become efficient: they can specialize in producing different outputs. In efficiency analysis this may lead sometimes to results that are not plausible: for example, it is likely that we—as customers—strongly prefer a hospital specialized on excellence in medical treatments to one that is specialized in excellence in administrations. The latter is an important factor as well. In the literature there exist some approaches to overcome these difficulties, but they require some partial price information to be included into the analysis—which, as we concluded, may be difficult.

Several DEA extensions have been introduced to deal with the situations where value-free specialization is not acceptable. The models are often inspired by real-life applications where there has emerged a need to avoid unrealistic specialization. They aim at introducing some *preference information* into the analysis of technical efficiency. The term "preference information" refers to the additional information based on market prices, expert opinion, preferences, values, or judgment of a DM having the control over the units whose performance is under evaluation.

Technically preference information is in most of the existing approaches incorporated into the analysis via restrictions placed on weighting parameters in a mathematical optimization problem. These weights have the economic interpretation of prices for inputs and outputs. Although in these approaches no exact price information is needed, they still require the DM to think in terms of prices for example, how many master's degrees are equivalent to one Ph.D. degree? What is the price of a medical treatment x with respect to treatment y? Thus these approaches share some of the problems related to the definition of the prices themselves. Although there is not necessarily a need to figure out the price level, we need to have some idea of relative prices or marginal rates of substitution. They may be practically or politically very difficult to determine.

In the book, we will also introduce another approach which is based on the idea to combine multiple objective linear programming (MOLP) and DEA. In MOLP, the purpose is to help a DM find the most preferred solution (MPS) on the efficient frontier. The MPS is the solution on the efficient frontier which pleases the DM most. It can be a real unit or a hypothetical unit (=a point on the efficient frontier). Sometimes, we use the term most preferred unit (MPU) as a synonym to MPS, when we would like to emphasize that the solution is a real DMU, especially in the context of non-convex models. No price or weight information is needed in advance to determine the MPS. The system may help the DM to search the efficient frontier until the MPS is found. By making general assumptions about the *value function* of the DM, we may introduce a new concept: a *value efficiency score* or *value inefficiency score* depending on which one is more convenient to use. The value efficiency score behaves like efficiency score, but it may be very low to the technically efficient unit very "far" from the MPS. The analysis in which preference information is incorporated into the DEA in the way described above is called value efficiency analysis (VEA).

In this chapter we first briefly discuss the key concepts of efficiency and production analysis relating DEA to this framework. Then we reproduce the basic DEA models as well as introduce some generalizations. Coelli et al. (2005) is a good source for a more comprehensive introduction to efficiency and productivity analysis. Charnes et al. (1994) and Cooper et al. (2007) provide a thorough presentation on DEA.

1.2 Preliminary Considerations

In efficiency and productivity analysis the aim is to evaluate the performance of firms, public organizations, or more generally DMUs that convert *inputs* into *outputs*.

1.2.1 Decision-Making Units, Inputs, and Outputs

The term DMU refers to the units whose performance is evaluated. They may be firms or parts of firms such as branches or public sector entities. Possible examples range from production facilities, supermarkets, and banks to schools, hospitals, and government agencies. What is essential is that the DMUs have control over their operations and that they are comparable: they perform essentially the same task using similar inputs to produce similar outputs and operate in similar environmental conditions.

Inputs are the resources consumed by the DMUs. The inputs can be, e.g., working hours, number of physicians or teachers, or sales space. Respectively, outputs are the goods and services produced by the DMUs. Number of products produced, number of customers served, sales volume, and number of students graduating are typical examples.

1.2.2 Productivity and Efficiency

The *productivity* of a DMU is defined as the ratio of the output(s) that it produces to the input(s) that it uses:

Definition 1.1 Productivity $= \frac{\text{Output(s)}}{\text{Input(s)}}$

When there is only a single input and a single output, the ratio is trivial. With the presence of multiple inputs and/or outputs, both the inputs and the outputs must be aggregated into a single index. Typically, the definition of the productivity is expanded to a ratio of the weighted sum of outputs over the weighted sum of inputs:

Definition 1.2 Productivity $= \dfrac{\sum_{r=1}^{s} \mu_r * \text{Output}_r}{\sum_{i=1}^{m} v_i * \text{Input}_i}$,

where s is the number of outputs and m the number of inputs.

Sometimes the weighted sums are referred to as a *virtual input* and a *virtual output*. How to select the weights? Traditionally evaluating DMUs with multiple inputs and/or outputs has required information on the prices and the price interpretation of the weights. DEA offers one possibility to come up with a single aggregated index without the need of having a priori price information. We discuss this later in this section when relating DEA into the framework of production economics. In our terminology, productivity refers to *total factor productivity*, which is a productivity measure involving all factors of production. The measures like labor productivity in a factory are known as *partial* measures of productivity. These partial productivity measures can provide a misleading indication of overall productivity when considered in isolation (Coelli et al. 2005).

It is important to make a clear distinction between productivity and *efficiency*. Productivity is an absolute measure of performance. Based on productivity measure, it is possible to construct the *production frontier* enveloping the production possibility set (PPS). The production frontier represents the maximal output attainable from each input level. Efficiency[1] on the other hand tells whether DMUs are operating on the production frontier or beneath it. The units operating on the frontier are *technically efficient* and those operating beneath it are *technically inefficient*. To illustrate the difference between the terms, consider a single input and a single output. The concept of efficiency goes back to Pareto (1906) who first defined the concept of efficiency. Since a point on the efficient frontier is also called a *Pareto optimal* point. Actually, Koopmans (1951) defined the technical efficiency in the context of the production analysis.

Figure 1.1 illustrates the situation, where one input and one output are assumed. DMUs 1 and 2 are technically efficient whereas DMU_0 is inefficient. The curve going through DMUs 1 and 2 represents the production frontier and the shaded is the PPS. The productivity of DMU_2 is less than DMU_1, but there is no other DMU at the same input level with higher productivity. DMU_0 is inefficient because it uses the same amount of input as DMU_2, but its output level is lower.

---

[1] We formally define efficiency later on.

Fig. 1.1 Efficiency and productivity

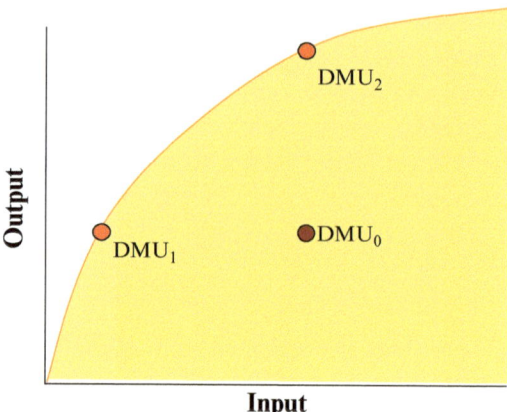

1.2.3 Technical, Overall, Allocative Efficiency

Assume we are evaluating DMUs consuming two inputs to produce the same amount of one output (or consuming the same amount of one input to produce two outputs). Figure 1.2 illustrates the classical concepts of efficiency with the above assumptions in two pictures. In each picture, the curve going through DMU_1 illustrates the production frontier. DMU_0 is technically inefficient in each picture: it does not operate on the production frontier. The tangent line for the production frontier at DMU_1 is the isocost (isorevenue) line containing the information on input (output) prices. In the left side picture the approach is called *input oriented* and in the right side picture the approach is called *output oriented*. As we can see DMU_1 is the unit on the production frontier having minimum costs (maximum profits). Thus among all technically efficient units, DMU_1 is the only one that is *overall efficient* (currently often called *economic efficiency*).

For DMU_0 the ratio[2] $TE = \frac{O\text{-}DMU_0^T}{O\text{-}DMU_0}$ reflects technical efficiency, and ratio OE $= \frac{O\text{-}DMU_0^O}{O\text{-}DMU_0}$ overall efficiency. (The letter "O" refers to the origin.) *Allocative efficiency* is defined as the ratio $AE = \frac{O\text{-}DMU_0^O}{O\text{-}DMU_0^T}$. Thus the overall efficiency can be decomposed into technical and allocative efficiency: $OE = TE \times AE$, where technical efficiency addresses DMU distance from the production frontier, and allocative efficiency its distance from the optimal input (output) allocation. The decomposition was first proposed by Farrell (1957).

---

[2] Notation of type $O \text{-} DMU_0^T$ refers to the length of the line between the origin and point DMU_0^T.

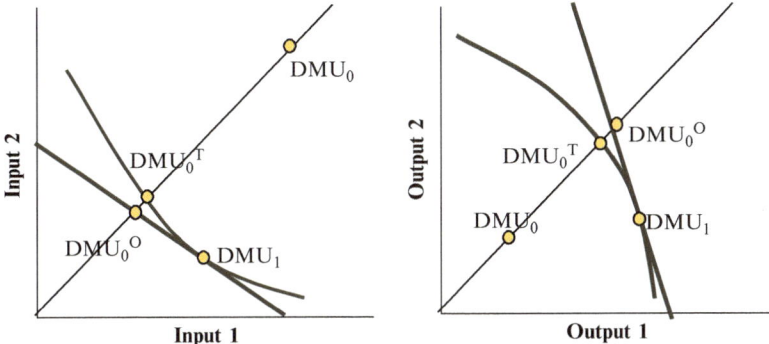

Fig. 1.2 Technical and overall efficiency: input and output orientations

1.2.4   Radial Projection

In illustrations of efficiency in Fig. 1.2, we used a so-called radial projection to project an inefficient unit DMU_0 onto the efficient frontier. The radial projection is determined either by increasing outputs proportionally subject to given input levels or by decreasing inputs proportionally subject to given output levels. We also use the term radial projection, when inputs are proportionally decreased and outputs increased simultaneously. Variables are proportionally improved until the boundary of the PPS is achieved. Farrell (1957) used the radial projection in his seminal paper as well. However, Farrell was not the first person who proposed its use. Debreu (1951) used the radial projection and showed that it also implicitly defines prices for the inputs and outputs. The prices that correspond to a radially projected point are thus such that using those, the unit is allocatively efficient. If the true prices are unknown, the technical efficiency is a conservative approximation of the overall efficiency and the radial projection sets an efficient target based on the implicit prices. This aspect is discussed more later on.

Unfortunately, the radial projection does not guarantee that the boundary point is efficient. The point can be *weakly efficient*. The weakly efficient point is inefficient, but there is no possibility to improve all inputs and outputs simultaneously.

1.2.5   Returns to Scale and Scale Efficiency

In Fig. 1.3, we have three DMUs that all operate on the production possibility frontier. In Fig. 1.3, we have drawn three rays starting from the origin and passing through the units DMU_1, DMU_2, and DMU_3. The slopes of these rays are standing for the ratio output/input. Thus the slopes are measures for productivity. Because the ray passing through DMU_2 is a tangent to the production frontier at this point, it has the greatest slope indicating DMU_2 has the best possible productivity—its

Fig. 1.3 Scale efficiency

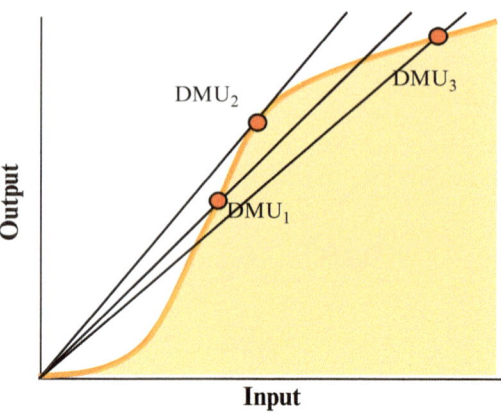

output/input—ratio is maximal. It is operating at the *optimal scale* size. If all DMUs had the same slope on the production frontier, then we should say that the production frontier specifies constant returns to scale (CRS); otherwise it specifies variable returns to scale (VRS). The returns to scale of DMU_1 is clearly lower than that of DMU_2. If VRS is assumed, then DMU_2 is efficient, but for becoming optimal it has to improve its productivity. It cannot happen unless it decreases its input and/or output as well. It is said to operate on the area of increasing *returns to scale*. The returns to scale of DMU_3 is also lower than that of DMU_2, but DMU_3 operates on the area of decreasing returns to scale. If its input increases, it cannot preserve its current productivity level; it decreases. Thus even if the units are technically efficient, they may increase their productivity by exploiting *scale efficiency*.

1.3   Illustration of Basic Principles of Data Envelopment Analysis

1.3.1   Brief Overview

DEA was developed by Charnes, Cooper, and Rhodes in their seminal paper Charnes et al. (1978) as a technique to measure *relative (technical) efficiency* of the DMU which uses multiple inputs and produces multiple outputs. The term decision-making unit was used for the first time in their article. In DEA each unit is freely allowed to select the weights so that the ratio of the weighted sum of outputs to the weighted sum of inputs (Definition 1.2) is maximized. The only limitation is that with the selected weights the ratio cannot exceed 1 (unity, 100 %) for any unit evaluated. The selection of the weights is done via a linear programming algorithm as suggested by Charnes et al. (1978). Thus DEA offers a method to measure technical efficiency: not only do we know which units are technically efficient and which are inefficient, but the ratio also indicates the measure for the inefficiency.

Fig. 1.4 Theoretical and empirical production frontiers

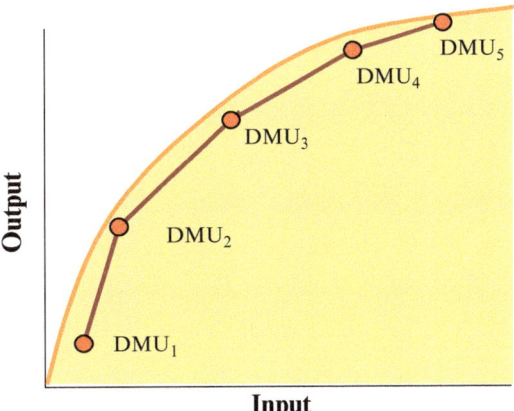

In DEA spirit we can relate the technical and overall efficiency so that if there exists any isocost (isorevenue) line, i.e., if there exists any set of prices leading the unit to have minimum costs (maximum revenues), it is technically efficient. Thus DEA does not require any a priori pricing information and is often advertised as a *value-free* approach (see, e.g., Charnes et al. 1994, p. 8).

Actually, DEA only provides an approximation to technical efficiency because we do not know the *actual efficient frontier*. DEA will empirically estimate the efficient frontier based on the set of available DMUs. Thus DEA does not aim to estimate the true *theoretical production frontier*, but uses instead an *empirical production frontier* based on the observed efficient DMUs. Figure 1.4 illustrates the difference. The theoretical frontier is the north-west surface of the shaded area. Instead, the estimated frontier (*best practice*) is a piecewise linear curve from DMU$_1$ to DMU$_5$.

More precisely, the empirical production frontier in DEA is usually based on the postulates of (*strong*) *free disposability* and *convexity*. (Strong) free disposability means that each DMU can "destroy" extra inputs without costs or produce less outputs than an efficient unit at a certain input level. Convexity assumption implies that convex combinations of observed DMUs are all feasible and thus belongs to the PPS.

Figure 1.5 illustrates the postulates. The lines connecting the DMUs represent their convex combinations often referred as *virtual* DMUs. In DEA it is assumed that these virtual units can be attained. When the convexity assumption is not made, the PPS is referred to as the term free disposable hulls (FDHs) (see, e.g., Deprins et al. 1984). The point belongs to that set if it is dominated at least by one given DMU.

A DMU is efficient (*nondominated*) if there is no other comparable unit— existing or virtual—that can produce at least the same amount of all outputs and use at most the same amount of all inputs. In addition, at least one output has

Fig. 1.5 DEA postulates

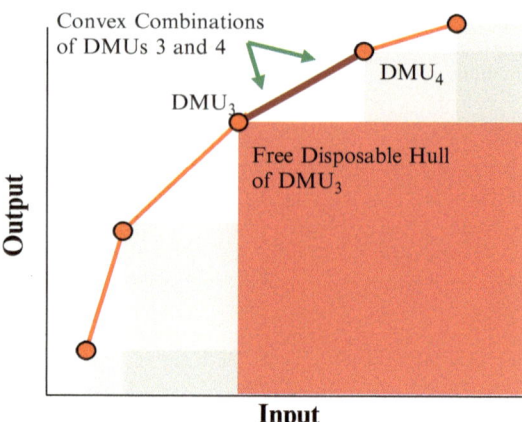

to be higher or one input has to be lower than the unit under evaluation.
(The exact definition is given later on.) The former approach is referred to as the
output-oriented and the latter as the input-oriented DEA. If a DMU is not efficient
(nondominated), it is inefficient (dominated). Note that on the "ends" (in this
two-dimensional illustration) the frontier is defined by the FDHs. These vertical
and horizontal areas of the frontier are only weakly efficient. See Definitions 2.3
and 2.4 for precise mathematical definitions.

DEA provides each unit with efficiency score that gives the DMU information
on its distance from the efficient frontier and with *target unit* (shortly *target*) a
virtual unit that is the projection of the unit evaluated to the efficient frontier. Target
is a combination (convex or linear—see Fig. 1.7) of some existing units, and these
units are referred to as the *reference units* or the *reference set* of the unit evaluated.
From the efficiency score, it is possible to see the percentage by which the unit
should decrease its inputs (input-oriented case) or increase its outputs (output-
oriented case). The target on the other hand gives the input and output levels that
the unit should attain to become efficient. The results of the DEA analysis,
especially the efficiency scores, are used in practical applications as performance
indicators of DMUs.

The most widely used DEA formulations are the CCR model with CRS by
Charnes et al. (1978) and BCC model with VRS by Banker et al. (1984). As the
names indicate, these two models differ with respect to their assumptions on returns
to scale. Figure 1.6 illustrates the situation. With CRS, it is assumed that each
additional unit of input produces the same amount of output. With this assumption
only DMU_2 is efficient. The assumption on VRS in the BCC model allows the
additional output produced by a unit of additional input to vary (i.e., first increase
and then decrease) according to scale size. With this assumption all DMUs in
Fig. 1.6 are efficient.

Fig. 1.6 Constant and
variable returns to scale

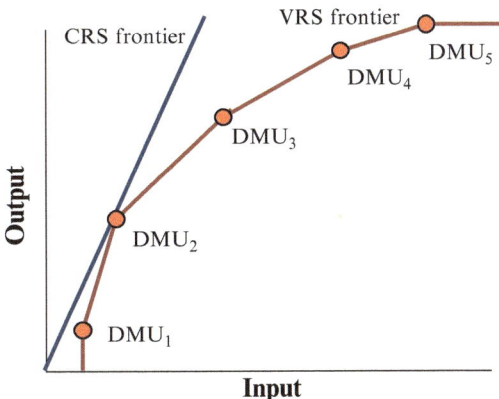

1.3.2   Projections, Efficiency Scores, and Targets

Figure 1.7 presents a situation with five DMUs ($DMU_0, \ldots, DMU_4$) each using one input to produce one output. DEA is used to estimate empirical efficient frontiers with the CCR and BCC models. The upward sloping line through DMU_1 represents the efficient frontier obtained by the CCR model, and the piecewise linear curve describes the efficient frontier by the BCC model.

If CRS assumption is used, only DMU_1 is efficient. All the points on the frontier and the points east from a point on the frontier belong to the PPS. In the input-oriented approach, the output level of DMU_0 is given, and the input level is tried to be reduced as much as possible. This principle leads to the target point $DMU_0*^{I\text{-}CCR}$. In the output-oriented approach, we fix the input level and try to increase the output. The target is denoted by $DMU_0*^{O\text{-}CCR}$. With input orientation the efficiency score for DMU_0 is ratio[3] $\frac{DMU_0{}^I - DMU_0*^{I\text{-}CCR}}{DMU_0{}^I - DMU_0}$ and with output orientation $\frac{DMU_0{}^O - DMU_0}{DMU_0{}^O - DMU_0*^{O\text{-}CCR}}$.

When VRS assumption is made, all DMUs except DMU_0 are efficient. The piecewise linear curve from $DMU_1{}^O$ through the efficient units represents the efficient frontier, and all the points on the frontier and the points east from a point on the frontier are contained in the PPS. Now the target unit for DMU_0 in the input-oriented case is $DMU_0*^{I\text{-}BCC}$, and in the output-oriented case $DMU_0*^{O\text{-}BCC}$. With input orientation the efficiency score for DMU_0 is ratio $\frac{DMU_0{}^I - DMU_0*^{I\text{-}BCC}}{DMU_0{}^I - DMU_0}$ and with output orientation $\frac{DMU_0{}^O - DMU_0}{DMU_0{}^O - DMU_0*^{O\text{-}BCC}}$. Note that the efficiency score is never better in the CRS approach than in the VRS approach.

---

[3] Notation of type $DMU_0{}^O - DMU_0$ refers to the length of the line between these two points.

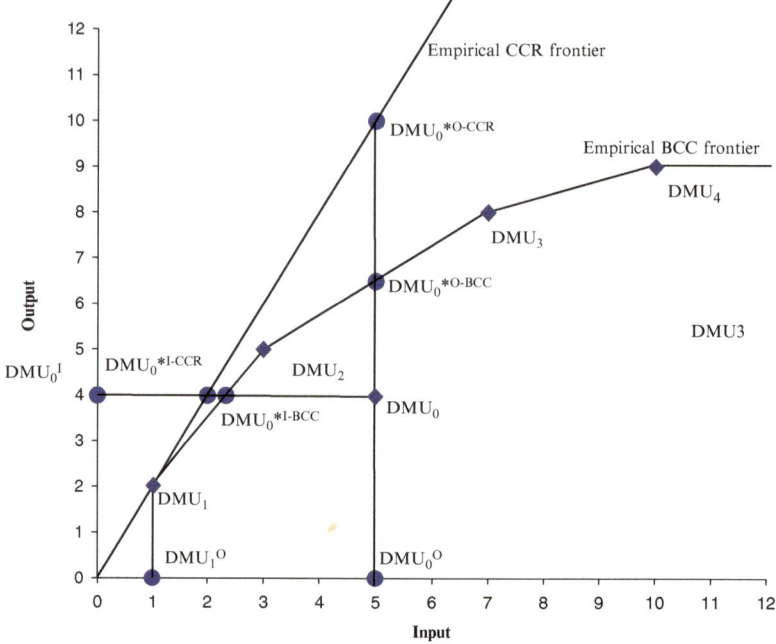

Fig. 1.7 Basic concepts of DEA

1.3.3 Slacks

The concept which plays an important role in DEA is a *slack*. As we described before in the input-oriented model, the purpose is to reduce inputs of an inefficient unit in the same proportion until we reach the boundary of the PPS. In the similar way in the output-oriented model, we increase the outputs of an inefficient unit in the same proportion until the boundary is reached. The radial projection is supposed to project the unit onto the efficient frontier. However, it does not always happen.

Figure 1.8 illustrates the empirical efficient frontier based on the VRS assumption. Consider first the inefficient unit DMU_1. In the input-oriented approach, we reduce the input by moving from its current position left until we reach the efficient frontier. Instead of using the output-oriented approach, we move up until the boundary is reached. Now we reach the weakly efficient part of the frontier. To get onto the efficient frontier, we have to move left to unit DMU_2. The difference between the weakly efficient point and DMU_2 is called the input slack.

Unit DMU_4 is weakly efficient. If we use the input-oriented approach, the unit seems to be efficient, because there is no possibility to move left from its current position. However, to become efficient it has to improve its output with no need to reduce its input. Thus DMU_4's target is DMU_3. The difference in the output between DMU_4 and DMU_3 is the output slack.

In later chapters slacks are considered in more detail.

Fig. 1.8 Slacks in DEA

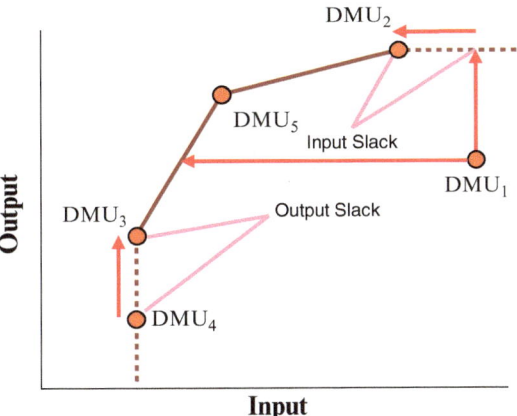

1.4   Incorporating Preference Information into Efficiency Analysis

Original DEA is value-free in the sense that all units on an efficient frontier are equally good. However, there are many problems in practice in which this assumption is not realistic. It is not sufficient that something is made efficiently; it is also important that right things are made.

In many practical applications (see, e.g., Allen et al. 1997 for discussion), there has been a need to incorporate price information, expert opinion, or preferences, values, or judgment of those into the analysis to achieve acceptable results.

Allocative efficiency proposed by Farrell (1957) is a classical example on the efficiency analysis in which all inputs are not equally important. The inputs are aggregated by using a linear function with prices as weights. The linear function is minimized in the PPS subject to the output level(s) of each unit and the efficiency is determined in relation to this hyperline at the optimum. Allocative efficiency measures how much the unit on the (technically) efficient frontier has to reduce its inputs to becoming optimal.

To operate with weights has been a dominating technique in DEA to incorporate preference information into the analysis. In some cases, the weights can be interpreted as prices, but it is not a necessity. The weights can, for example, be used to make some extreme values of inputs/outputs at the efficient frontier non-acceptable.

An important area, where preference information is needed, is benchmarking. In fact, DEA itself is a benchmarking technique in the sense that inefficient units are benchmarked against the efficient frontier. However, it is not the only way how benchmarking can be applied in the context of DEA. We may choose one or several units which are used as benchmarking units to other units. For this purpose, preference information is needed. On the other hand, we may have a need to find a good benchmarking unit for each unit separately. In the overall benchmarking an evaluator is often an "outsider" or a manager having a control over all units. Instead, in case of individual benchmarking, a unit itself is interested in seeing how to improve its performance. The use of the terms is adopted from Bogetoft and Nielsen (2005).

In later chapters, we will consider in more details the traditional and more recent technique to incorporate preference information. In addition, we will discuss the use of those methods in practice.

References

Allen R, Athanassopoulos A, Dyson RG, Thanassoulis E (1997) Weights restrictions and value judgements in data envelopment analysis: evolution, development and future directions. Ann Oper Res 73:13–34

Banker RD, Charnes A, Cooper WW (1984) Some models for estimating technical and scale inefficiencies in data envelopment analysis. Manag Sci 30:1078–1092

Bogetoft P, Nielsen K (2005) Internet based benchmarking. Group Decis Negotiation 14(3):195–215

Bragge J, Korhonen P, Wallenius H, Wallenius J (2012) Scholarly communities of research in multiple criteria decision making: a bibliometric research profiling study. Int J Inf Technol Decis Mak 11(02):401–426

Charnes A, Cooper WW, Rhodes E (1978) Measuring efficiency of decision making units. Eur J Oper Res 2:429–444

Charnes A, Cooper WW, Rhodes E (1979) Short communication: measuring efficiency of decision making units. Eur J Oper Res 3:339

Charnes A, Cooper W, Lewin AY, Seiford LM (1994) Data envelopment analysis: theory, methodology and applications. Kluwer Academic, Norwell, p 8

Coelli TJ, Rao DSP, O'Donnell CJ, Battese GE (2005) An introduction to efficiency and productivity analysis, 2nd edn. Springer, New York

Cooper WW, Seiford LM, Tone K (2007) Data envelopment analysis: a comprehensive text with models, applications, references and DEA-solver software, 2nd edn. Kluwer Academic, Boston

Debreu G (1951) The coefficient of resource utilization. Econometrica 19(3):273–292

Deprins D, Simar L, Tulkens H (1984) Measuring labour efficiency in post offices. In: Marchand M, Pestieau P, Tulkens H (eds) The performance of public enterprises: concepts and measurement. North-Holland, Amsterdam, pp 243–267

Färe R, Grosskopf S (2000) Theory and application of directional distance functions. J Prod Anal 13:93–103

Farrell MJ (1957) The measurement of productivity efficiency. J R Stat Soc Ser A 120:253–290

Koopmans TC (1951) Analysis of production as an efficient combination of activities. In: Koopmans TC (ed) Activity analysis of production and allocation. Cowles Commission monograph no. 13. Wiley, New York

Korhonen P, Stenfors S, Syrjänen M (2003) Multiple objective approach as an alternative to radial projection in DEA. J Prod Anal 20:305–321

Norton R (1994) Which offices or stores really perform best? A new tool tells. Fortune 31 Oct 1994, p 38

Pareto V (1906) Manuale di Economia Politica. Piccola Biblioteca Scientifica, Milan

Seiford LM (1996) Data envelopment analysis: the evolution and the state of the art (1978–1995). J Prod Anal 7(2–3):99–137

Simons R (1996) How DEA can be a spur to improved performance. OR Newsletter, December 1996, pp 11–13

Thanassoulis E, Dyson RG (1992) Estimating preferred target input-output levels using data envelopment analysis. Eur J Oper Res 56:80–97

Chapter 2
Data Envelopment Analysis

Basic Models with Input, Output, and Combined Orientation

2.1 Basic Data Envelopment Analysis Models

In this chapter we review the input- and output-oriented DEA models, and introduce the use of combined orientation.

Assume we have n DMUs each consuming m inputs and producing s outputs. Let $\mathbf{X} \in \mathfrak{R}_+^{m \times n}$ ($x_{ij} > 0, i = 1, 2, \ldots, m, j = 1, 2, \ldots, n$) and $\mathbf{Y} \in \mathfrak{R}_+^{s \times n}$ ($y_{rj} > 0, r = 1, 2, \ldots, s, j = 1, 2, \ldots, n$) be the matrices, consisting of positive elements, containing the observed input and output measures for the DMUs. We denote by x_j (the jth column of $\mathbf{X}$) the vector of inputs consumed by DMU$_j$, and by x_{ij} the quantity of input i consumed by DMU$_j$. A corresponding notation is used for outputs. Slack variable vector associated to inputs is denoted by s^- and that associated to outputs with s^+. See Thrall (1996) for a discussion. Furthermore, we denote $\mathbf{1} = [1, \ldots, 1]^T$ and refer by e_i to the ith unit vector in $\mathfrak{R}^n$.

2.1.1 Constant Returns to Scale Models

In DEA, each DMU's efficiency is considered via maximizing the ratio of a weighted sum of outputs and a weighted sum of inputs (or minimizing the inverse) subject to the condition that corresponding ratios for each DMU are less than or equal to 1 (or greater than or equal to 1 for the inverse). The model chooses nonnegative weights for the DMU whose performance is being evaluated in a way that is most favorable for it.

This leads to linear programming problems. In the models below, the weights ν_i and μ_r are assigned to ith input and rth output. Subscript "$_0$" refers to the unit under consideration in the functional, but preserves its original subscript in the constraints.

© Springer Science+Business Media New York 2015
T. Joro, P.J. Korhonen, *Extension of Data Envelopment Analysis with Preference Information*, International Series in Operations Research & Management Science 218, DOI 10.1007/978-1-4899-7528-7_2

Table 2.1 Original DEA models

Input-oriented model	Output-oriented model
$\max h_0 = \dfrac{\sum\limits_{r=1}^{s}\mu_r y_{r0}}{\sum\limits_{i=1}^{m}\nu_i x_{i0}}$	$\min f_0 = \dfrac{\sum\limits_{i=1}^{m}\nu_i x_{i0}}{\sum\limits_{r=1}^{s}\mu_r y_{r0}}$
s.t. $\qquad\qquad\qquad\qquad\qquad$ (2.1a)	s.t. $\qquad\qquad\qquad\qquad\qquad$ (2.1b)
$\dfrac{\sum\limits_{r=1}^{s}\mu_r y_{rj}}{\sum\limits_{i=1}^{m}\nu_i x_{ij}}\leq 1,\ j=1,2,\ldots,n$	$\dfrac{\sum\limits_{i=1}^{m}\nu_i x_{ij}}{\sum\limits_{r=1}^{s}\mu_r y_{rj}}\geq 1,\ j=1,2,\ldots,n$
$\mu_r,\ \nu_i \geq 0,\ r=1,2,\ldots,s,\ i=1,2,\ldots,m$	$\mu_r,\nu_i \geq 0,\ r=1,2,\ldots,s,\ i=1,2,\ldots,m$

The original model proposed by Charnes et al. (1978, 1979) for measuring the efficiency of unit DMU_0 was the so-called input-oriented model shown in the left column of Table 2.1. We may also consider the reciprocal model, where the numerator and denominator in the objective function and constraints have changed places. The objective is then to minimize the ratio of a weighted sum of inputs to a weighted sum of outputs subject to the condition that corresponding ratios for each DMU be greater than or equal to 1. Both models are described in Table 2.1.

Charnes et al. (1979) quickly recognized the problem of using nonnegativity conditions for the weights μ_r, ν_i and proposed that constraints μ_r, $\nu_i \geq 0$ should be replaced by strict positivity conditions by writing μ_r, $\nu_i \geq \varepsilon$ where $\varepsilon > 0$ is a *Non-Archimedean infinitesimal*; see Arnold et al. (1997) for discussion. If we do not force the weights to be strictly positive, the solutions might be only weakly efficient not efficient. The solution is only weakly efficient if it is possible to improve any of inputs or outputs, but not simultaneously all. In the sequel, we use the formulation that guarantees efficiency (see for more details in Chap. 3).

Models in Table 2.1 are based on the constant returns to scale assumption (CRS) and called the CCR models according to the developers Charnes et al. (1978). The vectors μ and ν are the optimal weights to inputs and outputs that maximize the efficiency score for the DMU in question. In the input orientation the optimal value of the objective function h_0 is the efficiency score, and in the output orientation, the efficiency scores are obtained as a reciprocal of the optimal value of the objective function $1/f_0$.

The formulations above are fractional linear programs that can be easily formulated and solved as linear programs. Let us consider the input-oriented model. By setting the nominator to unity, we obtain

$$\max \sum_{r=1}^{s} \mu_r y_{r0}$$

s.t.   (2.2)

$$\frac{\sum_{r=1}^{s} \mu_r y_{rj}}{\sum_{i=1}^{m} \nu_i x_{ij}} \leq 1, \quad j = 1, 2, \ldots, n$$

$$\sum_{i=1}^{m} \nu_i x_{i0} = 1$$

$$\mu_r, \nu_i \geq \varepsilon, \quad r = 1, 2, \ldots, s, \ i = 1, 2, \ldots, m$$

$$\varepsilon > 0 \ (\text{"Non-Archimedean"})$$

Next we multiply both sides of the first constraint by its nominator. This is possible, since the nominator is positive by definition. Thus we obtain

$$\max \sum_{r=1}^{s} \mu_r y_{r0}$$

s.t.   (2.3)

$$\sum_{r=1}^{s} \mu_r y_{rj} - \sum_{i=1}^{m} \nu_i x_{ij} \leq 0, \quad j = 1, 2, \ldots, n$$

$$\sum_{i=1}^{m} \nu_i x_{i0} = 1$$

$$\mu_r, \nu_i \geq \varepsilon, \quad r = 1, 2, \ldots, s, \ i = 1, 2, \ldots, m$$

$$\varepsilon > 0 \ (\text{"Non-Archimedean"})$$

The linearization of the output-oriented formulation is similar. The input- and output-oriented CCR models and their dual models are summarized in Table 2.2 using matrix notation. In DEA literature the primal formulation is referred to as *multiplier model* (M) and the dual formulations as *envelopment model* (E). To avoid confusion, we will use these names instead of the terms primal and dual.

Note that in input orientation, the optimal value of θ in the envelopment model is an efficiency score. Instead, in the output orientation, the efficiency score is obtained as a reciprocal of σ at the optimum ($=1/\sigma$). We may give the following definition for efficiency. Note that usually different efficiency scores are obtained in using an input-oriented model and an output-oriented model. However, the efficiency of the unit can be solved with any model.

Table 2.2 Multiplier and envelopment CCR models

Input-oriented CCR ($CCR_M - I$)	Input-oriented CCR ($CCR_E - I$)
max $W_I = \mu^T y_0$	min $Z_I = \theta - \varepsilon(\mathbf{1}^T s^+ + \mathbf{1}^T s^-)$
s.t.	s.t.
$\quad \mu^T Y - \nu^T X \leq 0$	$\quad Y\lambda - s^+ = y_0$
$\quad \nu^T x_0 = 1$	$\quad X\lambda - \theta x_0 + s^- = 0$
$\quad \mu, \nu \geq \varepsilon \mathbf{1}$	$\quad \lambda, s^-, s^+ \geq 0$
$\quad \varepsilon > 0$ ("Non-Archimedean")	$\quad \varepsilon > 0$ ("Non-Archimedean")
Output-oriented CCR ($CCR_M - O$)	Output-oriented CCR ($CCR_E - O$)
min $W_O = \nu^T x_0$	max $Z_O = \sigma + \varepsilon(\mathbf{1}^T s^+ + \mathbf{1}^T s^-)$
s.t.	s.t.
$\quad -\mu^T Y + \nu^T X \geq 0$	$\quad Y\lambda - \sigma y_0 - s^+ = 0$
$\quad \mu^T y_0 = 1$	$\quad X\lambda + s^- = x_0$
$\quad \mu, \nu \geq \varepsilon \mathbf{1}$	$\quad \lambda, s^-, s^+ \geq 0$
$\quad \varepsilon > 0$ ("Non-Archimedean")	$\quad \varepsilon > 0$ ("Non-Archimedean")

(2.4a) for the left input-oriented rows; (2.4b) for the right input-oriented rows; (2.5a) for the left output-oriented rows; (2.5b) for the right output-oriented rows.

Alternatively, we refer to models by using returns to scale assumption, e.g., CRS

Definition 2.1 DMU_0 is CCR efficient if $\exists\ \varepsilon > 0$ such that the optimal values $Z_O^* = Z_I^* = W_O^* = W_I^* = 1$; otherwise, DMU_0 is inefficient.

Correspondingly, we may define weak efficiency as follows:

Definition 2.2 DMU_0 is CCR inefficient, but weakly efficient, if $\exists\ \varepsilon > 0$ such that the optimal values $Z_O^* = W_O^* > 1$ and $Z_I^* = W_I^* < 1$, but $\theta = \sigma = 1$ at the optimum; otherwise, DMU_0 is not weakly efficient.

If DMU_0 is only weakly efficient, then the efficiency score is 1, but at least one element of slack vectors s^- or s^+ is positive. Note that the efficient DMU is weakly efficient, but not the other way round.

2.1.2   Variable Returns to Scale Models

Later on, Banker et al. (1984) considered the variable returns to scale (VRS) assumption and developed the so-called BCC model. In the BCC model, an extra variable u is added into the numerator. The variable u allows the change of scale. Assume that we have two units with inputs (2, 5) and outputs (1, 2). The productivity of the first unit is greater than that of the second unit: $1/2 > 2/5$. In terms of the CCR model, the latter unit is not efficient, but if we allow to add $u = 0.5$ into the numerator, then $1/2 = (2 + 0.5)/5$ making the latter one efficient under VRS assumption.

The input- and output-oriented BCC models are given in Table 2.3. The BCC models can also be presented as linear programming models like the CCR models.

Table 2.3 Original BCC models

Input-oriented model	Output-oriented model
$\max h_0 = \dfrac{\sum_{r=1}^{s} \mu_r y_{r0} + u}{\sum_{i=1}^{m} \nu_i x_{i0}}$	$\min f_0 = \dfrac{\sum_{i=1}^{m} \nu_i x_{i0} + u}{\sum_{r=1}^{s} \mu_r y_{r0}}$
s.t. $\qquad\qquad\qquad$ (2.6a)	s.t. $\qquad\qquad\qquad$ (2.6b)
$\dfrac{\sum_{r=1}^{s} \mu_r y_{rj} + u}{\sum_{i=1}^{m} \nu_i x_{ij}} \leq 1, \; j = 1, 2, \ldots, n$	$\dfrac{\sum_{i=1}^{m} \nu_i x_{ij} + u}{\sum_{r=1}^{s} \mu_r y_{rj}} \geq 1, \; j = 1, 2, \ldots, n$
$\mu_r, \nu_i \geq \varepsilon, \; r = 1, 2, \ldots, s, \, i = 1, 2, \ldots, m$	$\mu_r, \nu_i \geq \varepsilon, \; r = 1, 2, \ldots, s, \, i = 1, 2, \ldots, m$
$\varepsilon > 0$ ("Non-Archimedean")	$\varepsilon > 0$ ("Non-Archimedean")

Table 2.4 Multiplier and envelopment BCC models

Input-oriented BCC ($\text{BCC}_M - \text{I}$)	Input-oriented BCC ($\text{BCC}_E - \text{I}$)
$\max \; W_I = \boldsymbol{\mu}^T \boldsymbol{y}_0 + u$	$\min \; Z_I = \theta - \varepsilon(\mathbf{1}^T \boldsymbol{s}^+ + \mathbf{1}^T \boldsymbol{s}^-)$
s.t. $\qquad\qquad\qquad$ (2.7a)	s.t. $\qquad\qquad\qquad$ (2.7b)
$\boldsymbol{\mu}^T \mathbf{Y} - \boldsymbol{\nu}^T \mathbf{X} + u\mathbf{1}^T \leq \mathbf{0}$	$\mathbf{Y}\boldsymbol{\lambda} - \boldsymbol{s}^+ = \boldsymbol{y}_0$
$\boldsymbol{\nu}^T \boldsymbol{x}_0 = 1$	$\mathbf{X}\boldsymbol{\lambda} - \theta \boldsymbol{x}_0 + \boldsymbol{s}^- = \mathbf{0}$
$\boldsymbol{\mu}, \boldsymbol{\nu} \geq \varepsilon \mathbf{1}$	$\mathbf{1}^T \boldsymbol{\lambda} = 1$
$\varepsilon > 0$ ("Non-Archimedean")	$\boldsymbol{\lambda}, \boldsymbol{s}^-, \boldsymbol{s}^+ \geq \mathbf{0}$
	$\varepsilon > 0$ ("Non-Archimedean")
Output-oriented BCC ($\text{BCC}_M - \text{O}$)	Output-oriented BCC ($\text{BCC}_E - \text{O}$)
$\min \; W_O = \boldsymbol{\nu}^T \boldsymbol{x}_0 + u$	$\max \; Z_O = \sigma + \varepsilon(\mathbf{1}^T \boldsymbol{s}^+ + \mathbf{1}^T \boldsymbol{s}^-)$
s.t. $\qquad\qquad\qquad$ (2.8a)	s.t. $\qquad\qquad\qquad$ (2.8b)
$-\boldsymbol{\mu}^T \mathbf{Y} + \boldsymbol{\nu}^T \mathbf{X} + u\mathbf{1}^T \geq \mathbf{0}$	$\mathbf{Y}\boldsymbol{\lambda} - \sigma \boldsymbol{y}_0 - \boldsymbol{s}^+ = \mathbf{0}$
$\boldsymbol{\mu}^T \boldsymbol{y}_0 = 1$	$\mathbf{X}\boldsymbol{\lambda} + \boldsymbol{s}^- = \boldsymbol{x}_0$
$\boldsymbol{\mu}, \boldsymbol{\nu} \geq \varepsilon \mathbf{1}$	$\mathbf{1}^T \boldsymbol{\lambda} = 1$
$\varepsilon > 0$ ("Non-Archimedean")	$\boldsymbol{\lambda}, \boldsymbol{s}^-, \boldsymbol{s}^+ \geq \mathbf{0}$
	$\varepsilon > 0$ ("Non-Archimedean")

The input- and output-oriented multiplier BCC models and their duals (envelopment models) are given in Table 2.4. In the multiplier BCC models, the variable u appears in objective functions and in the first constraint. In the envelopment model, the convex combination constraint ($\mathbf{1}^T \boldsymbol{\lambda} = 1$) is a new constraint caused by the existence of variable u in the multiplier model. By setting various restrictions to variable u, other models can be introduced. They will be discussed in Chap. 5 when a general DEA model is introduced.

Like in case of the CCR models, we defined the BCC efficiency as follows:

Definition 2.3 DMU_0 is BCC efficient if $\exists\ \varepsilon > 0$ such that the optimal values $Z_O^* = Z_I^* = W_O^* = W_I^* = 1$; otherwise, DMU_0 is inefficient.

Actually, Definitions 2.1 and 2.3 coincide. They define that the unit under consideration is efficient if the solution of the corresponding model is in unity. However, they do not specify the same set of efficient units. If unit is CCR efficient, it is also BCC efficient, but not in the contrary. We will consider these questions more thoroughly later on.

The definition of the weak efficiency for the BCC model is also the same as for the CCR model.

2.1.3   Non-increasing and Non-decreasing Returns to Scale Models

In the BCC model presented in the previous subsection, an extra variable u was added into the numerator (Table 2.3). When the sign of u was not defined, we obtained a (general) VRS model. When restrictions $u \geq 0$ and $u \leq 0$ are added into the models in Table 2.3, we get the special types of VRS models: non-increasing and non-decreasing models. We use the abbreviations NIRS for a non-increasing returns to scale model and NDRS for a non-decreasing returns to scale model, respectively.

The models are introduced by assuming output orientation (Model 2.6b), but the considerations are similar for input-oriented models, and those ones are omitted here.

First, we assume that $u \geq 0$.

$$\min f_0 = \frac{\sum_{i=1}^{m} \nu_i x_{i0} + u}{\sum_{r=1}^{s} \mu_r y_{r0}}$$

s.t.

$$\frac{\sum_{i=1}^{m} \nu_i x_{ij} + u}{\sum_{r=1}^{s} \mu_r y_{rj}} \geq 1, \quad j = 1, 2, \ldots, n$$

$$\mu_r, \nu_i \geq \varepsilon, \quad r = 1, 2, \ldots, s, \quad i = 1, 2, \ldots, m$$
$$u \geq 0$$
$$\varepsilon > 0 \quad (\text{"Non-Archimedean"})$$

(2.9)

Now we get the following models (Table 2.5):

Table 2.5 Multiplier and envelopment nonincreasing models

Output-oriented BCC (BCC$_M$ – O)	Output-oriented BCC (BCC$_E$ – O)

min $W_O = \boldsymbol{\nu}^T \boldsymbol{x}_0 + u$
 s.t.   (2.10a)
    $-\boldsymbol{\mu}^T \mathbf{Y} + \boldsymbol{\nu}^T \mathbf{X} + u\mathbf{1}^T \geq \mathbf{0}$
    $\boldsymbol{\mu}^T \boldsymbol{y}_0 = 1$
    $u \geq 0$
    $\boldsymbol{\mu}, \boldsymbol{\nu} \geq \varepsilon\mathbf{1}$
    $\varepsilon > 0$
	max $Z_O = \sigma + \varepsilon\left(\mathbf{1}^T \boldsymbol{s}^+ + \mathbf{1}^T \boldsymbol{s}^-\right)$
	 s.t. (2.10b)
	    $\mathbf{Y}\boldsymbol{\lambda} - \sigma\boldsymbol{y}_0 - \boldsymbol{s}^+ = \mathbf{0}$
	    $\mathbf{X}\boldsymbol{\lambda} + \boldsymbol{s}^- = \boldsymbol{x}_0$
	    $\mathbf{1}^T \boldsymbol{\lambda} \leq 1$
	    $\boldsymbol{\lambda}, \boldsymbol{s}^-, \boldsymbol{s}^+ \geq \mathbf{0}$
	    $\varepsilon > 0$

Correspondingly, when we use the restriction $u \leq 0$ instead of $u \geq 0$, then nondecreasing models (Table 2.6) are obtained.

Table 2.6 Multiplier and envelopment nondecreasing models

Output-oriented BCC (BCC$_M$ – O)	Output-oriented BCC (BCC$_E$ – O)

min $W_O = \boldsymbol{\nu}^T \boldsymbol{x}_0 + u$
 s.t.   (2.11a)
    $-\boldsymbol{\mu}^T \mathbf{Y} + \boldsymbol{\nu}^T \mathbf{X} + u\mathbf{1}^T \geq \mathbf{0}$
    $\boldsymbol{\mu}^T \boldsymbol{y}_0 = 1$
    $u \leq 0$
    $\boldsymbol{\mu}, \boldsymbol{\nu} \geq \varepsilon\mathbf{1}$
    $\varepsilon > 0$
	max $Z_O = \sigma + \varepsilon\left(\mathbf{1}^T \boldsymbol{s}^+ + \mathbf{1}^T \boldsymbol{s}^-\right)$
	 s.t. (2.11b)
	    $\mathbf{Y}\boldsymbol{\lambda} - \sigma\boldsymbol{y}_0 - \boldsymbol{s}^+ = \mathbf{0}$
	    $\mathbf{X}\boldsymbol{\lambda} + \boldsymbol{s}^- = \boldsymbol{x}_0$
	    $\mathbf{1}^T \boldsymbol{\lambda} \geq 1$
	    $\boldsymbol{\lambda}, \boldsymbol{s}^-, \boldsymbol{s}^+ \geq \mathbf{0}$
	    $\varepsilon > 0$

Finally, we can provide a unified representation to the models based on CRS, VRS, NIRS, and NDRS assumptions. The models are given in Table 2.7.

The effect of the returns to scale assumption on a production possibility set is illustrated in Fig. 2.1.[1] The size of the production possibility set is the largest one consisting of areas I + II + III, when returns to scale is constant. Only unit B is efficient. If the returns to scale is variable, then all units—except A—are efficient. The production possibility set is the smallest one. In case of NIRS, PPS consists of areas I and II, and finally in case of NDRS, PPS consists of areas I and III.

2.2 How to Deal with ε in the DEA Models?

Because we cannot solve the optimization problems in Tables 2.2 and 2.4 in the open set by using the constraint $\varepsilon > 0$, we have to find other methods.

If we use the constraint $\varepsilon = 0$, it means that at least one of the weights μ_r, $r = 1$, 2, ..., s, and ν_i, $i = 1, 2, ..., m$ is allowed to be 0. However, this may lead to the solution that is weakly efficient, but not efficient. For example, DMU$_4$ in Fig. 1.8 is weakly efficient. When the input-oriented approach is used, the unit diagnosed is

---

[1]Briefly defined production possibility set is a set of possible solutions (see Chap. 4).

Table 2.7 The unified multiplier and envelopment models based on CRS, VRS, NIRS, and NDRS assumptions

Input-oriented multiplier model	Input-oriented envelopment model
$\max\ W_{\mathrm{I}} = \boldsymbol{\mu}^{\mathrm{T}}\boldsymbol{y}_0 + u$ s.t. $\qquad\qquad\qquad\qquad\qquad$ (2.12a) $\quad \boldsymbol{\mu}^{\mathrm{T}}\mathbf{Y} - \boldsymbol{\nu}^{\mathrm{T}}\mathbf{X} + u\mathbf{1}^{\mathrm{T}} \le \mathbf{0}$ $\quad \boldsymbol{\nu}^{\mathrm{T}}\boldsymbol{x}_0 = 1$ $\quad \boldsymbol{\mu},\boldsymbol{\nu} \ge \varepsilon\mathbf{1}$ $\quad \varepsilon > 0$ $u \begin{cases} = 0 & \text{if RTS is CRS} \\ = \text{free} & \text{if RTS is VRS} \\ \ge 0 & \text{if RTS is NDRS} \\ \le 0 & \text{if RTS is NIRS} \end{cases}$ Note! see NDRS vs. NIRS	$\min\ Z_{\mathrm{I}} = \theta - \varepsilon\big(\mathbf{1}^{\mathrm{T}}\boldsymbol{s}^+ + \mathbf{1}^{\mathrm{T}}\boldsymbol{s}^-\big)$ s.t. $\qquad\qquad\qquad\qquad\qquad$ (2.12b) $\quad \mathbf{Y}\boldsymbol{\lambda} - \boldsymbol{s}^+ = \boldsymbol{y}_0$ $\quad \mathbf{X}\boldsymbol{\lambda} - \theta\boldsymbol{x}_0 + \boldsymbol{s}^- = \mathbf{0}$ $\quad \mathbf{1}^{\mathrm{T}}\boldsymbol{\lambda} + \tau = 1$ $\quad \boldsymbol{\lambda}, \boldsymbol{s}^-, \boldsymbol{s}^+ \ge \mathbf{0}$ $\quad \varepsilon > 0$ $\tau \begin{cases} = 0 & \text{if RTS is VRS} \\ = \text{free} & \text{if RTS is CRS} \\ \ge 0 & \text{if RTS is NIRS} \\ \le 0 & \text{if RTS is NDRS} \end{cases}$
Output-oriented multiplier model	Output-oriented envelopment model
$\min\ W_{\mathrm{O}} = \boldsymbol{\nu}^{\mathrm{T}}\boldsymbol{x}_0 + u$ s.t. $\qquad\qquad\qquad\qquad\qquad$ (2.13a) $\quad -\boldsymbol{\mu}^{\mathrm{T}}\mathbf{Y} + \boldsymbol{\nu}^{\mathrm{T}}\mathbf{X} + u\mathbf{1}^{\mathrm{T}} \ge \mathbf{0}$ $\quad \boldsymbol{\mu}^{\mathrm{T}}\boldsymbol{y}_0 = 1$ $\quad \boldsymbol{\mu},\boldsymbol{\nu} \ge \varepsilon\mathbf{1}$ $\quad \varepsilon > 0$ $u \begin{cases} = 0 & \text{if RTS is CRS} \\ = \text{free} & \text{if RTS is VRS} \\ \ge 0 & \text{if RTS is NIRS} \\ \le 0 & \text{if RTS is NDRS} \end{cases}$	$\max\ Z_{\mathrm{O}} = \sigma + \varepsilon\big(\mathbf{1}^{\mathrm{T}}\boldsymbol{s}^+ + \mathbf{1}^{\mathrm{T}}\boldsymbol{s}^-\big)$ s.t. $\qquad\qquad\qquad\qquad\qquad$ (2.13b) $\quad \mathbf{Y}\boldsymbol{\lambda} - \sigma\boldsymbol{y}_0 - \boldsymbol{s}^+ = \mathbf{0}$ $\quad \mathbf{X}\boldsymbol{\lambda} + \boldsymbol{s}^- = \boldsymbol{x}_0$ $\quad \mathbf{1}^{\mathrm{T}}\boldsymbol{\lambda} + \tau = 1$ $\quad \boldsymbol{\lambda}, \boldsymbol{s}^-, \boldsymbol{s}^+ \ge \mathbf{0}$ $\quad \varepsilon > 0$ $\tau \begin{cases} = 0 & \text{if RTS is VRS} \\ = \text{free} & \text{if RTS is CRS} \\ \ge 0 & \text{if RTS is NIRS} \\ \le 0 & \text{if RTS is NDRS} \end{cases}$

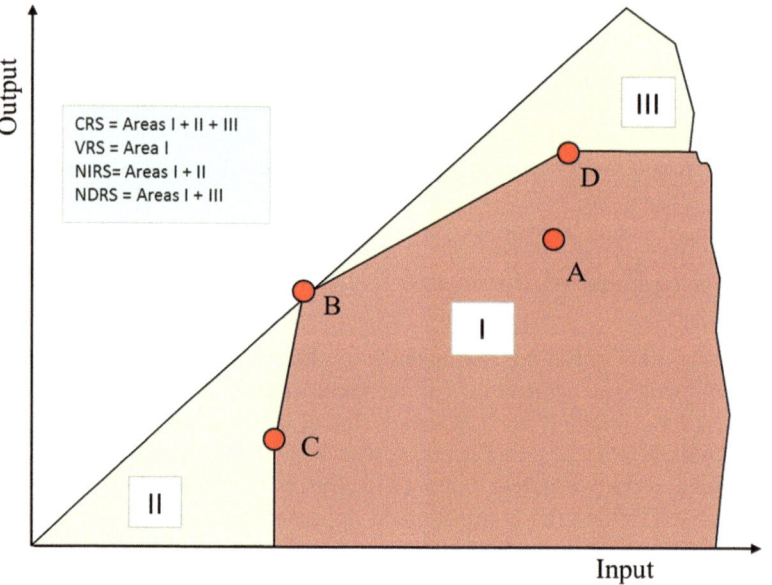

CRS = Areas I + II + III
VRS = Area I
NIRS= Areas I + II
NDRS = Areas I + III

Fig. 2.1 Illustration of the effect of returns to scale assumptions

efficient. In fact, its output is supposed to be improved without decreasing the input. If we use the output-oriented model, then its inefficiency is revealed.[2]

Another approach is to use a small positive value for ε. In most cases, the approach works, but some problems may emerge in certain circumstances. If ε (in practice) is too small in comparison to the input and output values of units, it has no meaning because of the rounding errors of computers. The solution may be diagnosed efficient, even if it is only weakly efficient. If ε is too big, some efficient solutions will be diagnosed inefficient, and sometimes there is no solution at all. See for more discussion, e.g., Ali and Seiford (1993).

The same problem has been recognized in the discipline of multiple criteria decision making. To avoid weakly efficient solutions, Sawaragi et al. (1985) and Steuer (1986) have proposed the use of a lexicographic approach. Later on, Charnes et al. (1992) independently proposed the same idea in the context of DEA. Currently, the use of the lexicographical approach is recommended (see also Ali 1989, 1994; Joro et al. 1998).

A solution to overcome the problem is to use the lexicographical formulation for the objective function. For instance, we may use the formulation

$$\text{lex } \max\{\sigma, \mathbf{1}^{\mathrm{T}} s^+ + \mathbf{1}^{\mathrm{T}} s^-\} \tag{2.14}$$

for the objective function, e.g., in the output-oriented CCR model (see Table 2.2). Notation lex max means that the objective function σ is first maximized and if the solution turns out not to be unique, the second objective function is maximized lexicographically subject to the constraint $\sigma \geq \sigma^*$ (σ^* is the maximum value of σ). When the optimal solution of the first objective function (σ) is unique, the second objective function is not needed.

The efficiency definition can also be in the following form (Charnes et al. 1994):

Definition 2.3 DMU_0 is CCR (BCC) efficient if $\sigma = 1$ and all slack variables s^-, s^+ equal to zero; otherwise, it is inefficient.

In the next chapter, we will consider efficiency concept in more detail.

2.3 Combined Model

In the input-oriented model, we assume that the DM is willing to control the inputs, but outputs are given. Correspondingly, in the output-oriented model, the role of inputs and outputs changes. However, there are situations where a DM may be willing to control all inputs and outputs simultaneously, or only a subset of inputs

---

[2]If unit is efficient or inefficient, but not weakly efficient, then to diagnose its status is independent of the value of ε (see for more details Korhonen and Luptacik 2004).

Table 2.8 Multiplier and envelopment combined models

Combined unified multiplier model	Combined unified envelopment model
$\min\ W_{\mathrm{C}} = \boldsymbol{\nu}^{\mathrm{T}}\boldsymbol{x}_0 - \boldsymbol{\mu}^{\mathrm{T}}\boldsymbol{y}_0 + u$ s.t. (2.15a) $\quad -\boldsymbol{\mu}^{\mathrm{T}}\mathbf{Y} + \boldsymbol{\nu}^{\mathrm{T}}\mathbf{X} + \mathbf{1}^{\mathrm{T}}u \geq \mathbf{0}$ $\quad \boldsymbol{\mu}^{\mathrm{T}}\boldsymbol{y}_0 + \boldsymbol{\nu}^{\mathrm{T}}\boldsymbol{x}_0 = 1$ $\quad \boldsymbol{\mu}, \boldsymbol{\nu} \geq \varepsilon\mathbf{1}$ $\quad \varepsilon > 0$ $u \begin{cases} = 0 & \text{if RTS is CRS} \\ = \text{free} & \text{if RTS is VRS} \\ \geq 0 & \text{if RTS is NIRS} \\ \leq 0 & \text{if RTS is NDRS} \end{cases}$	$\max\ Z_{\mathrm{C}} = \eta + \varepsilon\left(\mathbf{1}^{\mathrm{T}}\boldsymbol{s}^+ + \mathbf{1}^{\mathrm{T}}\boldsymbol{s}^-\right)$ s.t. (2.15b) $\quad \mathbf{Y}\boldsymbol{\lambda} - \eta\boldsymbol{y}_0 - \boldsymbol{s}^+ = \boldsymbol{y}_0$ $\quad \mathbf{X}\boldsymbol{\lambda} + \eta\boldsymbol{x}_0 + \boldsymbol{s}^- = \boldsymbol{x}_0$ $\quad \mathbf{1}^{\mathrm{T}}\boldsymbol{\lambda} + \tau = 1$ $\quad \boldsymbol{\lambda}, \boldsymbol{s}^-, \boldsymbol{s}^+ \geq \mathbf{0}$ $\quad \varepsilon > 0$ $\tau \begin{cases} = 0 & \text{if RTS is VRS} \\ = \text{free} & \text{if RTS is CRS} \\ \geq 0 & \text{if RTS is NIRS} \\ \leq 0 & \text{if RTS is NDRS} \end{cases}$

and outputs. In this subsection, we only deal with the first case. A more general model is given in Chap. 3.

A model considering simultaneously both input minimization and output maximization was introduced by Charnes et al. (1985). Their model was the so-called additive model. Other models considering simultaneous input minimization and output maximization exist; see, for example, Warwick DEA-User Manual (Thanassoulis 1992; Thanassoulis and Dyson 1992; Zhu 1996; Briec 1997; Joro et al. 1998). In distance function literature, a similar approach is presented using a directional distance function (see, e.g., Chambers et al. 1996, 1998; Färe and Grosskopf 1997; Chung et al. 1997).

In the following, we present the combined unified model. The modification of the basic models for the unified models is straightforward. In the model (Table 2.8), η is not an efficiency score, but an inefficiency score, i.e., $1 + \eta = \sigma \Rightarrow \eta = \sigma - 1$ for the σ in the output-oriented model (2.13b) and $-1 + \eta = -\theta \Rightarrow \eta = 1 - \theta$ for θ in the input-oriented model (2.12b). Thus η describes how much an inefficient unit has to improve (increase outputs and decrease inputs) proportionally its inputs and outputs, simultaneously, for becoming efficient. The combined model can be given to CRS, VRS, NIRS, and NDRS assumptions.

Analogously to the basic considerations, we may introduce the efficiency score as the following ratio, for instance, for the CCR model (2.15a):

$$\min\ g_0 = \frac{\sum_{i=1}^{m} v_i x_{i0} - \sum_{r=1}^{s} u_r y_{r0}}{\sum_{r=1}^{s} u_r y_{r0} + \sum_{i=1}^{m} v_i x_{i0}} \tag{2.16}$$

Subject to the constraints of the reciprocal model of (2.1b).

By dividing the numerator and denominator by $\sum_{r=1}^{s} u_r y_{r0}$, we obtain

$$g_0 = \frac{\dfrac{\sum_{i=1}^{m} v_i x_{i0}}{\sum_{r=1}^{s} u_r y_{r0}} - 1}{\dfrac{\sum_{r=1}^{s} v_i x_{i0}}{\sum_{r=1}^{s} u_r y_{r0}} + 1} = \frac{\rho_0 - 1}{\rho_0 + 1} \qquad (2.17)$$

where ρ_0 is the value of the ratio $\dfrac{\sum_{i=1}^{m} v_i x_{i0}}{\sum_{r=1}^{s} u_r y_{r0}}$ at the optimum of the models in Table 2.8.

From the models in Table 2.8 we see that ρ_0 is always nonnegative; for an efficient unit it is 0. It reflects the percentage by which a DMU should both decrease its inputs and increase its outputs to become efficient.

2.4 Concluding Remarks

In this chapter we represented basic DEA models. In the later chapters, we consider ideas to extend those models to deal with the preference information of the DM.

References

Ali AI (1989) Computational aspects of data envelopment analysis. CCS research report no. 640. University of Texas Center for Cybernetic Studies, Austin

Ali AI (1994) Computational aspects of DEA. In: Charnes A, Cooper WW, Lewin AY, Seiford LM (eds) Data envelopment analysis: theory, methodology and applications. Kluwer Academic, Boston, pp 63–88

Ali AI, Seiford LM (1993) Computational accuracy and infinitesimals in data envelopment analysis. INFOR 31:290–297

Arnold V, Bardhan I, Cooper WW, Gallegos A (1997) Primal and dual optimality in computer codes using two-stage solution procedures in DEA. In: Aronson J, Zionts S (eds) Operations research: models, methods and applications. Quorum Books, Westport, pp 57–96, A volume in honor of G.L. Thompson

Banker RD, Charnes A, Cooper WW (1984) Some models for estimating technical and scale inefficiencies in data envelopment analysis. Manag Sci 30:1078–1092

Briec W (1997) A graph-type extension of Farrell technical efficiency measure. J Prod Anal 8:95–110

Chambers R, Chung Y, Färe R (1996) Benefit and distance functions. J Econ Theory 70:407–419

Chambers RG, Chung Y, Färe R (1998) Profit, directional distance functions, and Nerlovian efficiency. J Optim Theory Appl 98(2):351–364

Charnes A, Cooper WW, Rhodes E (1978) Measuring efficiency of decision making units. Eur J Oper Res 2:429–444

Charnes A, Cooper WW, Rhodes E (1979) Short communication: measuring efficiency of decision making units. Eur J Oper Res 3:339

Charnes A, Cooper WW, Golany B, Seiford LM, Stutz J (1985) Foundations of data envelopment analysis for Pareto-Koopmans efficient empirical production functions. J Econom 30 (1/2):91–107

Charnes A, Rousseau JJ, Semple JH (1992) Non-Archimedean infinitesimals, transcendentals and categorical inputs in linear programming and data envelopment analysis. Int J Syst Sci 23:2401–2406

Charnes A, Cooper WW, Lewin AY, Seiford LM (1994) Data envelopment analysis: theory, methodology and applications. Kluwer Academic, Boston

Chung YH, Färe R, Grosskopf S (1997) Productivity and undesirable outputs: a directional distance function approach. J Environ Manage 51(3):229–240

Färe R, Grosskopf S (1997) Profit efficiency, Farrell decompositions and the Mahler inequality. Econ Lett 1997:283–287

Joro T, Korhonen P, Wallenius J (1998) Structural comparison of data envelopment analysis and multiple objective linear programming. Manag Sci 44(7):962–970

Korhonen P, Luptacik M (2004) Eco-efficiency analysis of power plants: an extension of data envelopment analysis. Eur J Oper Res 154(2):437–446

Sawaragi Y, Nakayama H, Tanino T (1985) Theory of multiobjective optimization. Academic, New York

Steuer RE (1986) Multiple criteria optimization: theory, computation and application. Wiley, New York

Thanassoulis E (1992) Warwick DEA user manual. Warwick Business School, Coventry

Thanassoulis E, Dyson RG (1992) Estimating preferred target input-output levels using data envelopment analysis. Eur J Oper Res 56:80–97

Thrall RM (1996) Duality, classification and slacks in DEA. Ann Oper Res 66:109–138

Zhu J (1996) Data envelopment analysis with preference structure. J Oper Res Soc 47:136–150

Chapter 3
Production Possibility Set and Efficiency

Efficiency in Production Possibility Set and General Model

3.1 Production Possibility Set

Many concepts used in DEA are adopted from production economics. One of those concepts is production function $f: \mathfrak{R}^m \to \mathfrak{R}(y = f(x))$, where vector x represents inputs and y is one-dimensional output. In this case, it is assumed that a DM can control inputs x. There are possibly other inputs, which are non-controllable. They are taken into account in the structure of function f. Moreover, the term cost function is used to refer to the case, in which there are many outputs and one input, and the DM is assumed to control the outputs, i.e., $c: \mathfrak{R}^s \to \mathfrak{R} \ (x = c(y))$.

In DEA, both the input and output can be vectors. In addition, the relationship between inputs and outputs is not assumed known. It is used to refer to a multi-input/multi-output case by the term production possibility set and we denote it by T:

$$\mathrm{T} = \big\{ (y, x) \,\big|\, x \text{ can be produced from } x \big\} \subset \mathfrak{R}_+^{s+m} \qquad (3.1)$$

where $x \in \mathfrak{R}_+^m$ and $y \in \mathfrak{R}_+^s$ denote the vector of inputs and outputs, respectively. The set consists of all feasible inputs and outputs. As usual, we assume more is better in outputs and less is better in inputs. It is also common to set up some additional properties to T in addition to the non-negativity of inputs and outputs:

(i) If $(y, x) \in \mathrm{T}$ and $y \neq 0 \Rightarrow x \neq 0$.
(ii) T is closed.
(iii) T is bounded.
(iv) $(y, x) \in \mathrm{T}$, if $\exists \ (y^*, x^*) \in \mathrm{T}$, such that $y^* \geq y$ and $x^* \leq x$.

For more information about a production possibility set, see, e.g., Coelli et al. (2005).

Set T is a theoretical production possibility set, which is not assumed to be known in practical problems. In practice we operate with an empirical production

© Springer Science+Business Media New York 2015
T. Joro, P.J. Korhonen, *Extension of Data Envelopment Analysis with Preference Information*, International Series in Operations Research & Management Science 218, DOI 10.1007/978-1-4899-7528-7_3

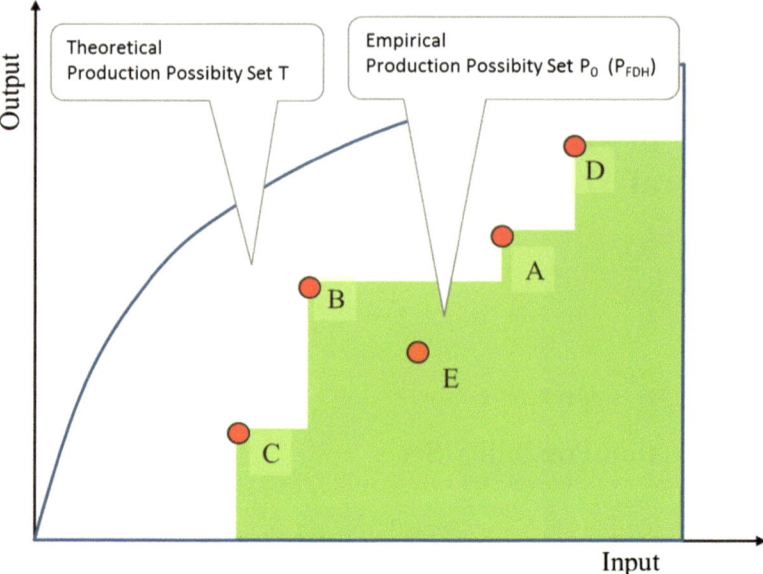

Fig. 3.1 Empirical PPS with minimal assumptions (FDH)

possibility set, which is characterized with the help of the sample consisting of n pairs $(\mathbf{y}_i, \mathbf{x}_i) \in \mathfrak{R}_+^{s+m}$, $i = 1, 2, \ldots, n$. Because the pairs are empirical data, it is justified to assume that $(\mathbf{y}_i, \mathbf{x}_i) \in \mathrm{T}$, $i = 1, 2, \ldots, n$. We denote $\mathrm{S}_0 = \{(\mathbf{y}_i, \mathbf{x}_i) \mid i = 1, 2, \ldots, n\}$, and further we refer to the matrix of outputs in the sample by $\mathbf{Y} = [\mathbf{y}_1, \mathbf{y}_2, \ldots, \mathbf{y}_n]$ and to the matrix of inputs by $\mathbf{X} = [\mathbf{x}_1, \mathbf{x}_2, \ldots, \mathbf{x}_n]$.

If we have no more information about T, we define the empirical production possibility set P_0 and call it the minimal production possibility set based on the sample set S_0:

$$\mathrm{P}_0 = \left\{ (\mathbf{y}, \mathbf{x}) \big| \exists (\mathbf{y}^*, \mathbf{x}^*) \in \mathrm{S}_0 \text{ such that } \mathbf{y}^* \geq \mathbf{y} \text{ and } \mathbf{x}^* \leq \mathbf{x} \right\} \qquad (3.2)$$

Set (3.2) is also used to call the *free disposal hull* (FDH). Occasionally, we alternatively use notation $\mathrm{P}_{\mathrm{FDH}}$ to refer to this set, which is illustrated in Fig. 3.1.

In addition to the sample set $\mathrm{S}_0 \subseteq \mathrm{P}_0$, P_0 includes the points which are based on the assumption: *without costs it is possible to produce less and/or to use resources more than any point in the sample* $(\mathbf{y}, \mathbf{x}) \in \mathrm{S}_0$. If additional information is available, we include it into set S_0. When it is not necessary to emphasize the type of additional information, we use generic notation S for expanded S_0 and call it the generator of a production possibility set—briefly a generator set. The corresponding notations P_0 and P are applied to the production possibility set as well.

Hence forward we refer to the empirical production possibility set by using the abbreviation PPS and dropping "empirical" off from the long name.

By defining new properties for set S_0, we can obtain an expanded generator set S_0^+.

(a) S_0^+ is the minimal convex hull containing points $(\boldsymbol{y}, \boldsymbol{x}) \in S_0$.
(b) If $(\boldsymbol{y}, \boldsymbol{x}) \in S_0 \Rightarrow (\delta\boldsymbol{y}, \delta\boldsymbol{x}) \in S_0^+$, $M \geq \delta \geq 0$, where M is a big number,
(c) If $(\boldsymbol{y}, \boldsymbol{x}) \in S_0 \Rightarrow (\delta\boldsymbol{y}, \delta\boldsymbol{x}) \in S_0^+$, $0 \leq \delta \leq 1$, and
(d) If $(\boldsymbol{y}, \boldsymbol{x}) \in S_0 \Rightarrow (\delta\boldsymbol{y}, \delta\boldsymbol{x}) \in S_0^+$, $M \geq \delta \geq 1$, where M is a big number.

It is possible to use any single property a) – d) or to pair each of the properties b) – d) with property a).

As "subscripts," we use the abbreviations which are used to refer to the corresponding models in DEA based on those generator sets. The sets in Table 3.1 have a hierarchy: $S_{CRS} \supseteq$ {no rank order between S_{NIRS} and S_{NDRS}} $\supseteq S_{VRS} \supseteq S_{FDH}$.

The same notation is used to refer to the production possibility set, i.e., P_{VRS} corresponds to S_{VRS}. Sets S_{VRS} and P_{VRS} are illustrated in Fig. 3.2.

Table 3.1 Expanded sample set S

Definitions of expanded sets	Generator set S_0 +
$S_{FDH} = \{(\boldsymbol{y}, \boldsymbol{x}) \mid \boldsymbol{Y}\lambda = \boldsymbol{y}, \boldsymbol{X}\lambda = \boldsymbol{x}, \mathbf{1}^T\lambda = 1, \lambda_i \in \{0, 1\}, i = 1, 2, \ldots, n\}$	–
$S_{VRS} = \{(\boldsymbol{y}, \boldsymbol{x}) \mid \boldsymbol{Y}\lambda = \boldsymbol{y}, \boldsymbol{X}\lambda = \boldsymbol{x}, \mathbf{1}^T\lambda = 1, \lambda \geq 0\}$	Property (a)
$S_{CRS} = \{(\boldsymbol{y}, \boldsymbol{x}) \mid \boldsymbol{Y}\lambda = \boldsymbol{y}, \boldsymbol{X}\lambda = \boldsymbol{x}, M \geq \lambda \geq 0\}$	Properties (a) and (b)
$S_{NIRS} = \{(\boldsymbol{y}, \boldsymbol{x}) \mid \boldsymbol{Y}\lambda = \boldsymbol{y}, \boldsymbol{X}\lambda = \boldsymbol{x}, \mathbf{1}^T\lambda \leq 1, \lambda \geq 0\}$	Properties (a) and (c)
$S_{NDRS} = \{(\boldsymbol{y}, \boldsymbol{x}) \mid \boldsymbol{Y}\lambda = \boldsymbol{y}, \boldsymbol{X}\lambda = \boldsymbol{x}, \mathbf{1}^T\lambda \geq 1, M \geq \lambda \geq 0\}$	Properties (a) and (d)

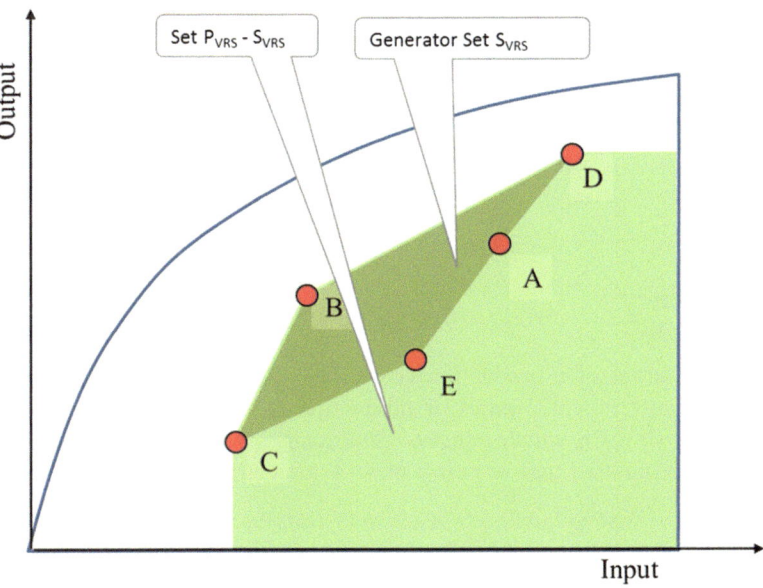

Fig. 3.2 Production possibility set P_{VRS}

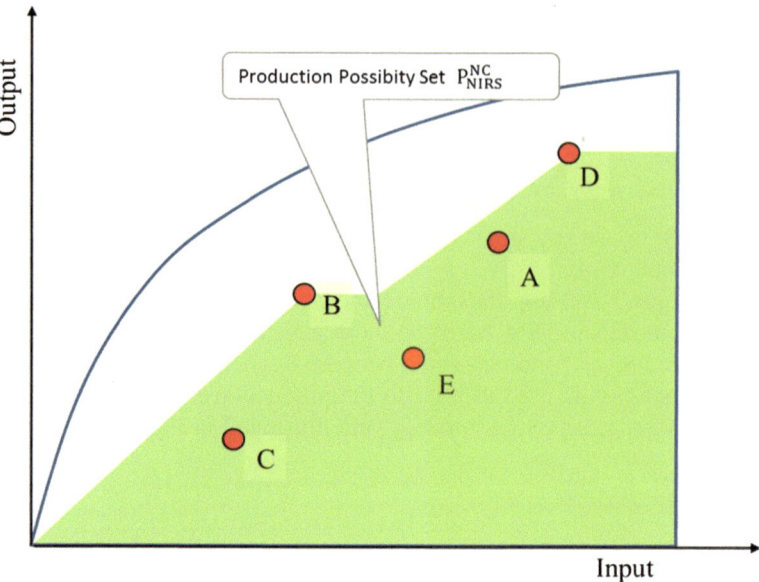

Fig. 3.3 Illustrating production possibility set P_{NIRS}^{NC}

Using properties without convex requirement, interesting sets can be defined. Those sets have also a reasonable interpretation. Consider for instance property (c). The corresponding set can be interpreted such as each unit in S_0 can be scaled downward by using constant returns to scale assumption. The corresponding set is as follows:

$$S_{NIRS}^{NC} = \left\{ (y,x) \,\middle|\, \mathbf{Y}(\delta\lambda) = y, \mathbf{X}(\delta\lambda) = x, \mathbf{1}^T\lambda = 1, \ \lambda_i \in \{0,1\}, \ i = 1,2,\ldots,n, \ \delta \le 1 \right\}$$

where the superscript (NC) means "not convex". Set P_{NIRS}^{NC} is illustrated in Fig. 3.3.

3.2 Efficiency

Most considerations of a production possibility set P are made in relation to its subset called an efficient frontier or production frontier. The terms refer to the subset E of P ($E \subseteq P$), which consists of efficient points, which are also called non-dominated points. *Efficient* points of set P are defined as follows:

Definition 3.1 Point $(y^*, x^*) \in S$ is *efficient* (*non-dominated*) iff there does not exist another $(y, x) \in S$ such that $y \ge y^*$, $x \le x^*$, and $(y, x) \ne (y^*, x^*)$.

Because set P∩–S by definition consists of only the points which are dominated by a point in set S, the efficiency definition can be given for points in set S. Note that the terms efficient and non-dominated have no difference in the DEA literature. Instead, in the multiple criteria decision making it is used to make a distinction between those concepts (see, e.g., Steuer 1986). The efficiency concept is used for points in decision (variable) space (see Chap. 4) and the term nondominance for points in a criterion space (cf. Definitions 4.1 and 4.2). In evolutionary multiple objective programming literature, the term Pareto optimal is used to refer to the points of the theoretical non-dominated frontier (see, e.g., Thiele et al. 2009). The term non-dominated is reserved to efficient points in a population, in which concept corresponds to the sample set in DEA. It means that in DEA literature we might also use different terms for the efficient points of the theoretical production possibility set T and that of the empirical production possibility set P.

If point $(y^*, x^*) \in$ S is not efficient, then it is *inefficient* or *dominated* by $(y, x) \in$ S. However, if an inefficient point is not an interior point in T, it may still be *weakly efficient*. Weak efficiency is defined as follows:

Definition 3.2 Point $(y^*, x^*) \in$ S is *weakly efficient* iff there does not exist another $(y, x) \in$ S such that $y > y^*, x < x^*$.

In some cases, we are also interested in the points $(y, x) \notin$ P. For those points, we define the concept *superefficiency* first proposed by Andersen and Petersen (1993), but did not use the term superefficiency. Here we give a general definition for the point (y^*, x^*) not belonging to the production possibility set, but are efficient in the set $P \cup \{(y^*, x^*)\}$:

Definition 3.3 $(y^*, x^*) \notin$ P is *superefficient* iff there does not point $(y, x) \in$ S such that $y \geq y^*, x \leq x^*$.

Note that $(y^*, x^*) \neq (y, x)$, because $(y^*, x^*) \notin$ P and $(y, x) \in S \subseteq$ P.

If point $(y^*, x^*) \in$ S (under consideration) is not weakly efficient, then it is said to be *strongly inefficient* or *strongly dominated* by $(y, x) \in$ S. An efficient point is also weakly efficient.

The efficiency concept is here defined in an empirical efficient set. In the same way, the corresponding concepts can be defined for the theoretical efficient set T as well. Actually, the frontier based on the generator set S is only an approximation. An empirical production frontier is also called (revealed) best-practice production frontier (see, e.g. Charnes et al. 1994). In DEA, the main goals of the analysis are:

1. To recognize efficient and inefficient points.
2. To project the inefficient points onto the efficient frontier.
3. To recognize the points which characterize the projection point on the efficient frontier.
4. To measure the degree of inefficiency of the inefficient points.

A key role in searching for ways to reach those goals plays a principle to project a given point onto the efficient frontier. The traditional DEA models use the Debreu–Farrell efficiency measure. It means that the projection onto the efficient frontier was carried out in proportion to the current values of input and/or output values. Variables are proportionally (radially) improved until the boundary of the production possibility set is achieved. In the combined model, the direction is given in which the unit has to improve its current input and output values. The total need for improvement is in proportion to this given direction.

It is worth noticing that the radial Debreu–Farrell measure of efficiency does not necessarily lead to an efficient target in DEA, but it may result a weakly efficient solution. For example, Färe and Lovell (1978) criticize the radial projection because of this and suggest the use of the so-called Russell measure to assess technical efficiency. Also, this is why the so-called two-stage procedure ∈ is commonly used (see 2.12). Two-stage procedure guarantees that the target (reference) point belongs to the efficient subset of the isoquant. This corresponds to Koopman's (1951) definition of efficiency. In addition to Russell measure, a number of other non-radial efficiency measures have been suggested. For discussion see, for example, Borger et al. (1998), Färe and Grosskopf (2000), and Thanassoulis and Dyson (1992).

Actually, the Debreu–Farrell measure is a good measure and also provides an efficiency score, which is a good way to measure efficiency. However, it is not able to recognize points which are only weakly efficient but not efficient. Using a lexicographic approach, it is easy to do, whether the point is only weakly efficient or efficient. In the first stage, the Debreu–Farrell measure is used and if the solution is not unique, in the second stage, the sum of slack variables or that of input and output variables is maximized in the set, where the Debreu–Farrell measure reached the optimum. This second stage optimization has no effect on the value of the measure, but it guarantees that the solution is efficient.

When the point on the efficient frontier is found, immediately we also know the points characterizing the projection point. That point is a kind of reference (target/benchmarking) point to the inefficient point. It is good to note that the procedure is general in the sense that it is working for a different generator sets. In the next subsection, we describe a general model, in which the projection direction can be chosen by the DM and $(y, x) \notin P$ is not necessary.

3.3 General Model

We use the term "general model" to refer to the model, which have two additional features in comparison to a standard DEA model:

1. The model makes it possible to project any point $g = \begin{bmatrix} g^y \\ g^x \end{bmatrix} \in \Re^{s+m}$ onto the efficient frontier.
2. The projection direction can be chosen by the DM.

The first feature is needed, for instance, when the DM would like to project a target point $g \in \Re^{s+m}$ onto the efficient frontier. It is not required that $g \in P$. The second feature is useful, when the DM is not willing to use the radial direction as a

Table 3.2 General multiplier and envelopment model

General multiplier DEA model	General envelopment DEA model
$\min\ W_C = \boldsymbol{v}^T\boldsymbol{g}^x - \boldsymbol{\mu}^T\boldsymbol{g}^y + u$ s.t. $\qquad\qquad\qquad\qquad\qquad$ (3.3a) $\quad -\boldsymbol{\mu}^T\mathbf{Y} + \boldsymbol{v}^T\mathbf{X} + \mathbf{1}^T u \geq \mathbf{0}$ $\quad \boldsymbol{\mu}^T\boldsymbol{w}^y + \boldsymbol{v}^T\boldsymbol{w}^x = 1$ $\quad \boldsymbol{\mu}, \boldsymbol{v} \geq \varepsilon\mathbf{1}$ $\quad \varepsilon > 0$ $u \begin{cases} = 0 & \text{if RTS is CRS} \\ = \text{free} & \text{if RTS is VRS} \\ \geq 0 & \text{if RTS is NIRS} \\ \leq 0 & \text{if RTS is NDRS} \end{cases}$	$\max\ Z_C = \eta + \varepsilon\left(\mathbf{1}^T\boldsymbol{s}^+ + \mathbf{1}^T\boldsymbol{s}^-\right)$ s.t. $\qquad\qquad\qquad\qquad\qquad$ (3.3b) $\quad \mathbf{Y}\boldsymbol{\lambda} - \eta\boldsymbol{w}^y - \boldsymbol{s}^+ = \boldsymbol{g}^y$ $\quad \mathbf{X}\boldsymbol{\lambda} + \eta\boldsymbol{w}^x + \boldsymbol{s}^- = \boldsymbol{g}^x$ $\quad \mathbf{1}^T\boldsymbol{\lambda} + \tau = 1$ $\quad \boldsymbol{\lambda}, \boldsymbol{s}^-, \boldsymbol{s}^+ \geq \mathbf{0}$ $\quad \varepsilon > 0$ $\tau \begin{cases} = 0 & \text{if RTS is VRS} \\ = \text{free} & \text{if RTS is CRS} \\ \geq 0 & \text{if RTS is NIRS} \\ \leq 0 & \text{if RTS is NDRS} \end{cases}$

projection direction. Then a DM can choose any vector $\boldsymbol{w} = \begin{bmatrix} \boldsymbol{w}^y \\ \boldsymbol{w}^x \end{bmatrix} \geq 0, \ \boldsymbol{w} \in \mathfrak{R}^{s+m}$, and $\boldsymbol{w} \neq 0$. The solution is always a weakly efficient, but if we use a standard requirement $\varepsilon > 0$ in the model, we obtain an efficient solution. The models are described in Table 3.2. Note that the formulation in always guarantees that the solution point is efficient.

In Theorem 3.1, we prove some results concerning the properties of projection direction and efficiency. To make the proof more readable, we simplify some notation.

We denote $\mathbf{U} = \begin{bmatrix} \mathbf{Y} \\ -\mathbf{X} \end{bmatrix}$, $\boldsymbol{s} = \begin{bmatrix} \boldsymbol{s}^+ \\ \boldsymbol{s}^- \end{bmatrix}$, $\boldsymbol{u}_0 = \begin{bmatrix} \boldsymbol{g}^y \\ -\boldsymbol{g}^x \end{bmatrix}$, and assume $\tau = 0$.

Using the notation above, we may present the BCC (VRS) model in the envelopment form:

$$\begin{aligned} \max\ Z_C &= \eta + \varepsilon\mathbf{1}^T\boldsymbol{s} \\ \text{s.t.} \qquad\qquad & \qquad\qquad\qquad\qquad (3.4) \\ \mathbf{U}\boldsymbol{\lambda} - \eta\boldsymbol{w} - \boldsymbol{s} &= \boldsymbol{u}_0 \\ \mathbf{1}^T\boldsymbol{\lambda} &= 1 \\ \boldsymbol{\lambda}, \boldsymbol{s} &\geq \mathbf{0} \\ \varepsilon &> 0 \end{aligned}$$

Let's consider a given point $\boldsymbol{u}_0$ in model (3.4). In Theorem 3.1, we demonstrate which kind of benefits we may obtain by varying the projection direction:

Theorem 3.1 The following results hold:

1. $\boldsymbol{u}_0$ is efficient $\Leftrightarrow$ for all $\boldsymbol{w} \geq \mathbf{0}$, $\boldsymbol{w} \neq \mathbf{0}$, $\eta^* = 0$ at the optimum.
2. $\boldsymbol{u}_0$ is strongly inefficient $\Leftrightarrow$ for all $\boldsymbol{w} \geq \mathbf{0}$, $\boldsymbol{w} \neq \mathbf{0}$, $\eta^* > 0$ at the optimum.

3. u_0 is inefficient, but weakly efficient $\Leftrightarrow \exists\ w_0 \geq 0$, $w_0 \neq 0$ such that $\eta^* = 0$ at the optimum $\wedge\ \exists\ w_1 \geq 0$, $w_1 \neq 0$ such that $\eta^* > 0$ at the optimum.

4. u_0 is superefficient $\Leftrightarrow$ for all $w \geq 0$, $w \neq 0$, $\eta^* < 0$ at the optimum, or there is no feasible solution for some $w \geq 0$, $w \neq 0$.

Proof 1.a u_0 is efficient $\Rightarrow$ for all $w \geq 0$, $w \neq 0$, $\eta^* = 0$ at the optimum.

Assume $\eta^* > 0$ for some $w \geq 0$, $w \neq 0$. Hence it follows that $U\lambda^* - \eta^* w \geq u_0 \Rightarrow U\lambda^* \geq u_0 \wedge U\lambda^* \neq u_0 \Rightarrow u_0$ is not efficient, which contradicts with the assumption.

1.b u_0 is efficient $\Leftarrow$ for all $w \geq 0$, $w \neq 0$, $\eta^* = 0$ at the optimum.

Assume u_0 is inefficient $\Rightarrow \exists u \in P$ such that $u \geq u_0 \wedge u \neq u_0$. Assume $u_j > u_{0j}$, $j \in \{1, 2, \ldots, s+m\}$. Choose $w_j = 1 \wedge w_i = 0$, $i = 1, 2, \ldots, s+m$, $i \neq j \Rightarrow u = U\lambda - \eta w \geq u_0 \wedge u \neq u_0$, when $\eta = u_j - u_{0j} > 0$, which contradicts with the assumption that for all $w \geq 0$, $w \neq 0$, $\eta^* = 0$ at the optimum.

2.a u_0 is strongly inefficient $\Rightarrow$ for all $w \geq 0$, $w \neq 0$, $\eta^* > 0$ at the optimum.

Assume u_0 is strongly inefficient $\Rightarrow \exists\ u$ such that $u > u_0 \Rightarrow$ for all $w \geq 0$, $w \neq 0\ \exists\ \eta > 0$ such that $u = U\lambda - \eta w > u_0 \Rightarrow \eta^* > 0$.

2.b u_0 is strongly inefficient $\Leftarrow$ for all $w \geq 0$, $w \neq 0$, $\eta^* > 0$ at the optimum.

Because for all $w \geq 0$, $w \neq 0$, $\exists \eta^* > 0$ at the optimum, we choose $w = [1, 1, \ldots, 1]$. Hence it follows that $\exists \eta^* > 0$ at the optimum such that $u^* = U\lambda^* - \eta^* w \geq u_0 \Rightarrow u^* > u_0$.

3.a u_0 is inefficient, but weakly efficient $\Rightarrow \exists\ w_0 \geq 0$, $w_0 \neq 0$ such that $\eta^* = 0$ at the optimum $\wedge\ \exists\ w_1 \geq 0$, $w_1 \neq 0$ such that $\eta^* > 0$ at the optimum.

Assume u_0 is weakly efficient $\Rightarrow$ for all u_1 for which $u_1 \geq u_0$, $\exists\ j \in \{1, 2, \ldots, s+m\}$ such that $u_{1j} - u_{0j} = 0$; otherwise u_0 is strongly inefficient. Because u_0 is inefficient, then $\exists\ i \in \{1, 2, \ldots, s+m\}$ such that $u_{1i} - u_{0i} > 0$. Choose $w_{0j} = 1$, if $u_{1j} - u_{0j} = 0$, $j \in \{1, 2, \ldots, s+m\}$ and $w_{0j} = 0$ otherwise $\Rightarrow \eta^* = 0$. On the other hand, choose $w_{1i} = 1$, if $u_{1i} - u_{0i} > 0$, $i \in \{1, 2, \ldots, s+m\}$ and $w_{1j} = 0$ otherwise $\Rightarrow \eta^* > 0$.

3.b u_0 is inefficient, but weakly efficient $\Leftarrow \exists\ w_0 \geq 0$, $w_0 \neq 0$ such that $\eta^* = 0 \wedge \exists\ w_1 \geq 0$, $w_1 \neq 0$ such that $\eta^* > 0$.

Assume $\exists\ w_0 \geq 0$, $w_0 \neq 0$ such that $\eta^* = 0 \Rightarrow u_0$ is not strongly inefficient (see 2. b). Moreover, assume $\exists\ w_1 \geq 0$, $w_1 \neq 0$ such that $\eta^* > 0 \Rightarrow u_0$ is inefficient. Hence it follows that u_0 is inefficient, but weakly efficient.

4.a u_0 is superefficient $\Rightarrow$ for all $w \geq 0$, $w \neq 0$, $\eta^* < 0$ at the optimum or there is no feasible solution for some $w \geq 0$, $w \neq 0$.

Assume that u_0 is superefficient $\Rightarrow \exists\ w \geq 0$, $w \neq 0$, such that $\eta^* \geq 0$ at the optimum. Because u_0 is superefficient, there exists no $u \in P$ such that $u \geq u_0$ and $u \neq u_0 \Rightarrow$ for each $u \in P$, $u_j < u_{0j}$ for at least one $j \in \{1, 2, \ldots, s+m\}$. Thus $u - \eta w = U\lambda - \eta w \geq u_0$ is true for component j: $u_j - \eta w_j \geq u_0$, $w_j \geq 0$, only if $w_j > 0$ and $\eta^* < 0$ at the optimum, which contradicts with the assumption that $\exists\ w \geq 0$, $w \neq 0$, such that $\eta^* \geq 0$ at the optimum.

4.b u_0 is superefficient $\Leftarrow$ for all $w \geq 0$, $w \neq 0$, $\eta^* < 0$ at the optimum or there is no feasible solution for some $w \geq 0$, $w \neq 0$.

Assume for all $w \geq 0$, $w \neq 0$, $\eta^* < 0$ at the optimum. We choose an arbitrary $w \geq 0$, $w \neq 0$, $w \in \mathfrak{R}^{s+m}$ and find an efficient point $u^* \in P$ as a feasible solution to a problem. Thus we have $U\lambda^* - \eta^* w - s^* = u^* - \eta^* w - s^* = u_0$, $s^* \geq 0$, and at least one $s_j^* = 0$, corresponding to $w_j > 0$, $j \in \{1, 2, \ldots, s+m\}$, because otherwise the solution is not optimal. Hence it follows that $u_j^* - \eta^* w_j = u_0 \Rightarrow u_j^* \leq u_{0j}$, because $\eta^* w_j < 0 \Rightarrow u^*$ does not dominate u_0. The result is valid for all $w \geq 0$, $w \neq 0$, $\eta^* < 0$ at the optimum which means that u_0 is superefficient.

Assume $\exists\, w \geq 0$, $w \neq 0$, such that the problem (3.4) has no feasible solution. If for $w_j = 0$, $j \in \{1, 2, \ldots, s+m\}$, $u_j \leq u_{0j}$, for all $u \in P$, then problem (3.4) has no solution $\Rightarrow u_0$ is superefficient. $\square$

Remarks

1. To check whether a point u_0 is inefficient, we may use any projection direction vector $w_0 \geq 0$, $w_0 \neq 0$. If $\eta^* > 0$, then u_0 is not efficient (1.a). On the other hand, if $\eta^* = 0$, then u_0 is not strongly inefficient (2.a). In both cases, it is necessary to study, if u_0 were inefficient, but weakly efficient.
2. Although $(y, x) \notin P$, it does not mean that (y, x) is superefficient. Point (y, x) might be less than zero. In this case, $\eta^* > 0$ for all $w \geq 0$, $w \neq 0$. It means that point $(y, x) \notin P$ is strongly inefficient, even if it is not feasible, i.e., $(y, x) \notin P$.

Let's consider the following example demonstrating the projection of point $\begin{bmatrix} g^y \\ -g^x \end{bmatrix} \notin P$ onto the efficient frontier:

$$\max\ \eta + \varepsilon(s^+ + s^-)$$
$$\text{s.t.} \tag{3.5}$$
$$5.2\lambda_1 + 3.1\lambda_2 + 2.3\lambda_3 + 6.0\lambda_4 + 4.3\lambda_5 + w^x\eta + s^- = g^x$$
$$4.2\lambda_1 + 3.5\lambda_2 + 1.5\lambda_3 + 5.5\lambda_4 + 2.6\lambda_5 - w^y\eta - s^+ = g^y$$
$$1^T\lambda = 1$$
$$s^-, s^+ \geq 0$$
$$\varepsilon > 0$$

in which we assume that the DM would like to project point $\begin{bmatrix} g^y \\ g^x \end{bmatrix} = \begin{bmatrix} 3 \\ 5 \end{bmatrix}$ onto the efficient frontier by using the vector $\begin{bmatrix} w^y \\ w^x \end{bmatrix} = \begin{bmatrix} 1 \\ 1 \end{bmatrix}$ as a projection vector. Figure 3.4 illustrates the problem. As we can see, $\begin{bmatrix} 3 \\ 5 \end{bmatrix} \notin P_{\text{FDH}}$. In case we would have defined $\varepsilon \geq 0$, then the solution would be B', which is only weakly efficient. Because we have the term $\varepsilon(s^+ + s^-)$, $\varepsilon > 0$, in the objective function, the solution is point B. The value of the term $\eta^* = -1.5$, which indicates that point g is superefficient.

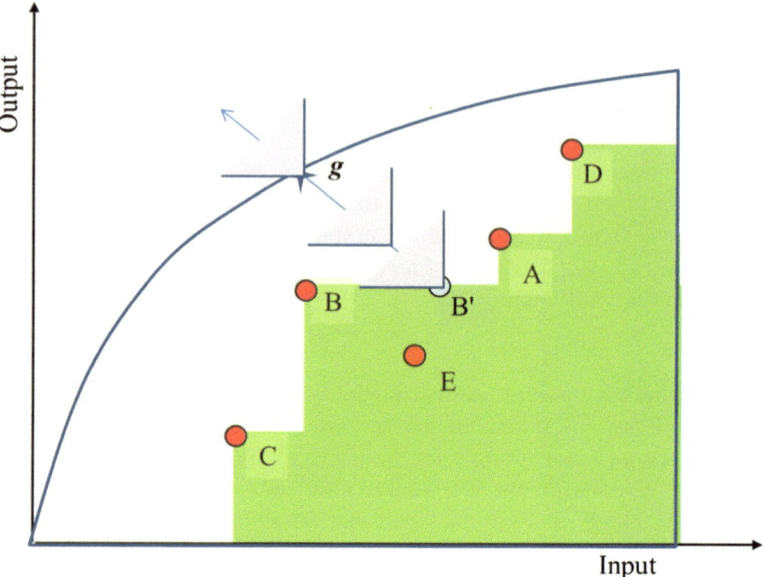

Fig. 3.4 Illustration on the use of a general model

3.4 Efficiency and Dimensionality

In DEA, there is often necessary to reduce the number of variables in the analysis. That's why it is important to know how efficiency may change in variable reduction. We illustrate with a simple example that all changes are possible for units, which are originally efficient and inefficient, but weakly efficient. The same result is not true for a strongly inefficient unit. Its status remains the same in reduction. The data set for the example is given in Table 3.1. For simplicity and without losing generality, we ignore inputs and make considerations in the output space, where all criteria are maximized.

The result is proven in Lemma 3.1.

Lemma 3.1 If vector $u = (u_1, u_2, \ldots, u_p) \in \Re^p$ dominates strongly vector $v = (v_1, v_2, \ldots, v_p) \in \Re^p$, then vector $u^- = (u_{j_1}, u_{j_2}, \ldots, u_{j_k}) \in \Re^k$ dominates strongly vector $v^- = (v_{j_1}, v_{j_2}, \ldots, v_{j_k}) \in \Re^k, j_i \in \{1, 2, \ldots, p\}, i = 1, 2, \ldots, k$.

Proof Because vector $u = (u_1, u_2, \ldots, u_p) \in \Re^p$ dominates strongly vector $v = (v_1, v_2, \ldots, v_p) \in \Re^p \Rightarrow u > v$, i.e., $u_i > v_i$, for all $i \in \{1, 2, \ldots, p\}$. Thus it is true for any subset of the components of vectors u and v: $u_{j_i} > v_{j_i}, j_i \in \{1, 2, \ldots, p\}, i = 1, 2, \ldots, k$ (Table 3.3). □

In Table 3.4, we have shown that dropping one or two dimensions from the original problem (Table 3.3), the status of inefficient, but weakly efficient unit (A)

Table 3.3 Data set for illustrating efficiency change in dimension reduction

Outputs	A	B	C	D
Output 1	1	2	3	1.5
Output 2	3	3	2	1.5
Output 3	2	2	2	1

Table 3.4 Effect of change in dimensionality on efficiency

Unit	Before	Dominance	Change	After	Dominance
A	WEff	B ≥ A	Drop 3	WEff	B ≥ A
A	WEff	B ≥ A	Drop 1	Eff	B = A
A	WEff	B ≥ A	Drop 2 and 3	SInEff	B > A
B	Eff	–	Drop 3	Eff	–
B	Eff	–	Drop 2	WEff	C ≥ B
B	Eff	–	Drop 2 and 3	SInEff	C > B
D	SInEff	C > D	Drop any	SInEff	C > D

Notations: *Eff* efficient, *WEff* only weakly efficient, *SInEff* strongly inefficient, ≥ dominates only weakly, > dominates strongly, *Drop <n>* variable *<n>* is dropped

and efficient unit (B) may be efficient, only weakly efficient, or strongly inefficient after variable reduction. For curiosity, we have also demonstrated that strongly inefficient unit (D) remains its status under reduction.

3.5 Returns to Scale

In classical economics, returns to scale have typically been defined only for a production function and single output situations. Let $\alpha > 0$ represent the proportional increase in all the inputs and $\beta > 0$ the resulting proportional increase in the single output. Increasing returns to scale prevail $\beta > \alpha$; decreasing returns to scale prevail $\beta < \alpha$. If $\beta = \alpha$, then returns to scale called constant.

In DEA, the relationship between inputs and outputs is not assumed to be known. Instead of operating with a production function, the considerations are made in the production possibility set. The returns to scale is also defined for inefficient points, not only points on the efficient frontier. In the following, we consider the PPSs: P_{CRS}, P_{VRS}, P_{NIRS}, and P_{NDRS}. As we mentioned in Sect. 3.1, the following rank order is true to generator sets S and it is the same to the PPSs as well: $P_{CRS} \supseteq \{$no rank order between P_{NIRS} and $P_{NDRS}\} \supseteq P_{VRS}$.

Färe et al. (1985, 1994) proposed a simple method based on the efficiency score of the CRS model and VRS model to characterize the returns to scale of a point.

The characterization is given below. We use inefficiency score instead of efficiency score:

- If $\theta_{CRS} = \theta_{VRS}$, then returns to scale of the point is constant.
- If $\theta_{CRS} \neq \theta_{VRS}$, then

  - if $\theta_{CRS} = \theta_{NIRS}$, then the constant returns to scale of the point is increasing.
  - if $\theta_{CRS} > \theta_{NIRS}$, then the constant returns to scale of the point is decreasing.

Banker et al. (2004) have studied the problem of alternate optima, which may happen, when the returns to scale of the inefficient unit is in question. Actually, returns to scale has an ambiguous meaning for inefficient points. That's why we only consider efficient points. It means that the returns to scale of an inefficient point depend on the projection direction. In projection, we may use input, output, combined, or even general orientation. The only requirement is that at least one element of the projection direction vector is strictly positive and none of the components are not negative. Thus for our purposes the approach by Färe et al. (1985) is sufficient.

For instance, in Fig. 3.2 we see that point B is the only efficient point of the CCR (CRS) model. Depending on whether we use input-oriented or output-oriented model, point E is projected onto line (B, C) or (B, D). For all points on the line (B, C), except B, returns to scale is increasing and for points (B, D), except B, it is decreasing.

References

Andersen P, Petersen NC (1993) A procedure for ranking efficient units in data envelopment analysis. Manage Sci 39(10):1261–1264

Banker RD, Cooper WW, Seiford LM, Thrall RM (2004) Returns to scale in different DEA models. Eur J Oper Res 154:345–362

Borger BD, Ferrier GD, Kerstens K (1998) The choice of a technical efficiency measure of the free disposal hull reference technology: a comparison using US banking data. Eur J Oper Res 105 (3):427–446

Coelli TJ, Rao DSP, O'Donnell CJ, Battese GE (2005) An introduction to efficiency and productivity analysis, 2nd edn. Springer, New York

Charnes A, Cooper WW, Lewin AY, Seiford LM (1994) Data envelopment analysis: theory, methodology, and application. Kluwer, USA

Färe R, Grosskopf S (2000) Theory and application of directional distance functions. J Prod Anal 13:93–103

Färe R, Lovell CAK (1978) Measuring the technical efficiency of production. J Econ Theory 19:150–162

Färe RS, Grosskopf S, Lovel CAK (1985) The measurement of efficiency of production. Kluwer, Boston

Färe RS, Grosskopf S, Lovel CAK (1994) Production frontiers. Cambridge University Press, Cambridge

Koopmans TC (1951) Analysis of production as an efficient combination of activities. In: Koopmans TC (ed) Activity analysis of production and allocation, Cowles Commission monograph no. 13. Wiley, New York

Steuer RE (1986) Multiple criteria optimization: theory, computation and application. Wiley, New York

Thanassoulis E, Dyson RG (1992) Estimating preferred target input–output levels using data envelopment analysis. Eur J Oper Res 56:80–97

Thiele L, Miettinen K, Korhonen P, Molina J (2009) A preference-based evolutionary algorithm for multi-objective optimization. Evol Comput 17(3):411–436

Chapter 4
Multiple Objective Linear Programming

Brief Introduction to MOLP

4.1 Motivation

Since the DEA approaches presented later in this study have a lot in common with multiple objective linear programming (MOLP), this chapter briefly reviews the basic concepts of the field.

The methods for solving single objective mathematical programming problems have been studied now for over 50 years since Dantzig introduced the simplex algorithm in 1947 (see, e.g., Foreword in Dantzig and Thapa (1997) for brief history of mathematical programming). However, often complex real-life decision-making problems involve several, conflicting objectives. Multiple objective mathematical programming, originating from goal programming (see Charnes and Cooper 1961), seeks to deal with these decision problems. This chapter concentrates on MOLP problems, i.e., multiple objective mathematical programming problems having both linear objective functions and linear constraints. This chapter first introduces key concepts of MOLP and after that reviews the different approaches to solve MOLP problems, focusing the reference point approach by Wierzbicki (1980) and reference direction approach by Korhonen and Laakso (1986).

Steuer (1986) is a good reference for a thorough presentation on MOLP and Miettinen (1994, 1999) for multiple objective nonlinear programming. MOLP and other multiple objective mathematical programming methods are part of the family of multiple criteria decision-making (MCDM) approaches. In addition to the term MCDM also abbreviations MCDA (multiple criteria decision analysis) and MCDS (multiple criteria decision support) are used in the literature. For an overview on MCDM, see, e.g., Korhonen et al. (1992), and for a further discussion on multiple objective programming and MCDM see Korhonen (2001).

© Springer Science+Business Media New York 2015   41
T. Joro, P.J. Korhonen, *Extension of Data Envelopment Analysis with Preference
Information*, International Series in Operations Research & Management
Science 218, DOI 10.1007/978-1-4899-7528-7_4

MOLP problem can be written in the general form as follows:

$$\text{"max" } \mathbf{C}x$$
$$\text{s.t.} \tag{4.1}$$
$$x \in X = \{x | \mathbf{A}x \leq b, x \geq 0\}$$

where $x \in \mathfrak{R}^n$, $b \in \mathfrak{R}^k$, the constraint matrix $\mathbf{A} \in \mathfrak{R}^{k \times n}$ is of full rank k, and the objective function matrix $\mathbf{C} \in \mathfrak{R}^{p \times n}$. Notation "max" indicates that we want to maximize all objectives simultaneously. Set X is a *feasible set*.

In MOLP there normally does not exist a single point of X that would simultaneously maximize all objectives. Instead, there exists a set of *efficient solutions*. The efficiency concept is defined using objective function vectors:

Definition 4.1 In (4.1), $x^* \in X$ is an *efficient* solution if there does not exist another $x \in X$ such that $\mathbf{C}x \geq \mathbf{C}x^*$ and $\mathbf{C}x \neq \mathbf{C}x^*$.

If $x^* \in X$ is not efficient, it is *inefficient*. However, an inefficient point may be *weakly efficient*:

Definition 4.2 In (4.1), $x^* \in X$ is *weakly efficient* if there does not exist another $x \in X$ such that $\mathbf{C}x > \mathbf{C}x^*$.

Let $Q = \{q = \mathbf{C}x \mid x \in X\}$ be the set of feasible objective (criterion) function vectors. Vectors $q \in Q$ corresponding to efficient solutions are called *nondominated* criterion vectors, and vectors $q \in Q$ corresponding to weakly efficient solutions are called *weakly nondominated* criterion vectors. The set of all efficient solutions is called the *efficient set* (denoted E), and the set of all nondominated criterion vectors is called the *nondominated set* (denoted N). For weakly efficient solutions, we use E^W and N^W, respectively. Note that $E^W \supseteq E$ and $N^W \supseteq N$. As we can see, the same concepts are used in DEA and MOLP (see Chap. 3).

At the conceptual level, we may write a general multiple objective programming problem as follows:

$$\max \ v(q)$$
$$\text{s.t.} \tag{4.2}$$
$$q \in Q$$

where Q is feasible region in the criterion space. It may be discrete, nonconvex, finite, infinite, etc. Function v is a value function, which has certain properties, but not assumed to be known (see Definition 4.2).

The following figures illustrate the principles of a MOLP. Assume we have two decision variables x_1 and x_2, five constraints that define the feasible set $\mathbf{X}(8x_1 - x_2 \geq 0, \frac{2}{11}x_1 - x_2 \leq 0, \frac{1}{2}x_1 + x_2 \leq 8.5, \frac{3}{2}x_1 + x_2 \leq 11.5, 6x_1 + x_2 \leq 64)$, and two objective functions $(x_1 + x_2, 10x_1 + x_2)$. Figure 4.1 shows the set of efficient solutions E in the decision space.

Fig. 4.1 Illustration of
MOLP: decision space

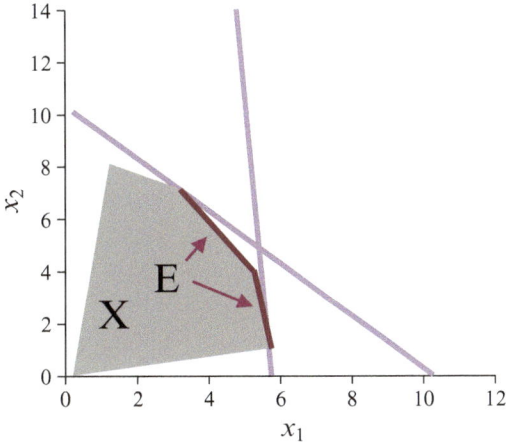

Fig. 4.2 Illustration of
MOLP: criterion space

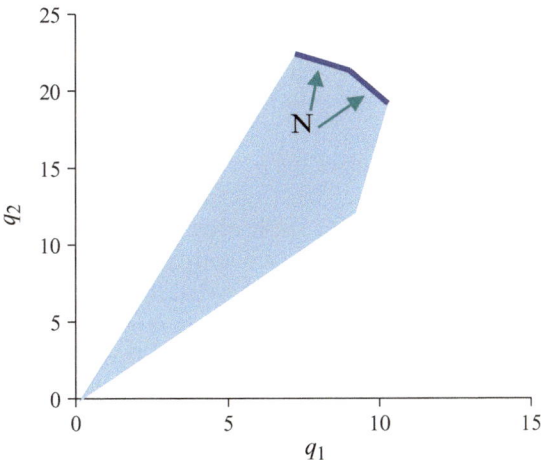

However, often MOLP problems are graphed in *criterion space*. This illustration can be more revealing with respect to conflicting criteria. Figure 4.2 illustrates the set of the nondominated criterion vectors N in the *criterion space*.

4.2   Different MOLP Approaches

Since in MOLP problems it is not usual to have a unique solution, we need to introduce two new concepts: a decision maker and his/her (underlying) value function.

Definition 4.3 A *decision maker* (DM) is a person or a group of persons who has ownership of the problem as well as the ability and authority to make the decision.

Definition 4.4 Function $v: \Omega \to \mathfrak{R}$, $\Omega \subseteq \mathfrak{R}^p$, $\mathfrak{R}^p \to \mathfrak{R}$ is called a *value function* if it has the following properties:

1. $v(x^*) > v(x)$, if x^* dominates x.
2. $v(x^*) > v(x)$, if x^* is preferred to x.
3. $v(x^*) \geq v(x)$, if x^* is at least as preferred as x.

Thus v represents a *rational* DM's preferences over the criterion vectors provided that x does not dominate x^* in 2 and 3.

In MOLP models, the DM aims at selecting among the efficient solutions the one that maximizes his/her value function, i.e., what he or she finds out to be the best. It is important to note that the approaches to solve MOLP problems do not usually aim on defining the value function itself; in many approaches only some rather general assumptions about the form of the function are made.

There are numerous methods to solve MOLP problems; see, e.g., Steuer (1986). In the early age of MOLP, the methods were typically based on the nonnegative criterion weights of a linear value function. The problem of this approach is that it limits the possible solutions to extreme point solutions. In terms of the problem illustrated in Figs. 4.1 and 4.2, this means that depending on weighting the approach would present one of the three extreme points from the set of efficient solutions as the best one.

Currently most of the approaches are based on aspiration levels and their projections to efficient surface with Tchebycheff-type achievement scalarizing functions developed by Wierzbicki (1980) (see Sect. 4.3). Steuer and Choo (1983) proposed a similar idea, which is not so general as Wierzbicki's approach. Wierzbicki's approach projects any feasible or infeasible point onto the efficient frontier. Korhonen and Laakso (1986) extended the approach by presenting the parameterization of the achievement scalarizing functions thus allowing the projection of a direction instead of a single point to the surface. Parameterization makes it possible to freely search the efficient frontier.

The approaches based on achievement scalarizing functions do not aim at determining the value function of the DM. Instead, they seek to search the best solution in interaction with him/her. Some assumptions on the form of the value function are made concerning the terminations of the search. There are several variations of this basic approach, as well as several computer implementations. Korhonen et al. (1992) classify them into three main categories:

1. The system generates a finite set of solutions for DM's evaluation. At each iteration, the size of the search area is reduced (Fig. 4.3).

   This approach is presented under the name of *weighted Tchebycheff procedure* in Steuer and Choo (1983).

Fig. 4.3 (**a, b**) Generating
efficient solutions

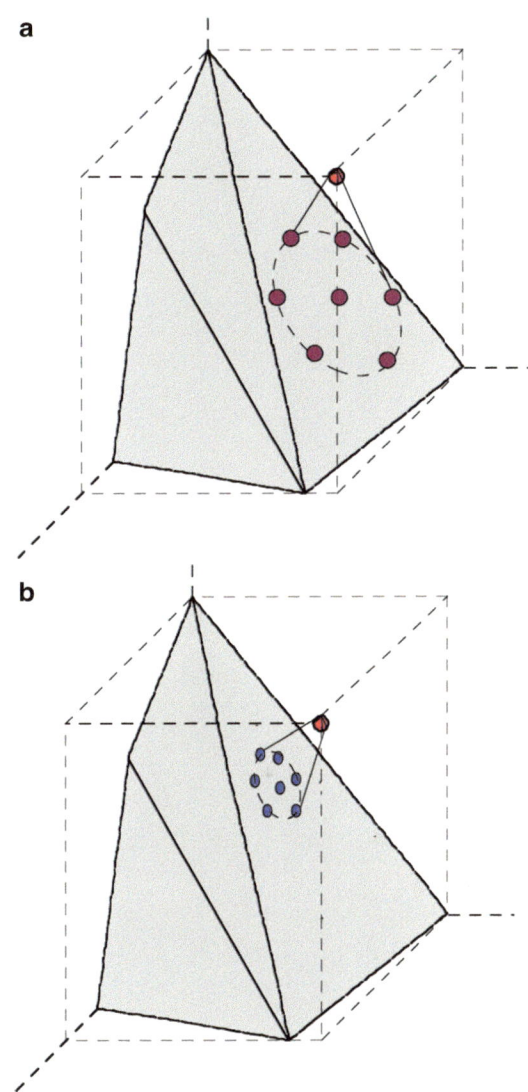

2. A DM freely specifies aspiration levels for the criteria, and the system projects them onto the set of efficient solutions (Fig. 4.4).

   This approach is implemented in DIDAS models; see Lewandowski et al. (1989).

3. A DM moves freely on the efficient frontier (Fig. 4.5).

   This approach is implemented in the VIG system (Korhonen 1987) under the name of Pareto Race (Korhonen and Wallenius 1988).

Fig. 4.4 (**a**, **b**) Projecting
an aspiration level point
onto efficient surface

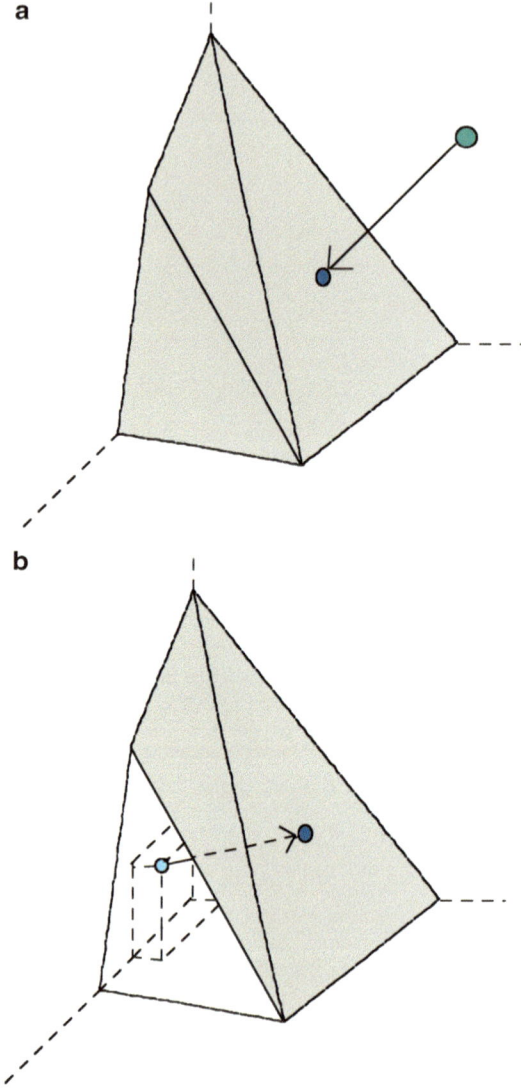

In this work we concentrate on the reference point approach by Wierzbicki (1980) and its extension, the reference direction approach by Korhonen and Laakso (1986). The reference point approach to solve MOLPs and DEA is structurally very similar, as we are going to show in Chap. 5. This finding is an important theoretical cornerstone when we later in this work introduce some MOLP-based DEA extension to incorporate preference information. The extension of the reference point approach, the reference direction approach, can provide flexibility and augmentations to DEA models, as discussed in Chap. 7.

Fig. 4.5 (**a**, **b**) Moving on the efficient frontier

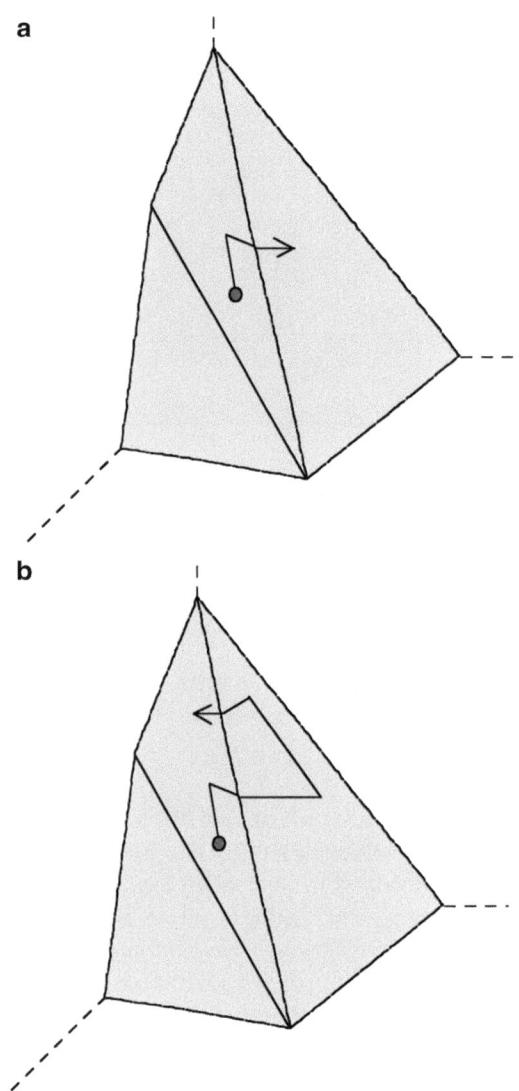

4.3   Reference Point Approach to Solving MOLP Problems

For characterizing the nondominated set, Wierzbicki (1980) suggested the use of an achievement (scalarizing) function (ASF). Consider the following problem:

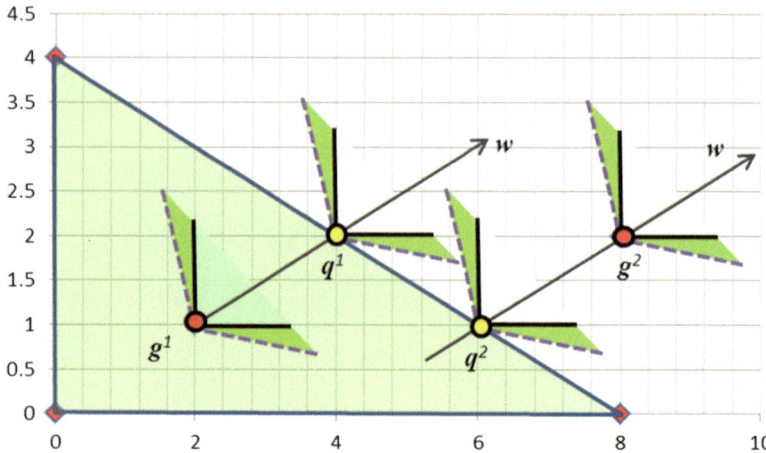

Fig. 4.6 Illustrating the projection of a feasible and infeasible aspiration level point onto the nondominated surface

$$\min \ s(\boldsymbol{g}, \boldsymbol{q}, \boldsymbol{w}, \rho) = \min \left\{ \max[(g_i - q_i)/w_i, \ i = 1, 2, \ldots, p] + \rho \sum_{i=1}^{p} (g_i - q_i) \right\}$$

s.t.
$$\boldsymbol{q} = Q = \left\{ \boldsymbol{q} = \mathbf{C}\boldsymbol{x} \middle| \boldsymbol{x} \in X \right\} \tag{4.3}$$

where s is the ASF, $\boldsymbol{w} > \boldsymbol{0}$, $\boldsymbol{w} \in \Re^p$, is a vector of weights, $\rho > 0$ is a scalar, and $P = \{1, 2, \ldots, p\}$. Vector $\boldsymbol{g} \in \Re^p$ is a given point in the objective function space, the components of which are called *aspiration levels*, and $\boldsymbol{q} \in Q$. Using (4.3), we may project any given (feasible or infeasible) point $\boldsymbol{g} \in \Re^p$ onto the set of nondominated solutions. The following two theorems provide the necessary theoretical basis.

The term $\rho \sum_{i=1}^{p}(g_i - v_i)$, $\rho > 0$, is required to guarantee that the solution of model (4.3) is efficient—not only weakly efficient. If $\rho = 0$, then the indifference curves of the scalarizing function should coincide with the coordinate axes, which define the positive orthant (see Fig. 4.6) where the positive orthant is defined with solid lines. If $\rho > 0$, it means that those axes are bent outward (see dotted lines in Fig. 4.6).

Theorem 4.1 Let $\boldsymbol{w} > \boldsymbol{0}$ be an arbitrary vector. Point $\boldsymbol{x}^* \in X$ is efficient if $\exists \, \boldsymbol{g} \in \Re^p$ and $\rho > 0$ such that $\boldsymbol{q}^* = \mathbf{C}\boldsymbol{x}^*$ is a solution of (4.3). If $\boldsymbol{x}^* \in X$ is efficient, then $\exists$ $\rho > 0$ such that $\boldsymbol{q}^* = \mathbf{C}\boldsymbol{x}^*$ is a solution of (4.3), when $\boldsymbol{g} = \boldsymbol{q}^*$. Then the optimal value of $s(\boldsymbol{g}, \boldsymbol{q}, \boldsymbol{w}, \rho)$ is zero.

Proof See, e.g., Wierzbicki (1986).   □

Theorem 4.2 Let $w > 0$ be an arbitrary vector. Point $x^* \in X$ is weakly efficient if $\exists$ $g \in \Re^p$ and $\rho \geq 0$ such that $q^* = Cx^*$ is a solution of (4.2). If $x^* \in X$ is weakly efficient, then $q^* = Cx^*$ is a solution of (4.2), when $g = q^*$ and $\rho = 0$. Then the optimal value of $s(g, v, w, 0)$ is zero.

Proof See, e.g., Wierzbicki (1986, Theorem 10).   □

   To illustrate the use of the ASF, consider a two-criterion problem from Arbel and Korhonen (1996) with a feasible region having three extreme points $\{(0, 0),$ $(8, 0),$ and $(0, 4)\}$, as shown in Fig. 4.6. Let us assume that the DM first specifies a feasible aspiration level point $g^1 = (2, 1)$. Using a weight vector $w = [2, 1]^T$, the minimum value of the ASF (-1) is reached at a point $q^1 = (4, 2)$ $(\min\{(2 - 4)/2,$ $(1 - 2)/1\} = -1)$ (cf. Fig. 4.6). Correspondingly, if an aspiration level point is infeasible, say $g^2 = (8, 2)$, then the minimum of the ASF $(+1)$ is reached at point $q^2 = (6, 1)$ $(\min\{(8 - 6)/2, (2 - 1)/1\} = 1)$.

   When a feasible point dominates the aspiration level point, then the value of the ASF is always negative; otherwise, it is nonnegative. It is zero if an aspiration level point is only weakly nondominated. Figure 4.6 illustrates the behavior of the achievement scalarizing function. If $\rho = 0$, then ASF consists of the first term:

$$\min\ s(g, q, w, \rho) = \min\{\max[(g_i - q_i)/w_i, \quad i = 1, 2, \dots, p]\} \qquad (4.4)$$

The solid lines up and right at points g^i and q^i, $i = 1, 2$, represent the values where function (4.4) has the same value as at the corresponding point. When $\rho > 0$, then those lines bend outward guaranteeing that the solution is not only weakly efficient. How much the lines bend depends on the magnitude of $\rho > 0$.

   Given $g \in \Re^p$ and $w > 0 \in \Re^p$, the minimum of $s(g, q, w, \rho)$ is found by solving the following LP problem (see, e.g., Wierzbicki 1980):

$$\min\ \varepsilon + \rho \sum_{i=1}^{p}(g_i - q_i)$$

$$\text{s.t.} \qquad\qquad\qquad\qquad\qquad\qquad\qquad\qquad (4.5)$$

$$x \in X$$
$$x \geq 0$$
$$\varepsilon \geq (g_i - C_i x)/w_i, \quad i = 1, 2, \dots, p$$

where C_i $(i = 1, 2, \dots, p)$ refers to the ith row of the objective function matrix C. Problem (4.5) can be further written as

$$\min \ \varepsilon + \rho \sum_{i=1}^{p} (g_i - q_i)$$

$$\text{s.t.} \tag{4.6}$$

$$x \in X$$
$$Cx + \varepsilon w - z = g$$
$$x, z \geq 0$$

Because $w_i \varepsilon = z_i + (g_i - C_i x) = z_i + (g_i - q_i)$, $i = 1, 2, \ldots, p$, we may write the objective function of (4.6) in the form

$$\varepsilon + \rho \sum_{i=1}^{p} (w_i \varepsilon - z_i) = \varepsilon(1 + \omega\rho) - \rho \sum_{i=1}^{p} z_i = (1 + \omega\rho) \left[\varepsilon - \frac{\rho}{1 + \omega\rho} \sum_{i=1}^{p} z_i \right],$$

where $\omega = \sum_{i=1}^{p} w_i$.

By writing $\delta = \frac{\rho}{1+\omega\rho}$, we may replace the objective function in (4.5) by

$$\varepsilon - \delta \mathbf{1}^T z$$

where $\delta > 0$ may assume to be a "non-Archimedean" such as in DEA as well (Chap. 2).

Thus we obtain

Table 4.1 The primal and dual formulation of the reference point approach

Original reference point primal (ORPP)		Original reference point dual (ORPD)	
min $\varepsilon - \delta \mathbf{1}^T z$		max $v^T g - u^T b$	
s.t.	(4.7a)	s.t.	(4.7b)
$\quad Cx + \varepsilon w - z = g$		$\quad v^T C - u^T A \leq 0$	
$\quad Ax \leq b$		$\quad v^T w = 1$	
$\quad x, z \geq 0$		$\quad v \geq \delta \mathbf{1}$	
$\quad \delta > 0$ ("Non-Archimedean")		$\quad u \geq 0$	
		$\quad \delta > 0$ ("Non-Archimedean")	

In the reference point approach, it is possible to scan the efficient frontier either by varying the weighting vector w or the aspiration level vector g (Table 4.1). In the first case, we have to use g with all components higher than or at least equal to the ideal values of the objectives (see, e.g., Fig. 4.3).

4.4 Reference Direction Approach to Solving MOLP Problems

In the reference direction approach by Korhonen and Laakso (1986), a direction d instead of a point is projected onto the efficient frontier. This is done through the parameterization of the achievement scalarizing function.

The reference direction models (4.8a) and (4.8b) are obtained from models (4.7a) and (4.7b) replacing g by $g + td$. Thus in the reference direction models (4.8a) and (4.8b) any direction d can be projected onto the efficient frontier. The reference direction formulation can be solved with the parametric linear programming technique: thus it is possible to provide the user with information in real time even when the problem is of realistic size. This guarantees true interactivity (Table 4.2).

As a solution model (4.8) generates an efficient path from the current solution to some corner point of the efficient frontier as shown in Fig. 4.7:

Table 4.2 The primal and dual models of the reference direction approach

Original reference direction primal (ORDP)	Original reference direction dual (ORDD)
$\min\ \varepsilon - \delta \mathbf{1}^{\mathrm{T}} z$ s.t. (4.8a) $\quad Cx + \varepsilon w - z = g + td$ $\quad Ax \le b$ $\quad x, z \ge 0$ $\quad t : 0 \to \infty$	$\min\ v^{\mathrm{T}}(g + dt) - u^{\mathrm{T}} b$ s.t. (4.8b) $\quad v^{\mathrm{T}} C - u^{\mathrm{T}} A \le 0$ $\quad v^{\mathrm{T}} w = 1$ $\quad v \ge \delta \mathbf{1}$ $\quad u \ge 0$ $\quad \delta > 0, t : 0 \to \infty$

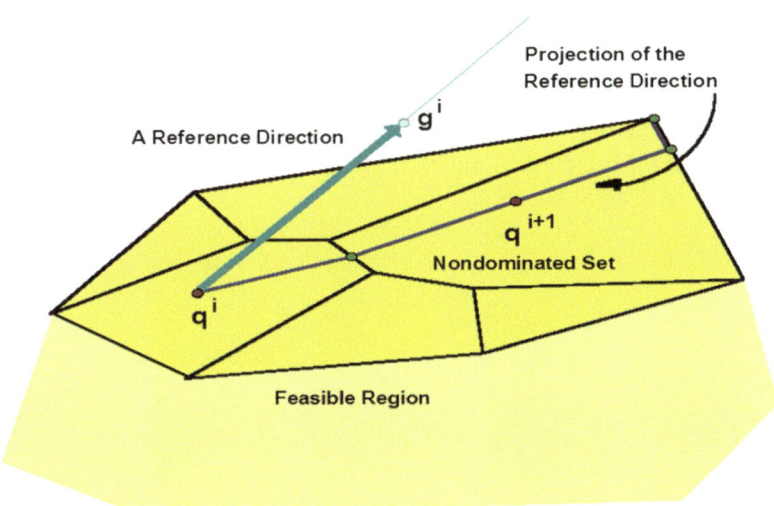

Fig. 4.7 Illustration of the reference direction approach

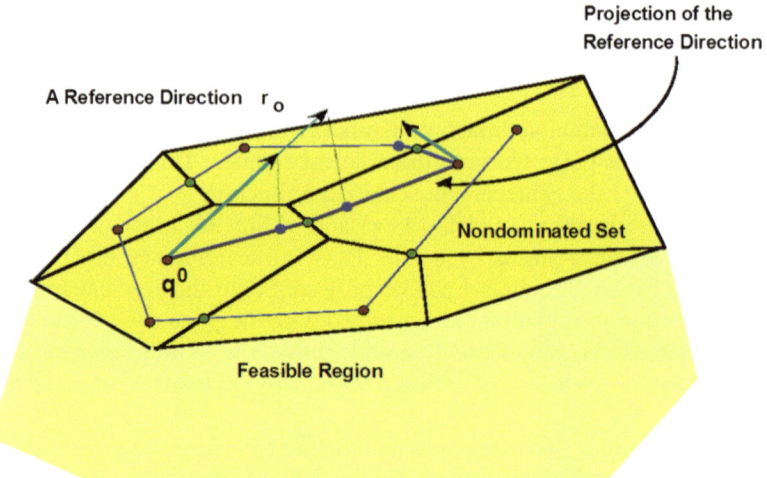

Fig. 4.8 Illustration of the dynamic version of the reference direction approach

Korhonen and Wallenius (1988) developed a dynamic version of the reference point approach that allows the DM to make a free search at any part of the efficient frontier as illustrated in Fig. 4.8:

The dynamic version, Pareto Race, is implemented in the VIG software (Korhonen 1987). With the software the DM can freely search the efficient frontier. The interface to control the speed and the direction of the movements is analogous to driving a car: he/she can accelerate, brake, and make turns. By using the interface to indicate which objectives he/she would like to improve and how strongly the DM implicitly specifies the reference direction. All the time he/she sees from the computer screen as figures and bar graphs how the values of the criteria, or the inputs and the outputs, change while he/she moves around the efficient frontier.

In terms of equation 4.8a, the right-hand side term td is used to control the movements along the efficient frontier: reference vector d controls the direction of movements, and scalar t the speed.

Figure 4.9 shows a Pareto Race screen where the values of criteria, or inputs and outputs with DEA terminology, are shown in numeric form and as bar graphs.

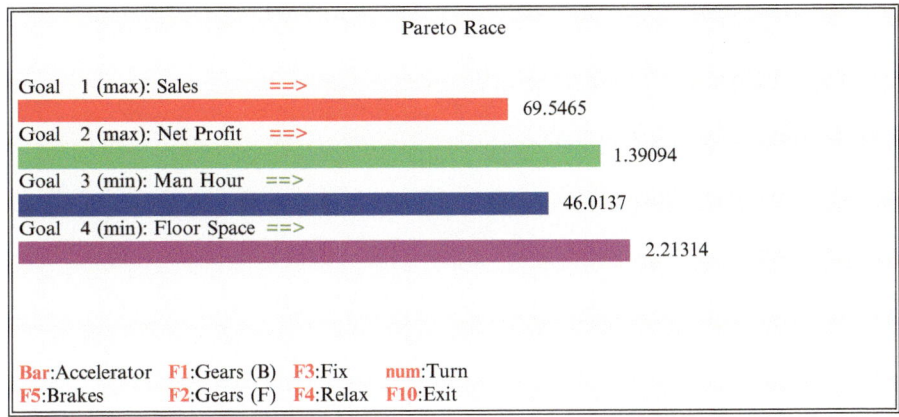

Fig. 4.9 Pareto Race screen

References

Arbel A, Korhonen P (1996) Using aspiration levels in interactive interior multiobjective linear programming algorithm. Eur J Oper Res 89:193–201

Charnes A, Cooper WW (1961) Management models and industrial applications of linear programming. Wiley, New York

Dantzig GB, Thapa MN (1997) Linear programming 1: introduction. Springer, New York

Korhonen P (1987) VIG—a visual interactive support system for multiple criteria decision making. Belg J Oper Res Stat Comput Sci 27:3–15

Korhonen P (2001) Multiple objective programming support. In: Floudas A, Pardalos P (eds) Encyclopedia of optimization, vol III. Kluwer Academic, Dortrecht, pp 566–574

Korhonen P, Laakso J (1986) A visual interactive method for solving the multiple criteria problem. Eur J Oper Res 24:277–287

Korhonen P, Wallenius J (1988) A pareto race. Nav Res Log 35:615–623

Korhonen PH, Moskowitz A, Wallenius J (1992) Multiple criteria decision support—a review. Eur J Oper Res 63:361–375

Lewandowski A, Kreglewski T, Rogowski T, Wierzbicki A (1989) Decision support systems of DIDAS family (dynamic interactive decision analysis & support). In: Lewandowski A, Wierzbicki A (eds) Aspiration based decision support systems. Springer, Berlin, pp 21–47

Miettinen K (1994) On the methodology of multiobjective optimization with applications. Doctoral dissertation, University of Jyväskylä, Jyväskylä

Miettinen K (1999) Nonlinear multiobjective optimization. Kluwer Academic, Boston

Steuer RE (1986) Multiple criteria optimization: theory, computation and application. Wiley, New York

Steuer RE, Choo EU (1983) An interactive weighted Tchebycheff procedure for multiple objective programming. Math Program 26:326–344

Wierzbicki A (1980) The use of reference objectives in multiobjective optimization. In: Fandel G, Gal T (eds) Multiple objective decision making, theory and application. Springer, New York

Wierzbicki A (1986) On the completeness and constructiveness of parametric characterizations to vector optimization problems. OR Spektrum 8:73–87

Chapter 5
Comparison of Data Envelopment Analysis and Multiple Objective Linear Programming

Structural Similarities Between DEA and MOLP

5.1 Background

Charnes and Cooper have played a significant role in the development of both areas: they have been the initiators of DEA in the late 1970s, but they have also had a significant impact on the development of multiple objective linear programming (MOLP) through the development of goal programming (Charnes and Cooper 1961). Although the methods have shared origins, researchers in these two camps have generally not paid much attention to research performed in the other camps. Neither has Charnes nor Cooper attempted to tie the two fields together. This is unfortunate, since—despite differences in terminology—DEA and MOLP address similar problems and the corresponding models are structurally very close to each other.

   In both models, technically speaking, the purpose is to identify efficient points in a certain space and suggest projections of inefficient (or any given) points on the basis of such information. In DEA the projection is performed by letting some mathematical program determine weights that (in the envelopment side) associate the analyzed point with the best possible efficiency score. In MOLP, the direction of the projection is based on the use of weights (more generally, parameters), which the DM can directly or indirectly influence reflecting his/her preference structure.

   The main difference in MOLP and DEA has traditionally been the use of the models: MOLPs, as other MCDM methods, are considered to be ex ante planning tools, whereas DEA is considered to be an ex post evaluation tool (Cooper 1996). Lately however there have emerged DEA approaches that are to be used more in planning phase, e.g., helping the inefficient DMUs to set appropriate targets.

   The first attempts to combine the DEA and MOLP approaches were presented by Golany (1988). He proposed the use of an interactive procedure to generate efficient solutions for characterizing the efficient frontier in DEA in a way somewhat similar to the weighted Tchebycheff procedure by Steuer and Choo (1983). Kornbluth (1991) pointed out that DEA problems could be expressed as multiple objective

© Springer Science+Business Media New York 2015   55
T. Joro, P.J. Korhonen, *Extension of Data Envelopment Analysis with Preference Information*, International Series in Operations Research & Management Science 218, DOI 10.1007/978-1-4899-7528-7_5

linear fractional programming problems. Cook and Kress (1991) presented a DEA-based structure to aggregate ordinal preference rankings across multiple criteria.

Doyle and Green (1993) criticized the review article on MCDM by Stewart (1992) for ignoring the DEA literature; see also Stewart (1993). They considered DEA—correctly, in our opinion—as an MCDM method. For the same reason, Belton (1992) called DEA and MCDM researchers to communicate with each other. It is easy to agree with her that "the two approaches can be integrated to provide a more effective and easier way to understand approach to performance measurement...." Belton has discussed the role of weights in DEA and contrasted the weighting to the preference weighting in MCDM approaches. See also Belton and Vickers (1993).

Yu et al. (1996a, b) discussed the equivalence between DEA efficiency and the nondominated solutions of a corresponding multi-objective program. Tofallis (1996) criticized DEA for failing to provide discrimination between a small number of alternatives and proposed the use of a multicriteria approach. Stewart (1996) discussed the relationships between DEA and MCDM addressing especially the concepts of efficiency and Pareto optimality as well as the role of weights. Joro et al. (1998) pointed out the structural similarity between DEA formulations and reference point approach to solve MOLP models. Belton and Stewart (1999) discussed whether DEA and MCDM should be viewed as competing or complementary approaches and commented the use of weight restriction from MCDM viewpoint.

Li and Reeves (1999) introduced multiple objective data envelopment analysis model that aims improving discriminating power of DEA without a priori information on the weights. In their approach several different efficiency measures, including classical DEA, are defined under the same constraints. Each of these measures serves as a criterion to be optimized, and efficiencies are then evaluated under the framework of multiple objective linear programming. Post and Spronk (1999) suggested the use of interactive multiple goal programming approach (see Spronk (1981)) to set targets in DEA framework. Bouyssou (1999) criticized the use of DEA as an MCDM tool. Ballestero (1999) proposed a single-priced MCDA model to evaluate efficiency. Wei et al. (2000) proposed an inverse DEA model to solve how much more outputs a unit should produce when its inputs are increased in order to maintain the efficiency at the same level. The problem is solved as a multiple objective programming model.

5.2   Comparison of the Models and Their Use

One of the characteristics of the DEA discipline is that it sees itself as an *application-driven theory*. And indeed many DEA extensions are based on a need that emerged in a real-life application. DEA applications are found on various areas on both public and private sector: education, health care, industry, banking, etc. DEA being a method for evaluating the relative efficiency, a typical DEA application seeks to compare and contrast a set of units to identify the good and bad performers.

MCDM approaches such as an MOLP seek to solve problems that are characterized by a presence of several conflicting objectives. Inside the MCDM discipline a key role is given to a DM whose preferences are to be incorporated into the model. Steuer (1986) illustrates possible MOLP application areas by mentioning scheduling, production planning, portfolio selection, capital budgeting, forest management, reservoir release policies, allocation, transportation, and blending.

One traditional fundamental difference has been that MCDM approaches such as MOLP are based on revealing and modeling the values and preferences of a DM and seeking for interaction with him/her whereas DEA on the other hand has traditionally sought a value-free or value neutral approach. However, lately among DEA scholars there has been interest towards extensions that incorporate price and preference information (see Chap. 4 for a review on MOLP), and this tendency makes the dialogue between these two areas important.

The key difference in the terminology is that instead of DEA's input and output concepts, the MOLP deals with objectives that are to be maximized or minimized. With MOLP terminology the DEA model is either minimizing inputs with given output levels (input oriented), maximizing outputs with given input levels (output oriented) or simultaneously minimizing inputs and maximizing outputs (combined).

5.3   Structural Similarities Between DEA and MOLP

Let us first consider the output-oriented envelopment model (2.5b) and the reference point approach to solve MOLP problems ((4.7) and reproduced in (5.1) below):

$$\min \ \varepsilon - \delta \mathbf{1}^{\mathrm{T}} \mathbf{z}$$
$$\text{s.t.} \tag{5.1}$$
$$\mathbf{C}x + \varepsilon w - z = g$$
$$\mathbf{A}x \leq b$$
$$x, z \geq \mathbf{0}, \delta > 0$$

where $x \in \mathfrak{R}^n$, $w \in \mathfrak{R}^k_+$, $b \in \mathfrak{R}^k$, the constraint matrix $\mathbf{A} \in \mathfrak{R}^{k \times n}$ is of full rank k, and the objective function matrix $\mathbf{C} \in \mathfrak{R}^{p \times n}$. After inequality $\delta > 0$, we may write "non-Archimedean" as in DEA models. In practice, we have to give a small numerical value to $\delta > 0$.[1]

---

[1]Another way is to define an objective function lexicographically: lex min $\{ \varepsilon, -\delta \mathbf{1}^{\mathrm{T}} z \}$. The latter function is only needed if the solution of ε is not unique.

Table 5.1 Comparison of reference point and output-oriented CCR models

Reference point model	Output-oriented CCR model (envelopment)
max $\sigma + \varepsilon \mathbf{1}^T s^+$ s.t. (5.2a) $\mathbf{Y}\lambda - \sigma y_0 - s^+ = y_0$ $\mathbf{X}\lambda + s^- = x_0$ $\lambda,\ s^-, s^+ \geq \mathbf{0}$ $\varepsilon > 0$ (Non-Archimedean)	max $\sigma + \varepsilon(\mathbf{1}^T s^+ + \mathbf{1}^T s^-)$ s.t. (5.2b) $\mathbf{Y}\lambda - \sigma y_0 - s^+ = y_0$ $\mathbf{X}\lambda + s^- = x_0$ $\lambda,\ s^-, s^+ \geq \mathbf{0}$ $\varepsilon > 0$ (Non-Archimedean)

To compare the structures of the two models, we interpret the reference point model (4.7) as a model in which n DMUs use k inputs to produce p outputs. Accordingly, we change notation to correspond to the DEA model, i.e., $\mathbf{C} \to \mathbf{Y}, x \to \lambda, \mathbf{A} \to \mathbf{X}, b \to x_0, z \to s^+, w = y_0, g \to y_0, -\varepsilon \to \sigma, \delta \to \varepsilon$. Furthermore, we assume that $\mathbf{C} \in \mathfrak{R}_+^{p \times n}$ and $\mathbf{A} \in \mathfrak{R}_+^{k \times n}$. The reference point model and the output-oriented CCR model are compared in Table 5.1.

As we can see, there is only one difference between the models: in the DEA model, there is a slack vector associated with the inputs in the objective functions. It means that in the MOLP-model, "inefficiency" in the use of the constraints (here inputs) is not interesting, and the efficiency of point (y_0, x_0) does not depend on x_0. If point (y_0, x_0) is efficient, then point (y_0, x_1) is as well even if $x_1 > x_0$. Instead, in DEA model "inefficiency" in the use of the inputs makes the point (y_0, x_1) inefficient if $x_1 > x_0$.

On the other hand, we may use the analogy between reference point and DEA model and introduce the so-called general combined DEA model (cf. Table 3.3). We change the notation of the reference point model as follows:

$$\mathbf{C} \to \begin{bmatrix} \mathbf{Y} \\ -\mathbf{X} \end{bmatrix}, \quad x \to \lambda, \quad z \to \begin{bmatrix} s^+ \\ s^- \end{bmatrix} > 0, \quad g \to \begin{bmatrix} g^y \\ -g^x \end{bmatrix}, \quad w \to \begin{bmatrix} w^y \\ w^x \end{bmatrix} > 0,$$

$$-\varepsilon \to \sigma, \quad \delta \to \varepsilon$$

where $\mathbf{X} \in \mathfrak{R}_+^{m \times n}$, $\mathbf{Y} \in \mathfrak{R}_+^{s \times n}$, $s^+ \in \mathfrak{R}_+^s$, $s^- \in \mathfrak{R}_+^m$, $g^y \in \mathfrak{R}^s$, $g^x \in \mathfrak{R}_+^m$, $w^y \in \mathfrak{R}_+^s$, $w^x \in \mathfrak{R}_+^m$, and $m + s = p$. Thus we interpret the reference point model (5.1) as a model in which n DMUs use m inputs to produce s outputs ($m + s = p$) and try to simultaneously minimize the use of inputs and maximize the amount of outputs produced. In addition, we have some constraints in the model. In Table 5.2, we have the reference point model using DEA notation and its dual.

In the sequel, we will call the reference point primal model in Table 5.2 the *general combined envelopment model*, and the dual model is called the *general combined multiplier model*. The generalization means that we can:

1. Project any point belonging or not belonging to the production possibility set.

2. Use in the projection any vector $w = \begin{bmatrix} w^y \\ w^x \end{bmatrix} \geq \mathbf{0},\ w \neq \mathbf{0}$ as the projection vector.

3. Add some extra constraints $\mathbf{A}\lambda \leq b$ into the model.

Table 5.2 The primal and dual reference point model with DEA notation

Reference point primal model (RP$_p$)	Reference point dual model (RP$_D$)
max $\sigma + \varepsilon\left(\mathbf{1}^T s^+ + \mathbf{1}^T s^-\right)$ s.t. $\qquad\qquad\qquad\qquad$ (5.3a) $\qquad \mathbf{Y}\lambda - \sigma w^y - s^+ = g^y$ $\qquad \mathbf{X}\lambda + \sigma w^x + s^- = g^x$ $\qquad \mathbf{A}\lambda \leq b$ $\qquad \lambda, s^-, s^+ \geq 0$ $\qquad \varepsilon > 0$ (Non-Archimedean)	min $v^T g^x - \mu^T g^y + u^T b$ s.t. $\qquad\qquad\qquad\qquad$ (5.3b) $\qquad -\mu^T \mathbf{Y} + v^T \mathbf{X} + u^T \mathbf{A} \geq 0$ $\qquad \mu^T w^y + v^T w^x = 1$ $\qquad \mu, v \geq \varepsilon \mathbf{1}$ $\qquad u \geq 0$ $\qquad \varepsilon > 0$ (Non-Archimedean)

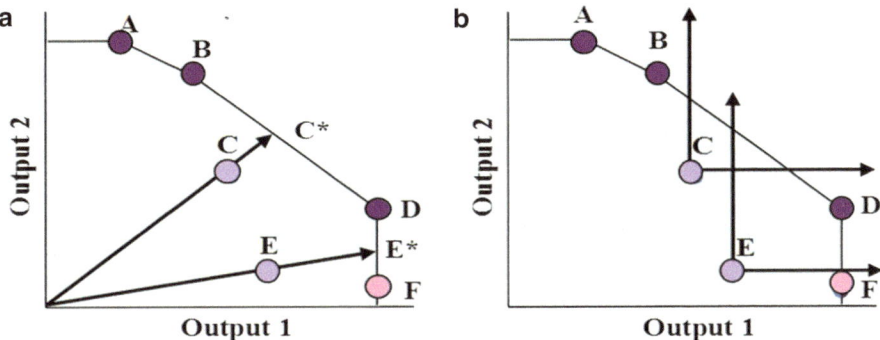

Fig. 5.1 (a, b) Illustrations of standard DEA and MOLP

The general combined model consists of, e.g., standard DEA models (CRS, VRS, NIRS, and NDRS) as special cases by choosing the constraints $\mathbf{A}\lambda \leq b$ in a suitable way. Furthermore, it provides a DM with a possibility to project a target point onto the efficient frontier. By carrying weighting vectors different efficient points can be generated. By setting suitable values to weights and aspiration levels, we can obtain different radial and models, as discussed in Chap. 3. Thus DEA formulations in Chap. 2 can be derived from the reference point formulation.

The ideas underlying the DEA and reference point models are illustrated in Fig. 5.1a, b. We assume that $m = 1$, $p = 2$, and $\mathbf{X} = \mathbf{1}^T$. In addition, in Fig. 5.1, we assume that $g = y_0$ and $b = b = 1$. In DEA (Fig. 5.1a), the projected point for C is C* and for E it is E*, or D, if it is required to be efficient (and not only weakly efficient). In MOLP (Fig. 5.1b), the projection of points C and E depends on the weighting vector used in the ASF. In any case, the projection is one of the (weakly) efficient points dominating points C and E, respectively. The vectors spanning the dominating cones are shown in Fig. 5.1.

In summary, DEA projects DMUs radially to the efficient frontier providing each unit with a target. In MOLP it is possible to project a DMU to any efficient point by changing either a projection vector w or aspiration levels (target) g.

Thus with reference point model, we may in addition to radial projections perform also nonradial projections. In Fig. 5.1 the points C and E belong to the

Table 5.3 The primal and dual reference direction approach models

Reference direction model primal (RD$_P$)	Reference direction model dual (RD$_D$)
max $\sigma + \varepsilon \mathbf{1}^{\mathrm{T}}(s^+ + s^-)$ s.t. $\qquad\qquad\qquad\qquad$ (5.4a) $\quad \mathbf{Y}\lambda - \sigma w^y - s^+ = g^y + t d^y$ $\quad \mathbf{X}\lambda + \sigma w^x + s^- = g^x + t d^x$ $\quad \mathbf{A}\lambda \leq b$ $\quad \lambda,\ s^-,\ s^+ \geq 0$ $\quad \varepsilon > 0$ (Non-Archimedean) $\quad t : 0 \rightarrow \infty$	min $v^{\mathrm{T}}(g^x + t d^x) - \mu^{\mathrm{T}}(g^y + t d^y) + u^{\mathrm{T}} b$ s.t. $\qquad\qquad\qquad\qquad$ (5.4b) $\quad -\mu^{\mathrm{T}}\mathbf{Y} + v^{\mathrm{T}}\mathbf{X} + u^{\mathrm{T}}\mathbf{A} \geq \mathbf{0}$ $\quad \mu^{\mathrm{T}} w^y + v^{\mathrm{T}} w^x = 1$ $\quad \mu,\ v \geq \varepsilon \mathbf{1}$ $\quad u \geq \mathbf{0}$ $\quad \varepsilon > 0$ (Non-Archimedean) $\quad t : 0 \rightarrow \infty$

production possibility set. The reference point approach does not require this property. The points to be projected onto the efficient frontier can be any points. The points can also be changed dynamically by using a parametric linear programming by using the model in Table 5.3. This property provides us with a practical tool to make a search on the efficient frontier (see Fig. 5.1).

By varying the scalar t and vector (d^x, d^y), this model can be used to investigate the efficient frontier in any scale assumption specified by $\mathbf{A}\lambda \leq b$.

5.4   An Example Demonstrating the Use of MOLP and DEA

In this section, we will demonstrate how MOLP and DEA together can be used to help a DM to analyze the efficiency of DMUs and find the ways to improve it. As we mentioned in Sect. 5.1, MOLPs, as other MCDM methods, are considered to be ex ante planning tool, whereas DEA is considered to be an ex post evaluation tool (Cooper 1996).

To illustrate the use of MOLP and DEA, let us consider the following example, which is originally extracted from a real application. The purpose was to analyze the performance of 25 firms (hypermarkets) and to reveal inefficient firms and find them guidelines to improve their performance. The original application consisted of more variables, but in our illustrative example only two outputs and two inputs are used. The outputs are "sales" (in money units) and "net profit" (in money units). The inputs are "man hours" (10^3 h) and floor space (10^3 m^2). "Man hours" refer to labor force available within a certain period and "floor space" is the total area of the market. The data set is given in Table 5.4. The example is adopted from Korhonen et al. (2002).

To make the considerations illustrative, throughout this section we will apply output-oriented BCC models, i.e., $\Lambda = \{\lambda \mid \lambda \in \mathfrak{R}_+^n$ and $\mathbf{1}^{\mathrm{T}}\lambda = 1\}$. The technical efficiency scores obtained by the standard output-oriented BCC model are in the last column of Table 5.4. Nine firms are efficient and the lowest efficiency score is 0.673 (DMU13).

Table 5.4 The values of output and input variables of 25 DMUs and their efficiency scores with the BCC model

DMUS	Outputs		Inputs		
	Sales	Net profit	Man hour	Floor space	Eff. scores
DMU1	115.266	1.708	79.056	4.986	0.821
DMU2	75.191	1.811	60.096	3.3	0.772
DMU3	225.454	10.393	126.699	8.117	1
DMU4	185.581	10.417	153.857	6.695	1
DMU5	84.52	2.357	65.684	4.735	0.769
DMU6	103.328	4.347	76.83	4.083	0.806
DMU7	78.755	0.162	50.157	2.531	1
DMU8	59.327	1.299	44.771	2.47	1
DMU9	65.718	1.485	48.058	2.324	1
DMU10	163.178	6.261	89.702	4.911	1
DMU11	70.679	2.802	56.923	2.24	1
DMU12	142.648	2.745	112.637	5.42	0.824
DMU13	127.767	2.701	106.869	6.281	0.673
DMU14	62.383	1.418	54.932	3.135	0.736
DMU15	55.225	1.375	48.809	4.43	0.803
DMU16	95.925	0.742	59.188	3.979	0.978
DMU17	121.604	3.059	74.514	5.318	0.93
DMU18	107.019	2.983	94.596	3.691	0.817
DMU19	65.402	0.618	47.042	3.001	0.969
DMU20	70.982	0.005	54.645	3.865	0.804
DMU21	81.175	5.121	90.116	3.31	0.858
DMU22	128.303	3.887	95.241	4.245	0.876
DMU23	134.989	4.728	80.079	3.786	1
DMU24	98.931	1.861	68.703	2.985	0.973
DMU25	66.743	7.409	62.282	3.1	1

Suppose that the manager of DMU13 would like to analyze possibilities to improve its performance. In addition to the technical efficiency score, DEA provides him/her with the reference values of the virtual unit, which will be found by projecting the output values of DMU13 onto the efficient frontier. The projection is carried out radially; the output values of DMU13 are improved proportionally until the boundary of the production possibility set is reached. In this case, the virtual unit found in this way is not efficient; it is only weakly efficient. The final efficient reference values are found by increasing "net profit" and decreasing "man hours" until the efficient frontier is reached. That point can be presented as a convex combination of DMU3 and DMU10 (the first row (A) Table 5.5).

However, the (virtual) unit (on row A) is only one possible benchmark for DMU13. Any convex combination between the values of A and B and that of B and C provides a possible benchmark for DMU13 to become efficient. The output values of those possible benchmarks are also displayed in Fig. 5.2.

Table 5.5 Alternative reference values for DMU13

Extreme points	DMU3	DMU4	DMU10	DMU25	Sales	Net profit	Man hour	Floor space
A	0.427		0.573		189.79	8.027	105.51	6.281
B	0.41	0.031	0.559		189.41	8.085	106.87	6.281
C	0.575	0.082		0.343	167.79	9.373	106.87	6.281

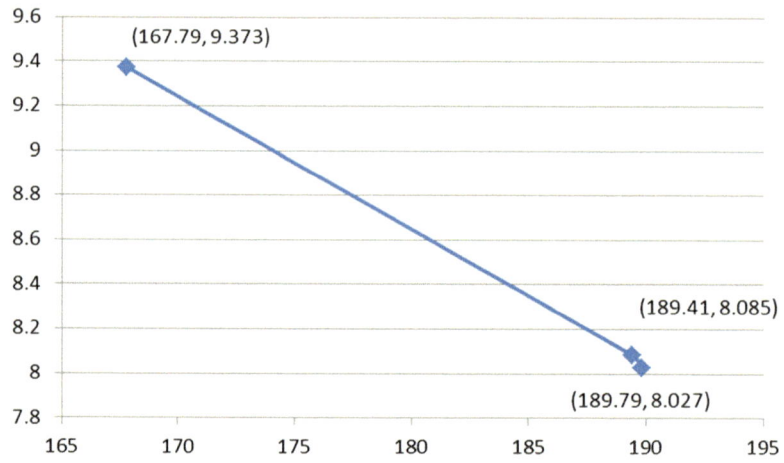

Fig. 5.2 Possible output benchmark values for the inefficient DMU13

If the manager of DMU13 would also like to control input values, then in the corresponding MOLP-model, the output values are maximized as before, but in addition to that, the input values are maximized. It means that the manager is looking for the benchmark for the DMU13 by varying output and input values simultaneously. To perform the search on the efficient frontier in case of four objective functions, a good software is required. Reflecting on our own bias, we use the VIG software (Korhonen 1987). VIG implements Pareto Race (see Fig. 5.2), a dynamic and visual free search type of interactive procedure for multiple objective linear programming (see, e.g., Korhonen and Wallenius 1988).

Pareto Race enables a DM to freely search any part of the efficient frontier by controlling the speed and direction of motion. The objective function values are represented in numeric form and as bar graphs on the computer screen (Fig. 5.3 see, for more details, Korhonen and Wallenius 1988).

In Table 5.6, we have summarized the main differences between reference point and DEA models.

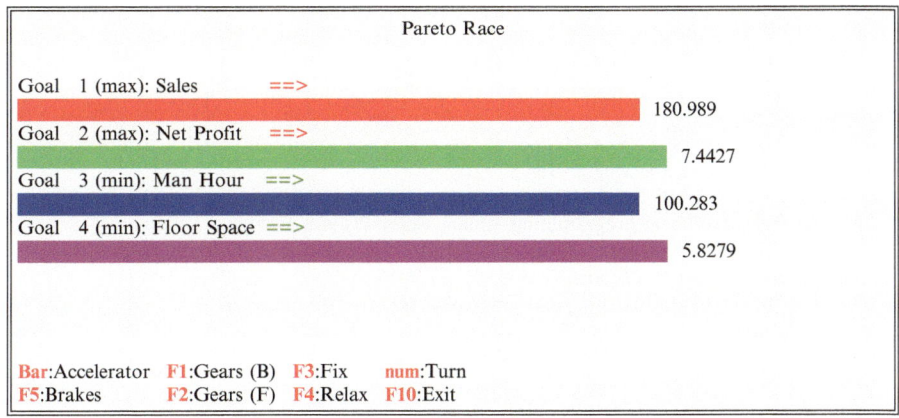

Fig. 5.3 Searching for the most preferred values for inputs and outputs

Table 5.6 Differences between a reference point and DEA model

DEA model	Reference point model
The "reference point" is a given and feasible point	Any point
Projection direction is based on the values of the "reference point" (=the point under consideration)	Projection direction is any nonnegative vector with at least one strictly positive element
Slack variables in the objective function are related to all inputs and outputs	Slack variables in the objective function are related to the rows corresponding to the original objectives
The amount of radial improvement of the current values of inputs and/or outputs is interesting (=an efficient score)	The amount of radial change is not interesting

References

Ballestero E (1999) Measuring efficiency by a single price system. Eur J Oper Res 115(3):616–623

Belton V (1992) An IDEA—integrating data envelopment analysis with multiple criteria decision analysis. In: Goicoechea A, Duckstein L, Zionts S (eds) Multiple criteria decision making. Proceedings of the ninth international conference. Springer, Berlin, pp 71–79

Belton V, Stewart T (1999) DEA and MCDA: competing or complementary approaches? In: Meskens N, Roubens M (eds) Advances in decision analysis. Kluwer, Dordrecht, pp 87–104

Belton V, Vickers SP (1993) Demystifying DEA—a visual interactive approach based on multiple criteria analysis. J Oper Res Soc 44:883–896

Bouyssou D (1999) DEA as a tool for MCDM: some remarks. J Oper Res Soc 50:974–978

Charnes A, Cooper WW (1961) Management models and industrial applications of linear programming. Wiley, New York

Cook WD, Kress M (1991) A multiple criteria decision model with ordinal preference data. Eur J Oper Res 54:191–198

Cooper WW (1996) Personal communication. Commentary letter on the manuscript of the article "Structural comparison of data envelopment analysis and multiple objective linear programming" by Joro T, Korhonen P, Wallenius J

Doyle RH, Green JR (1993) Data envelopment analysis and multiple criteria decision making. Omega 6:713–715

Golany B (1988) An interactive MOLP procedure for the extension of DEA to effectiveness analysis. J Oper Res Soc 39:725–734

Joro T, Korhonen P, Wallenius J (1998) Structural comparison of data envelopment analysis and multiple objective linear programming. Manag Sci 44(7):962–970

Korhonen P (1987) VIG—a visual interactive support system for multiple criteria decision making. Belg J Oper Res Statist Comput Sci 27:3–15

Korhonen P, Wallenius J (1988) A pareto race. Nav Res Log 35:615–623

Korhonen P, Siljamäki A, Soismaa M (2002) On the use of value efficiency analysis and further developments. J Prod Anal 17(1/2):49–64

Kornbluth JSH (1991) Analysing policy effectiveness using cone restricted data envelopment analysis. J Oper Res Soc 42:1097–1104

Li X-B, Reeves GR (1999) A multiple criteria approach to data envelopment analysis. Eur J Oper Res 115:507–517

Post T, Spronk J (1999) Performance benchmarking using interactive data envelopment analysis. Eur J Oper Res 115:472–487

Spronk J (1981) Interactive multiple goal programming: applications to financial planning. Kluwer, Boston

Steuer RE (1986) Multiple criteria optimization: theory, computation and application. Wiley, New York

Steuer RE, Choo EU (1983) An interactive weighted Tchebycheff procedure for multiple objective programming. Math Program 26:326–344

Stewart TJ (1992) A critical survey on the status of multiple criteria decision making theory and practice. Omega 20:569–586

Stewart TJ (1993) Data envelopment analysis and multiple criteria decision making: a response. Omega 22:205–206

Stewart TJ (1996) Relationships between data envelopment analysis and multicriteria decision analysis. J Oper Res Soc 47:654–665

Tofallis C (1996) Improving discernment in DEA using profiling. Omega 24(3):362–364

Wei Q, Zhang J, Zhang X (2000) An inverse DEA model for input/output estimate. Eur J Oper Res 121:151–163

Yu G, Wei Q, Brockett P (1996a) A generalized data envelopment model: a unification and extension of existing methods for efficiency analysis of decision making units. Ann Oper Res 66:47–89

Yu G, Wei Q, Brockett P, Zhou L (1996b) Construction of all DEA efficient surfaces of the production possibility set under the generalized data envelopment analysis model. Eur J Oper Res 95:491–510

Chapter 6
Incorporating Preference Information to Data Envelopment Analysis

Review and Classification of Preference-Based Approaches

6.1 Classification of Approaches

As discussed, DEA provides the DMUs under evaluation with an efficiency score and a projection point on the efficient frontier. The prior one describes the unit's performance with respect to the empirical efficient or best practice frontier, reflecting the distance from it. The latter one identifies the unit's projection on the efficient frontier and thus acts as a target point or a benchmark that the DMU should achieve in order to become efficient through radial output expansion and/or input reductions. Preference information can be incorporated to adjust both the efficiency scores and the targets.

However, before entering the details on incorporating preference information and especially before discussing the weight restriction methods, it is important to examine their role in DEA literature. One commonly faced problem in some practical DEA applications is that relatively many DMUs are diagnosed as efficient, when the number of inputs and/or outputs is relatively large with respect to the number of DMUs. In these cases DEA fails to discriminate between DMUs.

The problem is addressed often in weight restriction models but from two rather different viewpoints (see also Roll and Golany 1993; Cook et al. 1992):

1. Based on the weights resulted by the unbounded DEA model, some extreme weighting schemes are eliminated by restricting the acceptable variation of weights. This aims on maintaining the "value-free" concept of DEA.
2. The variation of weights is restricted based on preference information.

In this chapter we concentrate on incorporating preference information and thus share the way of thinking of the latter approach. It is important to note that when incorporating preference information into the model, the goal is not merely to increase discrimination between efficient DMUs. Instead, the purpose is to produce efficiency scores that also reflect the preferences that the DM has over different inputs and outputs. Especially important is to note that, in fact, some inefficient

© Springer Science+Business Media New York 2015
T. Joro, P.J. Korhonen, *Extension of Data Envelopment Analysis with Preference Information*, International Series in Operations Research & Management Science 218, DOI 10.1007/978-1-4899-7528-7_6

Table 6.1 Performance of students in exams

Students	EG	GG
A	6	1
B	6	2
C	5	4
D	3	5
E	1	7

Fig. 6.1 Illustration of weight restrictions

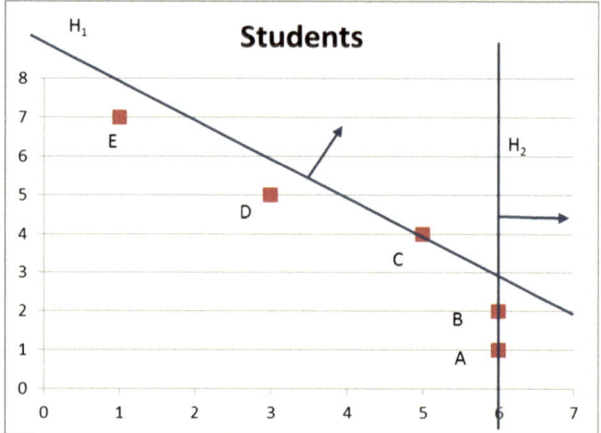

units may be "better" to the DM than some technically efficient units that are specialized against DM's preferences, or price their inputs and/or outputs against DM's perception of prices.

Let us consider a short example demonstrating the weight restrictions:

Example 6.1 Assume that a DM would like to evaluate the performance of students by using the outputs "the number of excellent grades" (EG) and "the number of good grades" (GG). The students have taken a different number of exams. The data of the example is shown in Table 6.1. We may assume a single constant input ($=1$) and the output-oriented constant returns to scale DEA model. The production possibility set is assumed convex.

As we can see from Fig. 6.1, students B, C, and E are efficient, A is only weakly efficient, and D is inefficient, but obviously efficient B, C, and E are not equal performers. Student C has most exams, five excellent grades and four good grades. Student E has more good grades, but less excellent grades. C is thus clearly better than E. To include this preference information into the model, we require that the weight of good grades is not higher than that of excellent grades (see Example 6.2). In Fig. 6.1, we have displayed two extreme "hyperplanes" H_1 and H_2. All other weights can be presented as the positive linear combination of these extreme weights: α [1,0] + β [0.5, 0.5] and $\beta \geq 0$. Note that $\alpha > 0$ because the only weakly efficient A is not allowed to be as good as B. Thus the potential best candidates are B and C.

There exist also other approaches that aim at increasing discrimination and producing rankings of efficient units but do not incorporate preference information. See, e.g., the above mentioned paper by Cook et al. (1992). See also Andersen and Petersen (1993) and Wilson (1995) for superefficiency models; Sexton et al. (1986) and also, e.g., Doyle and Green (1994) for cross-evaluation matrix approaches; and Torgersen et al. (1996) for slack-adjusted efficiency measures. See also Anderson et al. (2002) for a discussion on cross-evaluation model and fixed weighting in DEA. Various multivariate statistic tools have also been used to increase discrimination in DEA, first by Sinuany-Stern et al. (1994). See Adler et al. (2002) and Angulo-Meza and Lins (2002) for reviews on ranking methods.

6.1.1 Efficiency Scores with Preference Information

DEA, measuring the technical efficiency of DMUs, considers all the DMUs operating on the production frontier—i.e., being technically efficient—to be equally good. Thus the underlying assumption of the original DEA is that it is equally acceptable to specialize in producing any output or consuming any input. With respect to multiplier models, this means that the units may freely choose the weights for inputs and outputs. If the weights are interpreted as stable prices, this means that the units can use any prices for inputs or outputs.

However, in many cases free specialization or pricing is not acceptable or desirable. If we want to apply DEA in these situations, we need to be able to restrict the undesired specialization—i.e., we need to have a mechanism to *incorporate preferences over different inputs and outputs* into the model. With preference information we refer to the additional information based on price information, expert opinion, or preferences, values, or judgments of those having the control over the units whose performance is under evaluation.

With the price interpretation of the weights, this is a step from the analysis of technical efficiency into the direction of the analysis of overall efficiency: instead of complete price information, we incorporate some partial price information into the model. Another possible way to see these models is that based on the expert opinion, they move the empirical efficient frontier closer to the theoretical efficiency frontier. This interpretation is appealing especially in the approaches where unobserved DMUs are added into the model. We discuss the various weight restriction models in Sect. 6.2 and models based on adding artificial observations in Sect. 6.3. Furthermore, we will discuss the connections between weight restriction models and the approaches based on artificial observations in that section.

6.1.2   Setting Targets with Preference Information

DEA provides each inefficient DMUs with a target, a virtual unit from the efficient surface. In traditional DEA the targets are obtained by projecting the inefficient DMU radially to the efficient surface. The production theoretical argument for this principle is that the DMU preserves its current input and/or output mixes.

However, from a managerial point of view, it is possible that some other solutions on the efficient surface might be a more preferable target, i.e., there exists an input–output mix that is more suitable for the inefficient unit than the one obtained through radial projection.

One line of research in DEA concentrates on defining the targets for the inefficient DMUs. The DMU can use the targets as goals or benchmarks when working its way toward efficiency. In the target setting framework, the (management of the) inefficient DMU is often considered to be the decision makers that seek the best target; however, the DM can also be some other persons or entity having control over the DMUs.

In Sect. 6.4 our main focus is on approaches that firstly aim on *setting* a target for an existing or new DMU *reflecting the preferences* of the DM and secondly work within the DEA framework setting targets to inputs and outputs simultaneously with formulation resembling basic DEA models.

As we discussed in Chap. 4, MCDM approaches can be used for target setting. Consequently, in MCDM and goal programming literature, there are papers that relate to target setting in DEA, starting with the early paper by Golany (1988a). However generally these papers only share the terminology with DEA, and thus their detailed review does not serve the purpose of this chapter. Likewise, we do not review nonradial DEA-like models that do not seek to incorporate preference information.

However, it is worth of noticing a link between target setting models and the nonradial Färe–Lovell measure (Färe and Lovell 1978—also known as the Russell measure). Unlike DEA, the Färe–Lovell measure yields to efficient (instead of weakly efficient) targets. Although the standard Färe–Lovell measure does not use a priori preference information, certain target setting models can be interpreted as Färe–Lovell measure with preference weighting.

6.2   Weight Restrictions

In their review of different approaches to incorporate preference information in DEA, Allen et al. (1997) concluded that the approaches found from the literature are very application driven: in real-world applications there have emerged situations where some preference information is needed, and this has dictated the way it has been incorporated. This explains the wide variety of different approaches.

In this section the existing weight restriction approaches to incorporate preference information into DEA models are divided into three categories:

1. Direct and relative weight restriction approaches where restrictions are based to absolute values or ratios of weights in the multiplier DEA model
2. Cone ratio DEA, which can be seen as a generalization of the relative weight restrictions
3. Contribution restriction approaches where absolute or relative restrictions are based on products of the dual weights and the input and/or output quantities

We conclude the section by discussing the general notion of using weights to capture preferences in both DEA and MCDM approaches.

For reviews on different weight restriction models, see the above mentioned article by Allen et al. (1997); Pedraja-Chaparro et al. (1997); and Roll and Golany (1993). In Joro and Viitala (2004) some weight restriction models are compared with an application to Finnish forestry data.

6.2.1 Absolute and Relative Weight Restrictions

The weight restriction approaches can be further divided into the following categories:

- Upper and lower bounds to the weights
- Ordinal relationships among weights
- Assurance ratio models

With price interpretation the idea of weight restrictions is to include some partial price information into the model. Thus the weight restriction approaches can be seen as an intermediate between the analysis of technical and overall efficiency defining a group of possible cost/revenue lines.

6.2.2 Upper and Lower Bounds on Weights

The most straightforward weight restrictions are the absolute upper of lower bounds set to the input or output weights. The absolute bounds are given as additional constraints of type (6.1). Here δ, ϕ, γ, and φ are bounds specified by a DM:

$$\delta_i \leq v_i \leq \phi_i \quad \text{and} \quad \gamma_r \leq \mu_r, \leq \varphi_r, \quad i = 1, 2, \ldots, m, \quad r = 1, 2, \ldots, s \quad (6.1)$$

Direct weight restrictions for one input and several output cases were introduced in Dyson and Thanassoulis (1988).

The problem with direct weight restrictions is that magnitude of the weights depends on the scale of the inputs and the outputs. Due to the scaling of the efficiency scores, the weights are typically rather small, and it may be quite difficult and unintuitive for a DM to find the restrictions that capture his/her preferences by introducing boundaries to scaled weights. To overcome this, Roll et al. (1991) proposed the following primal and dual formulations to incorporate absolute bounds to weights. Here $T_0 = \frac{1}{v^T x_0}$ is the transformation factor for DMU_0 so that $m_0 = T_0 \mu_0$ and $n_0 = T_0 \nu_0$. With this formulation the upper and lower bound vectors δ, ϕ, γ, and φ specified for weights—or prices—can be expressed with respect to the original scale of inputs and outputs.

$$\max \ m_0^{\mathrm{T}} y_0$$

s.t.

$$m_0^{\mathrm{T}} \mathbf{Y} - n_0^{\mathrm{T}} \mathbf{X} \leq \mathbf{0}$$
$$n_0^{\mathrm{T}} x_0 = 1$$
$$T_0 \gamma \leq m_0 \leq T_0 \varphi$$
$$T_0 \delta \leq n_0 \leq T_0 \phi$$

Podinovski and Athanassopoulos (1998) and Podinovski (1999) suggested the use of maximin formulations (whose results coincide with CCR DEA in unrestricted case and also with assurance region restrictions reviewed later in this chapter) to accommodate absolute weight restrictions. See also Podinovski (2001a, b, 2004) for discussion on absolute weight restrictions. There are numerous applications of absolute weight restrictions in literature.

6.2.3 Ordinal Relationships Among Weights

Golany (1988b) introduced an approach using a weak ordering for some weights:

$$v_{i_1} \geq v_{i_2} \geq \cdots \geq v_{i_a} \geq \varepsilon, \quad \text{for } 2 \leq a \leq m$$
$$\mu_{r_1} \geq \mu_{r_2} \geq \cdots \geq \mu_{r_b} \geq \varepsilon, \quad \text{for } 2 \leq b \leq s$$

The idea of the approach is to eliminate extreme weightings. Golany (1988b) illustrated the approach with an application to advertising budgets.

Ali et al. (1991) suggested the use of strict rather than weak ordering:

$$v_{i_1} > v_{i_2} > \cdots > v_{i_a} > \varepsilon, \quad \text{for } 2 \leq a \leq m$$
$$\mu_{r_1} > \mu_{r_2} > \cdots > \mu_{r_b} > \varepsilon, \quad \text{for } 2 \leq b \leq s$$

The advantage of this approach is that with data transformation the calculations can be carried out using the original DEA models.

6.2.4 Assurance Region Models

Another approach is to restrict the relations of weights of the inputs and/or outputs. These approaches are known as assurance regions (AR). The idea is to exclude from the model virtual multiplier vectors that are not reasonable. Assurance regions were first introduced in Thompson et al. (1986). In their paper Thompson et al. (1990) introduced AR I–AR II classifications.

In the AR I model, the ratios of the output weights are restricted. Especially for the outputs these restrictions reflect the marginal rates of substitution. Different AR I restrictions found from the literature are of type (6.2):

$$\delta_i v_i + \delta_{i+1} v_{i+1} = v_{i+2}, \quad \gamma_r \mu_r + \gamma_{r+1} \mu_{r+1} = \mu_{r+2} \tag{6.2}$$

$$\delta_i \leq \frac{v_i}{v_{i+1}}, \quad \phi_i \geq \frac{v_i}{v_{i+1}}, \quad \gamma_r \leq \frac{\mu_r}{\mu_{r+1}}, \quad \varphi_r \geq \frac{\mu_r}{\mu_{r+1}}$$

We can present a full AR I weighting scheme in the following vector form (see Thompson et al. 1990, 1992) where weights of other outputs/inputs are related to the weight of the first output/input. Thus the following $s + m - 2$ equations

$$\delta_i \leq \frac{v_i}{v_1} \leq \phi_i, \quad i = 2, 3, \ldots, m \tag{6.3}$$

$$\gamma_r \leq \frac{\mu_r}{\mu_1} \leq \varphi_r, \quad r = 2, 3, \ldots, s$$

can be written as

$$v_1 \delta_i \leq v_i \Rightarrow -v_1 \delta_i + v_i \geq 0 \quad \text{and} \quad v_i \leq v_1 \phi_i \Rightarrow v_1 \phi_i - v_i \geq 0, \quad i = 2, 3, \ldots, m$$
$$\mu_1 \gamma_r \leq \mu_r \Rightarrow -\mu_1 \gamma_r + \mu_r \geq 0 \quad \text{and} \quad \mu_r \leq \mu_1 \varphi_r \Rightarrow \mu_1 \varphi_r - \mu_r \geq 0, \quad r = 2, 3, \ldots, s$$

and further

$$\mathbf{F} w \geq \mathbf{0}, \quad w \geq \mathbf{0}, w \neq \mathbf{0} \tag{6.4}$$

where

$$\mathbf{F} = \begin{bmatrix} \mathbf{D} & \mathbf{0} \\ \mathbf{0} & \mathbf{C} \end{bmatrix}, w = \begin{bmatrix} \mu \\ v \end{bmatrix}, \mathbf{D} = \begin{bmatrix} -\gamma_2 & 1 & 0 & \cdots & 0 \\ \varphi_2 & -1 & 0 & \cdots & 0 \\ -\gamma_3 & 0 & 1 & \cdots & 0 \\ \varphi_3 & 0 & -1 & \cdots & 0 \\ \cdots & \cdots & \cdots & \cdots & \cdots \\ -\gamma_s & 0 & 0 & \cdots & 1 \\ \varphi_s & 0 & 0 & \cdots & -1 \end{bmatrix}, \mathbf{D} \in \mathfrak{R}^{2(s-1) \times s},$$

Table 6.2 Input-oriented multiplier and envelopment CCR formula for the assurance region method (AR I)

Input-oriented CCR ($\text{CCR}_\text{M} - \text{I}$)	Input-oriented CCR ($\text{CCR}_\text{E} - \text{I}$)
max $W_\text{I} = \boldsymbol{\mu}^\text{T} \boldsymbol{y}_0$ s.t. $\quad$ (6.5a) $\quad \boldsymbol{\mu}^\text{T} \boldsymbol{Y} - \boldsymbol{v}^\text{T} \boldsymbol{X} \leq \boldsymbol{0}$ $\quad \boldsymbol{v}^\text{T} \boldsymbol{x}_0 = 1$ $\quad \boldsymbol{\mu}^\text{T} \boldsymbol{D}^\text{T} \geq \boldsymbol{0}$ $\quad \boldsymbol{v}^\text{T} \boldsymbol{C}^\text{T} \geq \boldsymbol{0}$ $\quad \boldsymbol{\mu}, \boldsymbol{v} \geq \varepsilon \boldsymbol{1}$ $\quad \varepsilon > 0$	min $Z_\text{I} = \theta - \varepsilon(\boldsymbol{1}^\text{T} \boldsymbol{s}^+ + \boldsymbol{1}^\text{T} \boldsymbol{s}^-)$ s.t. $\quad$ (6.5b) $\quad \boldsymbol{Y}\boldsymbol{\lambda} - \boldsymbol{D}^\text{T} \boldsymbol{\tau} - \boldsymbol{s}^+ = \boldsymbol{y}_0$ $\quad \boldsymbol{X}\boldsymbol{\lambda} - \theta \boldsymbol{x}_0 + \boldsymbol{C}^\text{T} \boldsymbol{\pi} + \boldsymbol{s}^- = \boldsymbol{0}$ $\quad \boldsymbol{\lambda}, \boldsymbol{\tau}, \boldsymbol{\pi}, \boldsymbol{s}^-, \boldsymbol{s}^+ \geq \boldsymbol{0}$ $\quad \varepsilon > 0$

$$
\mathbf{C} = \begin{bmatrix}
-\delta_2 & 1 & 0 & \cdots & 0 \\
\phi_2 & -1 & 0 & \cdots & 0 \\
-\delta_3 & 0 & 1 & \cdots & 0 \\
\phi_3 & 0 & -1 & \cdots & 0 \\
\cdots & \cdots & \cdots & \cdots & \cdots \\
-\delta_m & 0 & 0 & \cdots & 1 \\
\phi_m & 0 & 0 & \cdots & -1
\end{bmatrix}; \text{ and } \mathbf{C} \in \mathfrak{R}^{2(m-1) \times m}.
$$

We may now formulate the DEA models by restricting the ratios of weights as presented above. In Table 6.2, we have shown how input-oriented model can be presented as a multiplier and envelopment model.

Example 6.2 Consider Example 6.1 and add the constraint $\mu_1 \geq \mu_2 \Rightarrow \mu_1 - \mu_2 \geq 0$ into the model, i.e., the weight of the first output (the number of "excellent grades") is required to be higher than that of the second output (the number of "good grades"). It means that $\mathbf{D} = [1, -1]$ and $\mathbf{C} = 0$. The constant inputs are 1. We solve the problem by using the input-oriented envelopment model in Table 6.2 to study the efficiency of student E. Without using any constraints for weights, student E is efficient.

$$\min \; \theta + \varepsilon(s^+ + s^-)$$

$$\text{s.t.} \qquad\qquad\qquad\qquad\qquad\qquad\qquad (6.6)$$

$$6\lambda_1 + 6\lambda_2 + 5\lambda_3 + 3\lambda_4 + \lambda_5 - \tau - s_1^+ = 1$$

$$1\lambda_1 + 2\lambda_2 + 4\lambda_3 + 5\lambda_4 + 7\lambda_5 + \tau - s_2^+ = 7$$

$$\lambda_1 + \lambda_2 + \lambda_3 + \lambda_4 + \lambda_5 - \theta + s^- = 0$$

$$\lambda_i \geq 0, \quad i = 1, 2, \ldots, 5$$

$$s_1^+, s_2^+, s^-, \tau \geq 0$$

$$\varepsilon > 0$$

By taking the weight restriction $\mu_1 - \mu_2 \geq 0$ into account and solving model (6.6), we obtain that $\theta = 0.889$, which means that student E is not efficient. Its efficiency

Fig. 6.2 Illustrating the assurance region method (Example 6.2)

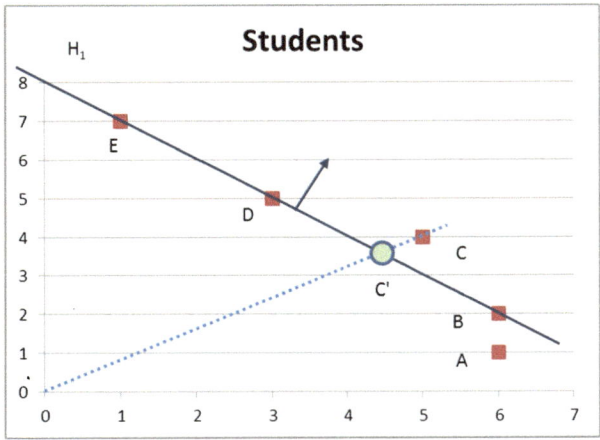

is 0.889. The values of the variables not zeroes are $\lambda_3 = 0.889$ and $\tau = 3.444$. The value $\lambda_3 = 0.889$ tells that if we radially reduce the input value (1) of student C by 11.1 % (C → C′ in Fig. 6.2), point C′ is "equally good" as student E.

The restrictions can also be set up on the ratios between inputs and outputs. This kind of models are called assurance ratio II models. Especially in the case of a single input and multiple outputs, the AR II restrictions reflect the relative prices, the price in terms of input:

$$\delta_i v_i \geq \mu_r, \quad i = 1, 2, \ldots, m, \quad r = 1, 2, \ldots, s$$
$$\phi_i v_i \leq \mu_r, \quad i = 1, 2, \ldots, m, \quad r = 1, 2, \ldots, s$$

The matrix forms for complete AR II restrictions can be presented in matrix form by adjoining

$$[\mathbf{F}_1, \mathbf{F}_2]w = \mathbf{F}_1\mu + \mathbf{F}_2 v \geq \mathbf{0}, \quad \mathbf{F}_1 \in \mathfrak{R}^{k \times s} \text{ and } \mathbf{F}_2 \in \mathfrak{R}^{k \times m}(k > 0)$$

where $\mathbf{F}_1$ and $\mathbf{F}_2$ are non-null matrices; see Thompson et al. (1990). Thus in the presence of both AR I and II, we have three groups of constraints:

- $D\mu \geq 0$, $\mu \geq 0$ defines the output cone U.
- $Cv \geq 0$, $v \geq 0$ defines the input cone V.
- $\mathbf{F}_1\mu + \mathbf{F}_2 v \geq 0$ defines the linkage constraints; see Thompson et al. (1990).

AR I and AR II models are sometimes referred to as separate cone AR, or just AR, and linked cone (LC) AR.

Another use for AR II is to divide some observed variables into input and output variables in DEA. See Thanassoulis et al. (1995) and Halme et al. (2002).

6.2.5 General Weight Restriction Formulation

Golany and Thore (1997) pointed out that AR constraints could also be used with the envelopment side formulation. They concluded that AR constraints define a set of linear constraints to λ variables and that in general such constraints can be represented as $\mathbf{A}\lambda \leq \mathbf{b}$. This formulation is similar to the one that Halme et al. (1999) suggested for a generalization of different scale assumptions (see for discussion in Chap. 5).

Halme and Korhonen (2000) have generalized the absolute and relative weight restrictions into the following form:

$$\boldsymbol{\mu}^{\mathrm{T}}\mathbf{R}^y - \boldsymbol{v}^{\mathrm{T}}\mathbf{R}^x \leq \boldsymbol{c} \tag{6.7}$$

where $\mathbf{R}^y \in \mathfrak{R}^{s \times k}, \mathbf{R}^x \in \mathfrak{R}^{m \times k}(k > 0)$, and $\boldsymbol{c} \in \mathfrak{R}^k$ (row vector). With the help of vector $\boldsymbol{c}$, it is possible to present both the absolute ($\boldsymbol{c} \neq \mathbf{0}$) and relative ($\boldsymbol{c} = \mathbf{0}$) weight restrictions. The absolute ($\boldsymbol{c} \neq \mathbf{0}$) weight restrictions are typically imposing a range for an individual weight. This approach was developed by Dyson and Thanassoulis (1988) and generalized by Roll et al. (1991). Also virtual weight restrictions introduced by Wong and Beasley (1990) belong to this category.

The class of relative ($\boldsymbol{c} = \mathbf{0}$) weight restrictions includes, among others, the assurance region models by Thompson et al. (1990) as well as cone ratio DEA models (e.g., Charnes et al. 1989). Golany and Roll (1994) introduced standards in DEA which resulted in a model where the upper and lower bounds of the weights are treated as variables.

Roll et al. (1991) showed that the linear weight restrictions work as artificial units. This can be easily seen by adding the weight restrictions into the multiplier model and writing the weight-restricted envelopment DEA models (see, e.g., Halme and Korhonen 2000). In Table 6.3, the generalization is presented in input-oriented CCR framework—naturally it can be done to all DEA models.

Table 6.3 Input-oriented multiplier and envelopment CCR formula for general weight restrictions

Input-oriented CCR ($\mathrm{CCR_M} - \mathrm{I}$)	Input-oriented CCR ($\mathrm{CCR_E} - \mathrm{I}$)
max $W_{\mathrm{I}} = \boldsymbol{\mu}^{\mathrm{T}}\boldsymbol{y}_0$ s.t. $\qquad\qquad\qquad\qquad$ (6.8a) $\qquad \boldsymbol{\mu}^{\mathrm{T}}\mathbf{Y} - \boldsymbol{v}^{\mathrm{T}}\mathbf{X} \leq \mathbf{0}$ $\qquad \boldsymbol{v}^{\mathrm{T}}\boldsymbol{x}_0 = 1$ $\qquad \boldsymbol{\mu}^{\mathrm{T}}\mathbf{R}^y - \boldsymbol{v}^{\mathrm{T}}\mathbf{R}^x \leq \boldsymbol{c}$ $\qquad \boldsymbol{\mu}, \boldsymbol{v} \geq \varepsilon \mathbf{1}$ $\qquad \varepsilon > 0$	min $Z_{\mathrm{I}} = \theta - \varepsilon(\mathbf{1}^{\mathrm{T}}\boldsymbol{s}^+ + \mathbf{1}^{\mathrm{T}}\boldsymbol{s}^-) + \boldsymbol{c}\boldsymbol{\omega}$ s.t. $\qquad\qquad\qquad\qquad$ (6.8b) $\qquad \mathbf{Y}\lambda + \mathbf{R}^y\boldsymbol{\omega} - \boldsymbol{s}^+ = \boldsymbol{y}_0$ $\qquad \mathbf{X}\lambda - \theta\boldsymbol{x}_0 + \mathbf{R}^x\boldsymbol{\omega} + \boldsymbol{s}^- = \mathbf{0}$ $\qquad \lambda, \boldsymbol{\omega}, \boldsymbol{s}^-, \boldsymbol{s}^+ \geq \mathbf{0}$ $\qquad \varepsilon > 0$

Table 6.4 The CR formulation of input-oriented multiplier and envelopment CCRM

Input-oriented CCR ($\text{CCR}_M - I$)	Input-oriented CCR ($\text{CCR}_E - I$)
max $W_I = \boldsymbol{\mu}^T \boldsymbol{y}_0$ s.t. $\qquad\qquad\qquad\qquad$ (6.9a) $\qquad \boldsymbol{\mu}^T Y - \boldsymbol{v}^T X \in K$ $\qquad \boldsymbol{v}^T \boldsymbol{x}_0 = 1$ $\qquad \boldsymbol{\mu} \in U$ $\qquad \boldsymbol{v} \in V$	min $Z_I = \theta$ s.t. $\qquad\qquad\qquad\qquad$ (6.9b) $\qquad -Y\lambda + \boldsymbol{y}_0 \in U^*$ $\qquad X\lambda - \theta \boldsymbol{x}_0 \in V^*$ $\qquad \lambda \in K^*$
$V \subseteq \mathfrak{R}_+^m, U \subseteq \mathfrak{R}_+^s$ and $K \subseteq \mathfrak{R}_-^n$ are closed convex cones	V^*, U^*, and K are the polar cones of V, U and K

6.2.6 Cone Ratio DEA

The elegant cone ratio (CR) DEA formulation (Charnes et al. 1989) generalized the basic DEA model by requiring that the weights $\boldsymbol{v}$ and $\boldsymbol{\mu}$ of the dual formulation belong to closed cones. In this section, we simply consider the model, where there are no cross restrictions between $\boldsymbol{v}$ and $\boldsymbol{\mu}$. The CR formulation (6.9a) and (6.9b) for input orientation is presented in Table 6.4 (see Yu 1974).

If $V = \mathfrak{R}_+^m$, $U = \mathfrak{R}_+^s$, and $K = \mathfrak{R}_-^n$, then the above model is equivalent to a CCR model (see Charnes et al. 1990).

From hence on, we assume that $K = \mathfrak{R}_-^n$ and U and V are polyhedral cones:

$$V = \left\{ \boldsymbol{v} \middle| \boldsymbol{v} = \mathbf{A}^T \boldsymbol{\alpha}, \ \boldsymbol{\alpha} \geq \mathbf{0} \right\}, \boldsymbol{\alpha} \in \mathfrak{R}_+^p, \mathbf{A}^T = \left(\boldsymbol{a}_1, \boldsymbol{a}_2, \ldots, \boldsymbol{a}_p \right), \boldsymbol{a}_i \in \mathfrak{R}_+^m,$$
$$i = 1, 2, \ldots, p$$
$$U = \left\{ \boldsymbol{\mu} \middle| \boldsymbol{\mu} = \mathbf{B}^T \boldsymbol{\beta}, \ \boldsymbol{\beta} \geq \mathbf{0} \right\}, \boldsymbol{\beta} \in \mathfrak{R}_+^k, \mathbf{B}^T = (\boldsymbol{b}_1, \boldsymbol{b}_2, \ldots, \boldsymbol{b}_k), \boldsymbol{b}_i \in \mathfrak{R}_+^s,$$
$$r = 1, 2, \ldots, k$$

and $V* = \{x | \mathbf{A}x \leq \mathbf{0}\}$ and $U* = \{y | \mathbf{B}y \leq \mathbf{0}\}$. Actually, the assurance region method is a special case of the cone ratio method (see Cooper et al. 2007).

The cone ratio types of restrictions into a DEA model can now simply be included by replacing the weights $\boldsymbol{\mu}$ and $\boldsymbol{v}$ in model (6.9a) by $\boldsymbol{\mu} = \mathbf{B}^T \boldsymbol{\beta}$ and $\boldsymbol{v} = \mathbf{A}^T \boldsymbol{\alpha}$. It is worth noting that the spanning directions $\boldsymbol{\alpha}$ and $\boldsymbol{\beta}$ must be nonnegative, i.e., $V \subseteq \mathfrak{R}_+^m$ and $U \subseteq \mathfrak{R}_+^s$.

As we can see from Table 6.5, the cone ratio model means that a singular or non-singular linear transformation is applied to original input and output variables by using the spanning directions of the cones for this purpose.

Figure 6.3 illustrates the input preference cone:

In most of the CR papers, the emphasis has been in input and output preference cones V and U. The K-cone, the predilection cone that allows the decision maker to represent preferences for a selected set of DMUs, is discussed in Wei and Yu (1997).

Table 6.5 The CR formulation of input-oriented multiplier and envelopment CCR model, when the cone is presented as a polyhedral cone

Input-oriented CCR (CCR$_M$ – I)	Input-oriented CCR (CCR$_E$ – I)
max $W_I = \beta^T(\mathbf{B}y_0)$ s.t. (6.10a) $\quad \beta^T(\mathbf{BY}) - \alpha^T(\mathbf{AX}) \le \mathbf{0}$ $\quad \alpha^T(\mathbf{A}x_0) = 1$ $\quad \beta, \alpha \ge \mathbf{0}$	min $Z_I = \theta$ s.t. (6.10b) $\quad (\mathbf{BY})\lambda - (\mathbf{B}y_0) \ge \mathbf{0}$ $\quad (\mathbf{AX})\lambda - \theta(\mathbf{A}x_0) \le \mathbf{0}$ $\quad \lambda \ge \mathbf{0}$

Fig. 6.3 Illustrating the cones in input space

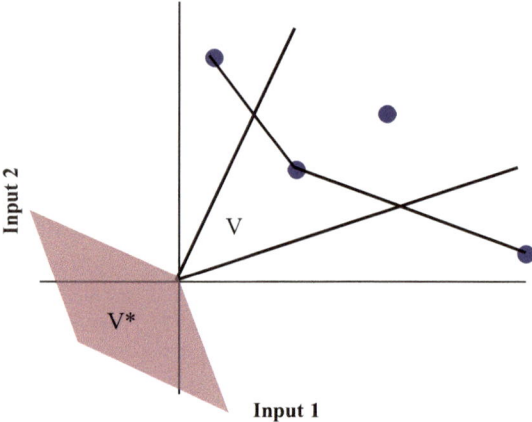

6.2.7   Contribution Restrictions

Wong and Beasley (1990) have introduced a weight restriction scheme for multiple inputs and outputs. In their model lower and upper bounds (6.11) are placed to the *contribution* of each input and/or output, i.e., the product of the input and/or output and its weight:

$$\delta_i \le \frac{v_i x_{ij}}{v^T x_j}, \quad \phi_i \ge \frac{v_i x_{ij}}{v^T x_j}, \quad \gamma_r \le \frac{\mu_r y_{rj}}{\mu^T y_j}, \quad \varphi_r \ge \frac{\mu_r y_{rj}}{\mu^T y_j} \tag{6.11}$$

In these inequalities x_j is the jth columns of matrix $\mathbf{X}$ and y_j is the jth columns of matrix $\mathbf{Y}$. The interpretation of the restrictions is how low/high can the importance of input i (output r) be.

The restrictions are DMU specific. Thus, e.g., introducing minimum and maximum restrictions for the contribution of each output for each DMU would lead to $2mn$ additional restrictions. Due to computational expensiveness of this approach, Wong and Beasley (1990) have presented modifications where only the contributions of the DMU in question are constrained, or constrains are placed to DMU in question and to an average DMU:

$$\delta_i \leq \frac{v_i x_i}{v^T x}, \quad \phi_i \geq \frac{v_i x_i}{v^T x}, \quad \gamma_r \leq \frac{\mu_r y_r}{\mu^T y}, \text{ and } \varphi_r \geq \frac{\mu_r y_r}{\mu^T y},$$

where $x = \mathbf{X1}, y = \mathbf{Y1}$.

Pedraja-Chaparro et al. (1997) and Sárrico and Dyson (2004) have extended the idea of contribution restrictions by introducing absolute as well as AR I- and AR II-type restrictions for contributions.

6.2.8   Weights and Preferences

Lately, AR and CR approaches have become a rather standard part of any DEA application.

Preference weighting has also been intensively studied in MCDM community, and Belton and Stewart (1999) criticize strongly the existing DEA weighting schemes. It is easy to agree with them that, e.g., expressing preference information on some complex and rather intangible issues in a form of a priori absolute restrictions to (scaled) weights may be difficult—if not impossible.

However it is important to remember that in many DEA applications, the preference information may arise from, e.g., DM's perception on market prices and that in these cases, e.g., the relative weight restriction schemes perform well.

Also, it is important to remember that when eliciting preference weights, MCDM weighting approaches face partly the same problems as DEA ones and thus do not necessarily provide any miracle medicine. In fact, in the MCDM literature, we can also find numerous arguments against using importance weights as a means to elicit and represent DM's preference information in MCDM approaches (e.g., Steuer 1986, pp. 193–200; Korhonen and Wallenius 1989; Wierzbicki 1986). Korhonen et al. (2013) studied the connection between the importance of criteria and the weights of criteria in a linear value function, and they found that there is no obvious link between those two concepts.

Later in this study, in Chap. 9, we introduce some novel approaches as an alternative to the existing ones reviewed in this chapter. In these approaches one of the major emphases has been on facilitating the DM to express his/her preferences over such abstract, complex, and often intangible outputs and inputs that are not easy to put a price tag on.

6.3   Models Based on Artificial DMUs

Adding artificial DMUs into the data set is another approach to incorporate preference information to DEA. Whereas the weight restriction models set limits to
multipliers, these models aim to shape the efficient frontier by introducing DMUs
that are not parts of the original data set. The artificial DMUs can be existing units
from outside of the original data, typically benchmarking units, or new DMUs that
are designed to alter the efficiency frontier either in order to reflect some performance standards or in some cases to provide better envelopment.

As Golany and Roll (1994) point out, the approaches that are based on artificial
DMUs have two major benefits. Firstly, they do not change the constraint set of the
standard DEA formulation, but just enlarge the reference set. Secondly, with weight
restrictions, in some cases the bounds might have been set so tight that the problem
becomes infeasible. With artificial DMUs, this cannot happen.

6.3.1   Weight Restrictions and Artificial DMUs

Roll et al. (1991) first observed the connection between restricting weight flexibility
and adding unobserved DMUs into a data set. They pointed out that each weight
restricted to be positive is equivalent to adding an unobserved DMU into the data
set. Figure 6.4 provides a simple illustration on the connection of weight restrictions
and artificial units. Assume we have DMUs that consume the same amount of one
output to produce two outputs, and that there are two additional weight restrictions.
Now introducing two unobserved DMUs (circles on x- and y-axes) as illustrated
would attain the same results than placing the additional restrictions.

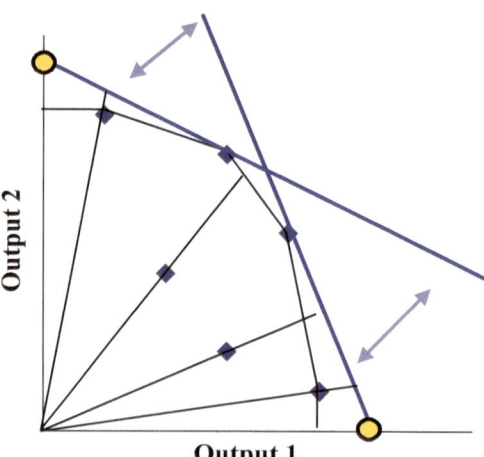

Fig. 6.4 Weight
restrictions and
artificial DMUs

Later Thanassoulis and Allen (1998) generalized the concept by showing the equivalence between placing AR I and II weight restrictions and simulating unobserved DMUs.

In Table 6.3, there is a generalization of the connection between the weight restrictions and artificial units. In the multiplier model, the matrices $\mathbf{R}^y$ and $\mathbf{R}^x$ define general constraints within and between weights $\boldsymbol{\mu}$ and $\boldsymbol{\nu}$. In the envelopment model, we see that matrix $\begin{bmatrix} \mathbf{R}^y \\ \mathbf{R}^x \end{bmatrix}$ is standing for k new units provided that $\mathbf{R}^y \in \mathfrak{R}_+^{s \times k}$ and $\mathbf{R}^x \in \mathfrak{R}_+^{m \times k}$. If some of the elements $\mathbf{R}^y$ and $\mathbf{R}^x$ are negative, then nonnegative assumptions of new "inputs" and "outputs" are not valid anymore.

6.4 Target Setting with Preferences

The origins of target setting models are in multiple criteria decision making (MCDM). The first approach that concentrates on producing preferred targets in DEA framework is IMOLP, interactive MOLP procedure by Golany (1988a). In this approach the DMU is presented with $s + 1$ optimal targets for a given resource vector. The DMU may use some of them as the most preferred target, or indicate which of them is the best, and proceed with the search. As Golany (1988a) pointed out, the idea of the procedure is somewhat similar to the approach by Steuer and Choo (1983): at each iteration it presents the DMU with $s + 1$ efficient targets that are existing DMUs, and from one iteration to another, it reduces the area the targets cover.

Given that the principle idea in target setting is to locate a point from the efficient frontier according to preferences of a DM, the task resembles the core problem addressed by most MCDM tools. The use of MCDM models and more specifically MOLP to explore the efficient frontier was discussed in Chaps. 3 and 4 where analyzing the efficient surface was discussed.

Section 6.4.1 of this chapter addresses goal programming-based target setting models. Section 6.4.2 describes target setting in DEA framework—these models that have connections to nonradial Färe–Lovell efficiency measure (Färe and Lovell 1978—also known as the Russell measure). In Sect. 6.4.3, we illustrate some target setting approaches as well as the use of the MOLP model.

6.4.1 Target Setting and Goal Programming

Pioneering work in preference-based target setting was done by Thanassoulis and Dyson (1992) where both goal programming-based models and models that resemble more the traditional DEA formulation were presented. In the goal programming-based model by Thanassoulis and Dyson (1992), the DMU in the first stage articulates an ideal target point (g^x, g^y) not necessarily feasible. Then the DMU assigns user-specified preference weight vectors $w_U^x \geq 0$ and $w_O^x \geq 0$ (at least one of the weights has to be strictly positive) for the deviation vectors s_U^x, s_O^x (under- and overachievements of inputs) and $w_U^y \geq 0, w_O^y \geq 0$ for the deviation vectors s_U^y, s_O^y (under- and overachievements of outputs). Then the model minimizes the weighted sum of the deviations. The more undesirable the deviation from the ideal level is, the larger weight is attached to it. With the under- and overachievement vectors, we can locate a feasible point (g^{xf}, g^{yf}) as close as possible to the target point.

Mathematically the model is the following:

$$\min \ w_U^{x^T} s_U^x + w_O^{x^T} s_O^x + w_U^{y^T} s_U^y + w_O^{y^T} s_O^y$$

$$\text{s.t.} \tag{6.12}$$

$$Y\lambda + s_U^y - s_O^y = g^y$$

$$X\lambda + s_U^x - s_O^x = g^x$$

$$\lambda, s_U^y, s_O^y, g^y, g^x, s_O^x, s_U^x \geq 0$$

This first stage of the model projects the given target point (g^x, g^y) to a feasible point (g^{xf}, g^{yf}), $g^{yf} = Y\lambda^* = g^y - s_U^{y*} + s_O^{y*}$ and $g^{xf} = X\lambda^* = g^x - s_U^{x*} + s_O^{x*}$, where λ^*, s_U^{y*}, s_O^{y*}, s_U^{x*} and s_O^{x*} are the optimal values of the solution of the model (6.12). The feasible point (g^{xf}, g^{yf}) is not usually efficient. Another model is required, which projects point (g^{xf}, g^{yf}) onto the efficient frontier. The corresponding model is

$$\max \ 1^T s_U + 1^T s_O$$

$$\text{s.t.} \tag{6.13}$$

$$Y\lambda - s_O = g^{yf}$$

$$X\lambda + s_U = g^{xf}$$

$$\lambda, s_O, s_U \geq 0$$

The optimal solution $Y\lambda^* = g^{y*} = g^{yf} + s_O^*$, $X\lambda^* = g^{x*} = g^{xf} - s_U^*$ is efficient, where λ^*, s_U^*, and s_O^* are the optimal values of λ, s_U, and s_O.

Assume that a DMU chooses $g^x = x_0$ and $g^y = y_0$ and wishes to reach the efficient frontier by improving inputs and outputs, simultaneously. Since the given point is an existing DMU, it belongs to the production possibility set and is thus feasible. Model (6.12) is not now needed to check feasibility, but we may directly use model (6.13) to find the final solution by setting $g^{yf} = y_0$ and $g^{xf} = x_0$.

6.4.2 Setting Targets Based on Preferences

Thanassoulis and Dyson (1992) and Zhu (1996) introduced several approaches to find targets for both inputs and outputs. In the preference weight-based model by Thanassoulis and Dyson (1992), the inputs and outputs are divided into two categories: those that the DMU wishes to improve and those that he/she wishes to maintain at their current levels. The $\mathbf{Y}$- and $\mathbf{X}$-matrices containing the input and output information of different DMUs are correspondingly divided into two matrices: $\mathbf{Y_I}$ and $\mathbf{X_I}$ contain the information on the inputs and outputs to be improved and $\mathbf{Y_C}$ and $\mathbf{X_C}$ the information on those to be maintained at the current level. Vectors y_{0I}, x_{0I}, y_{0C}, and x_{0C} contain the corresponding information on the DMU under consideration. $w^x \geq \mathbf{0}$ and $w^y \geq \mathbf{0}$ (at least one of the weights has to be strictly positive) are user-specified weighting vectors attached to coefficient vectors z and p. Here p is standing for the vector of proportions to which the inputs are decreased, and z refers to the vector of factors by which the different outputs are increased.

By varying the weights w^x and w^y, the DMU may search the efficient surface in the input–output space. As a result the DMU obtains coefficient vectors p and z that define the target corresponding to the preference weights used. By multiplying the current components of input and output vectors with the components of vectors p and z, the DMU obtains the target solution. If we assume $y_{0I} \geq \mathbf{0}$, $x_{0I} \geq \mathbf{0}$ and not ($y_{0I} = \mathbf{0}$ and $x_{0I} = \mathbf{0}$), then the formulation can be given in the form

$$\max \quad w^{y^T} z - w^{x^T} p + \varepsilon \left(\mathbf{1}^T s^+ + \mathbf{1}^T s^- \right)$$

$$\text{s.t.} \tag{6.14}$$

$$\mathbf{Y_I}\lambda - \mathbf{Y_{0I}}z - s_I^+ = \mathbf{0}$$
$$\mathbf{Y_C}\lambda - s_C^+ = y_{0C}$$
$$\mathbf{X_I}\lambda - \mathbf{X_{0I}}p + s_I^- = \mathbf{0}$$
$$\mathbf{X_C}\lambda + s_C^- = x_{0C}$$
$$\mathbf{Y_{0I}} = \text{diag}(y_{0I})^1$$
$$\mathbf{X_{0I}} = \text{diag}(x_{0I})$$
$$z \geq \mathbf{1}$$
$$p \leq \mathbf{1}$$
$$\lambda, p, s_I^+, s_C^+, s_I^-, s_C^- \geq \mathbf{0}$$
$$\varepsilon > 0$$

where $s^+ = \begin{bmatrix} s_I^+ \\ s_C^+ \end{bmatrix}$ and $s^- = \begin{bmatrix} s_I^- \\ s_C^+ \end{bmatrix}$.

---

[1]Notation diag(a) refers to the diagonal matrix with the elements of vector a on the diagonal.

The slack variables s_I^+ and s_I^- are redundant, i.e., $s_I^+ = \mathbf{0}$ and $s_I^- = \mathbf{0}$, if $\mathbf{w}^x > \mathbf{0}$, $\mathbf{w}^y > \mathbf{0}$, $\mathbf{y}_{0I} > \mathbf{0}$, and $\mathbf{x}_{0I} > \mathbf{0}$. We will make this assumption in the following considerations. Moreover, we modify the model (6.14) such that z is replaced by $(\sigma^y + 1)$ and p by $(1 - \sigma^x)$. The modified model looks as follows:

$$\max \ \mathbf{w}^{y^T} \boldsymbol{\sigma}^y + \mathbf{w}^{x^T} \boldsymbol{\sigma}^x + \mathbf{w}^{y^T} \mathbf{1} - \mathbf{w}^{x^T} \mathbf{1} + \varepsilon \left(\mathbf{1}^T s_C^+ + \mathbf{1}^T s_C^- \right)$$

$$\text{s.t.} \tag{6.15}$$

$$\mathbf{Y}_I \boldsymbol{\lambda} - \mathbf{Y}_{0I} \boldsymbol{\sigma}^y = \mathbf{y}_{0I}$$

$$\mathbf{Y}_C \boldsymbol{\lambda} - s_C^+ = \mathbf{y}_{0C}$$

$$\mathbf{X}_I \boldsymbol{\lambda} + \mathbf{X}_{0I} \boldsymbol{\sigma}^x = \mathbf{x}_{0I}$$

$$\mathbf{X}_C \boldsymbol{\lambda} + s_C^- = \mathbf{x}_{0C}$$

$$\mathbf{Y}_{0I} = \mathrm{diag}(\mathbf{y}_{0I})$$

$$\mathbf{X}_{0I} = \mathrm{diag}(\mathbf{x}_{0I})$$

$$\boldsymbol{\sigma}^x \leq \mathbf{1}$$

$$\boldsymbol{\lambda}, \boldsymbol{\sigma}^y, \boldsymbol{\sigma}^x, s_I^+, s_C^+, s_I^-, s_C^- \geq \mathbf{0}$$

$$\varepsilon > 0$$

If we further omit the constant from the objective function and redefine the notation, $s_I^+ = \mathbf{Y}_{0I} \boldsymbol{\sigma}^y \Rightarrow \boldsymbol{\sigma}^y = \mathbf{Y}_{0I}^{-1} s_I^+$ and $s_I^- = \mathbf{X}_{0I} \boldsymbol{\sigma}^x \Rightarrow \boldsymbol{\sigma}^x = \mathbf{X}_{0I}^{-1} s_I^-$, we get the model in Table 6.6 and compare it to the basic additive DEA model (see Charnes et al. 1985).

From Table 6.6, we see that modified goal programming model has only one difference in comparison to the basic additive DEA model: the weights of the slack variables s_I^+ and s_I^- are not equal to 1.

Table 6.6 Modified goal programming and basic additive DEA model

Modified goal programming model	Basic additive DEA model
$\max \ \mathbf{w}^{y^T} \mathbf{Y}_{0I}^{-1} s_I^+ + \mathbf{w}^{x^T} \mathbf{X}_{0I}^{-1} s_I^- + \varepsilon \left(\mathbf{1}^T s_C^+ + \mathbf{1}^T s_C^- \right)$ s.t. $\qquad\qquad\qquad\qquad\qquad\qquad\qquad$ (6.16) $\quad \mathbf{Y}_I \boldsymbol{\lambda} - s_I^+ = \mathbf{y}_{0I}$ $\quad \mathbf{Y}_C \boldsymbol{\lambda} - s_C^+ = \mathbf{y}_{0C}$ $\quad \mathbf{X}_I \boldsymbol{\lambda} + s_I^- = \mathbf{x}_{0I}$ $\quad \mathbf{X}_C \boldsymbol{\lambda} + s_C^- = \mathbf{x}_{0C}$ $\quad \mathbf{Y}_{0I} = \mathrm{diag}(\mathbf{y}_{0I})$ $\quad \mathbf{X}_{0I} = \mathrm{diag}(\mathbf{x}_{0I})$ $\quad s_I^- \leq \mathbf{X}_{0I}$ $\quad \boldsymbol{\lambda}, \boldsymbol{\sigma}^y, \boldsymbol{\sigma}^x, s_I^+, s_C^+, s_I^-, s_C^- \geq \mathbf{0}$ $\quad \varepsilon > 0$	$\max \ \mathbf{1}^T s^+ + \mathbf{1}^T s^-$ s.t. $\qquad\qquad\qquad\qquad\quad$ (6.17) $\quad \mathbf{Y} \boldsymbol{\lambda} - s^+ = \mathbf{y}_0$ $\quad \mathbf{X} \boldsymbol{\lambda} - s^+ = \mathbf{x}_0$ $\quad \boldsymbol{\lambda}, s^+, s^- \geq \mathbf{0}$

A DM can search alternative target values by varying the weights $w^x \geq 0$, $w^y \geq 0$ (at least one of the weights being strictly positive) in the objective function, e.g., in model (6.17). Like in the preference weight-based model by Thanassoulis and Dyson (1992), also here DMU gets coefficient vectors that define the target corresponding to the used preference weights, as a result of the model. For further information about target setting, see, e.g., Zhu (1996).

As Zhu (1996) pointed out, the above considerations have also a link to Färe–Lovell measure (Färe and Lovell 1978), where equal weights were used in the objective functions.

Since the sum of weights is scaled to unity, the Färe–Lovell measure reflects the average of the improvement needs of the inputs and outputs. Thus Färe–Lovell measure requires the units to be Pareto–Koopmans efficient instead of Debreu–Farrell efficient, measuring the distance from the true efficient surface (see, e.g., Lovell (1993) for discussion). Thus units or projections in the weakly efficient surface are penalized by their true distance from the true efficient frontier instead of an ε. Zhu's (1996) model is a generalization of the Färe–Lovell measure in two aspects. Firstly, it presents the measure in a combined framework allowing the improvements for inputs and outputs simultaneously, and secondly, since the selection of the weights is free, the model can be interpreted to be a weighted Färe–Lovell measure with preference weighting. Thus the value of the objective function has also an interpretation as a weighted Färe–Lovell efficiency score. (See also Ruggiero and Bretschneider 1998.) This enables a more flexible use of the target setting models: in addition to providing the DMU with a target, this way also the objective function value can be used as an efficiency score reflecting preferences.

To summarize our considerations, we present a generalization of the models reviewed in this subsection:

$$\max \ w^{y^T}\sigma^y - w^{x^T}\sigma^x + \varepsilon\left(\mathbf{1}^T s^+ + \mathbf{1}^T s^-\right)$$

s.t. $\hspace{10cm}$ (6.18)

$$\mathbf{Y}_I\lambda - \mathbf{Y}_{0I}\sigma^y - s_I^+ = g^y$$

$$\mathbf{Y}_C\lambda - s_C^+ = y_{0C}$$

$$\mathbf{X}_I\lambda - \mathbf{X}_{0I}\sigma^x + s_I^- = g^x$$

$$\mathbf{X}_C\lambda + s_C^- = x_{0C}$$

$$\mathbf{Y}_{0I} = \mathrm{diag}(y_{0I})$$

$$\mathbf{X}_{0I} = \mathrm{diag}(x_{0I})$$

$$\sigma^x \leq \mathbf{1}$$

$$\lambda, \sigma^y, \sigma^x, s_I^+, s_C^+, s_I^-, s_C^- \geq \mathbf{0}$$

$$\varepsilon > 0$$

where $s^+ = \begin{bmatrix} s_I^+ \\ s_C^+ \end{bmatrix}$ and $s^- = \begin{bmatrix} s_I^- \\ s_C^- \end{bmatrix}$. In addition, some constraints for $\sigma^y, \sigma^x, s_I^+$, and s_I^- can be set up. With the selection of the parameters g^y and g^x, it is possible to control the part of the efficient frontier from which the targets are searched. By setting $g^y = y_I^{\min}$ and $g^x = x_I^{\max}$, where $\begin{bmatrix} y^{\min} \\ x^{\max} \end{bmatrix}$ refers to the vector of the maximum observed values of inputs and minimum observed values of outputs to be improved, the model makes it possible to scan efficient solutions dominating $\begin{bmatrix} y^{\min} \\ x^{\max} \end{bmatrix}$, and it can be argued that it is probable that the realistic targets are to be found from this area.

The models suggested in Thanassoulis and Dyson (1992) and Zhu (1996) have been further developed and applied by various authors.

6.4.3 Illustration and Comparison

Below we apply the preference weight-based models by Thanassoulis and Dyson (1992) (with no additional restrictions) and by Zhu (1996) to the following simple example with both CCR and BCC assumptions. In the example, only DMU$_3$ is CCR efficient, and all DMUs except DMU$_6$ are BCC efficient. Table 6.7 and Fig. 6.5 show the targets that different models provide for DMU$_6$. Table 6.8 outlines the various targets. TD refers to the preference weight model by Thanassoulis and Dyson (1992). Zhu refers to the model by Zhu (1996). Which target is to be obtained depends on the weighting. The obtained targets are either existing units or solutions that lie on the edge of the part of the efficient frontier dominating the target (or being dominated by the target). This means that these models are generally not capable of providing a target that is located in the relative interior of a facet. Theoretically it is possible to obtain degenerated solutions, i.e., to have, for example, the whole line segment between DMU$_4$ and DMU$_3$ as a target. Since with CCR assumptions Zhu's model in this oversimplified example does not have any finite extreme points other than the origin, the target provided is either the origin or infinity.

A typical feature for the target setting models reviewed in previous subsections is that they—being linear programs with weighted sums as objective functions—are able to present only extreme points as solutions. However, it might be possible to have rather "long" efficient facets enveloping a large number of DMUs. In these cases it is possible that there is an efficient target located in the relative interior of such a facet that could in fact be the best target for an inefficient DMU. With the approaches presented above, such targets can be achieved by changing the right-hand side parameters, e.g., the vectors g^y and g^x, or by placing additional

Table 6.7 Example data for target setting

Unit	Input	Output
DMU$_1$	3	1
DMU$_2$	4	4
DMU$_3$	6	7
DMU$_4$	9	9
DMU$_5$	13	10
DMU$_6$	10	3

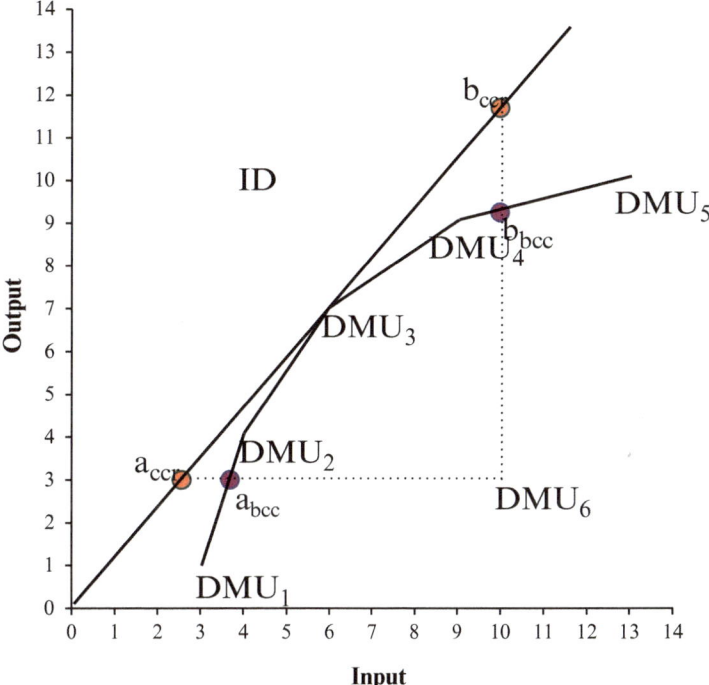

Fig. 6.5 Possible projections in input–output space

Table 6.8 Targets with various models

Model	Scale assumption	Possible targets
TD	CRS	a$_{ccr}$, b$_{ccr}$
	VRS	a$_{bcc}$, DMU$_4$, DMU$_3$, DMU$_2$, b$_{bcc}$
ZHU	CRS	Origin, infinity
	VRS	All efficient DMUs

restrictions. However, it may require several iterations to be able to "zoom in" to
the desired target area. Instead, a more preferable way is to use the reference point
and reference direction techniques.

Let us continue with the same example. The MOLP problem to search the
efficient frontier of the BCC model is the following bi-criteria problem:

$$\max \ \lambda_1 + 4\lambda_2 + 7\lambda_3 + 9\lambda_4 + 10\lambda_5 + 3\lambda_6$$
$$\min \ 3\lambda_1 + 4\lambda_2 + 6\lambda_3 + 9\lambda_4 + 13\lambda_5 + 10\lambda_6$$
$$\text{s.t.}$$
$$\mathbf{1}^T \lambda = 1$$
$$\lambda \geq \mathbf{0}$$

The reference point formulation to solve this problem is the following (see Chap. 4
for details of reference point approach):

$$\max \ \sigma + \varepsilon(s^+ + s^-)$$
$$\text{s.t.} \tag{6.19}$$
$$\lambda_1 + 4\lambda_2 + 7\lambda_3 + 9\lambda_4 + 10\lambda_5 + 3\lambda_6 - w^y\sigma - s^+ = g^y$$
$$3\lambda_1 + 4\lambda_2 + 6\lambda_3 + 9\lambda_4 + 13\lambda_5 + 10\lambda_6 + w^x\sigma + s^- = g^x$$
$$\mathbf{1}^T \lambda = 1$$
$$\lambda \geq \mathbf{0}$$
$$s^-, s^+ \geq 0$$
$$\varepsilon > 0$$

In the reference point approach, the efficient frontier can be scanned either by
changing the weights w^x and w^y or the aspiration levels g^x and g^y. In the following
example, we illustrate both approaches; however, in computational applications it is
more effective to fix the weighting vector and change the right-hand side parameters, i.e., the aspiration level vectors. We would like to emphasize that the formulation (6.19) is based on the use of the so-called achievement scalarizing function
which has the desirable property projects *any* point (feasible or infeasible) onto the
(weakly) efficient frontier.

Let us investigate what kind of targets this model gives in the example when the
weighting vector $\begin{bmatrix} w^y \\ w^x \end{bmatrix}$ is varied. As an aspiration level vector $\begin{bmatrix} g^y \\ g^x \end{bmatrix}$, we have used
vector of the inputs and outputs of DMU_6, i.e., vector $(10, 3)$. Six (6) targets have
been calculated (from a to f) both in the CCR and the BCC context. See Fig. 6.6 for
illustration and Table 6.9 for values of $\begin{bmatrix} w^y \\ w^x \end{bmatrix}$. If we wish to scan the whole part of

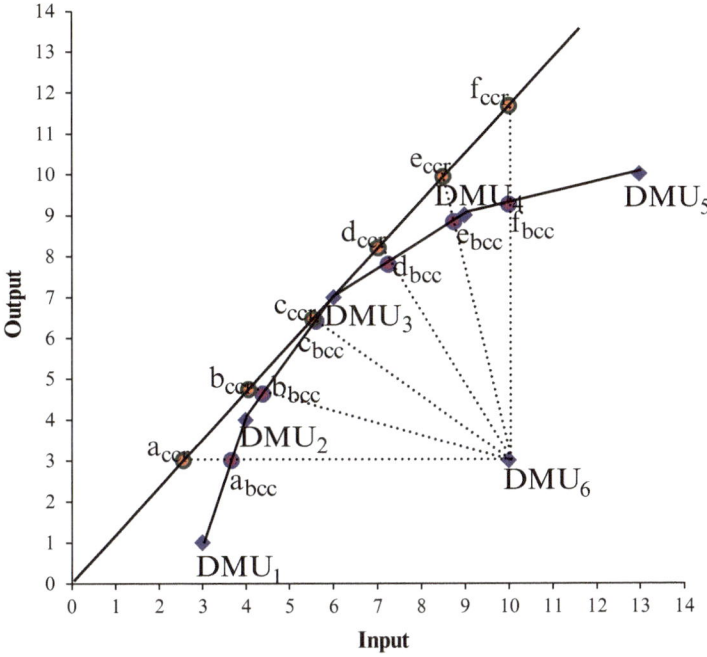

Fig. 6.6 Projections with various weighting vectors

the efficient frontier dominating the data set, we suggest the use of vector $\begin{bmatrix} y^{\min} \\ x^{\max} \end{bmatrix}$,

in this case (13, 1) as vector $\begin{bmatrix} g^y \\ g^x \end{bmatrix}$.

Same targets can be obtained by, i.e., fixing the weighting vector $\begin{bmatrix} w^y \\ w^x \end{bmatrix}$ to be

(0.5, 0.5) and changing the aspiration level vectors $\begin{bmatrix} g^y \\ g^x \end{bmatrix}$; see Fig. 6.7 and Table 6.10

for illustration. For BCC model we have used feasible aspiration levels, and for CCR infeasible ones, this is mainly to keep the figure readable. Naturally, for both models there is an infinite amount of aspiration levels leading to the same projection with a given weighting vector.

One notable advantage in using the reference point approach is that we can also find targets that are not *extreme point solutions*, but lie in the relative interior of some facet. In real data sets it is possible to have only few but rather large efficient facets. Thus limiting the targets to extreme point may result to targets having very different input and output mixes than unit's current one.

Table 6.9 Various weighting vectors

Weighting vectors	Aspiration level vector
(0.0, 1.0)	(10, 3) for all cases
(0.2, 0.8)	
(0.4, 0.6)	
(0.6, 0.4)	
(0.8, 0.2)	
(1.0, 0.0)	

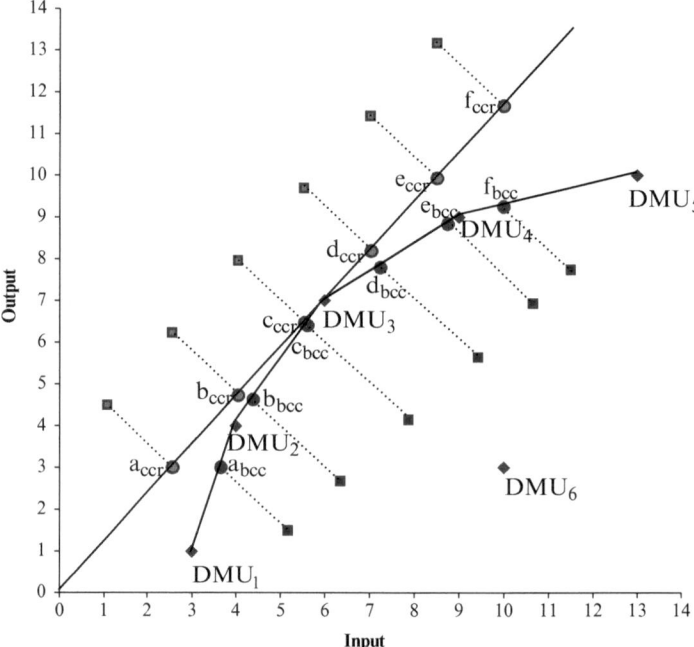

Fig. 6.7 Projections with various aspiration levels

Table 6.10 Aspiration levels

Aspiration level vectors	Weighting vectors	Aspiration level vectors	Weighting vectors
CRS assumptions		VRS assumptions	
(1.1, 4.5)	(0.5, 0.5) for all cases	(5.2, 1.5)	(0.5, 0.5) for all cases
(2.6, 6.2)		(6.4, 2.7)	
(4.0, 8v0)		(7.9, 4.2)	
(5.5, 9.7)		(9.4, 5.6)	
(7.0, 11.4)		(10.7, 6.9)	
(8.5, 13.2)		(11.5, 7.8)	

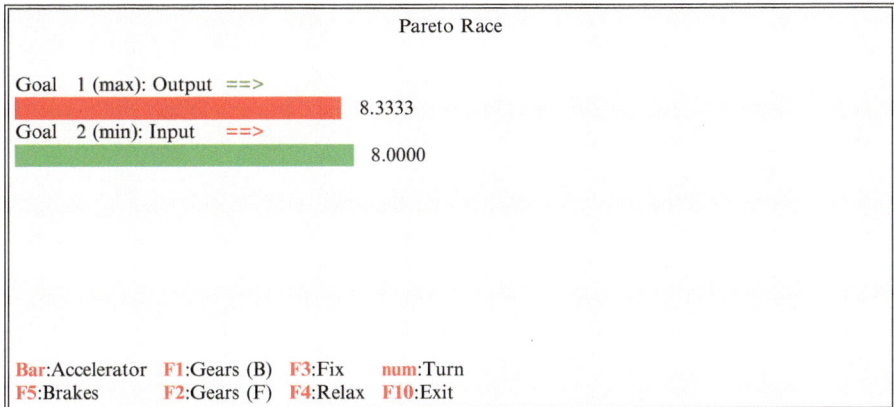

Fig. 6.8 A possible projection with reference direction approach

The reference direction model (Korhonen and Laakso 1986), an extension of the reference point model, is implemented in the VIG software (Korhonen 1987). An essential feature of VIG is its interface called Pareto Race developed by Korhonen and Wallenius (1988). Using Pareto Race DM is able to freely search the efficient frontier and investigate how input and output values change. Figure 6.8 illustrates the interface. The maximum number of the criteria which can be used at the same time is 10.

The example used here is rather naïve—with only one input and one output, a good graphical illustration would be sufficient for the search of the MP. However, this illustrates the principle of the Pareto Race and how the search can be carried out in applications of realistic size. See Korhonen (2001) for a thorough discussion and a real-life data example on the use of Pareto Race and VIG in the search of the efficient frontier in DEA.

6.5   Value Function

In the MCDM literature we can find numerous arguments against using importance weights as a means to elicit and represent DM's preference information (e.g., Steuer 1986, pp. 193–200, Korhonen and Wallenius 1989; Korhonen et al. 2013; Wierzbicki 1986). It seems particularly difficult to understand that the intuitively appealing notion "the greater the importance, the larger the weight" does not always work. When the weights have a straightforward interpretation, such as prices, their definition and use are also straightforward. However, this is not always the case. When inputs and outputs are some raw materials and produced goods, it is relatively easy to see the weights as prices. But when outputs are, for example, Ph.D. degrees and refereed publications or lives saved, it may be practically or politically impossible for the DM to give price estimates.

In Chap. 7 we present an approach where DM's preferences are incorporated into efficiency analysis by explicitly locating his/her most preferred input–output vector on the efficient frontier. We call this vector the DM's *most preferred solution* (MPS). It is a vector on the efficient frontier that he/she prefers to any other vector at the moment of the final choice. The MPS can be located by using an interactive MOLP search procedure as was described in Chap. 4. However, it is important to notice that the search can be also carried out by some other approaches as long as the approach used results in the MPS that is applicable for carrying out the proposed analysis.

Conceptually, an MPS can be defined as the point at which the DM's implicitly known value function reaches its maximum when the search terminates. Using the knowledge of the MPS, the DM's (unknown) value function is approximated using the so-called tangent cones at the MPS. The efficiency of each DMU is then determined with respect to this tangent cone. As a result we obtain scores that we call *value (in)efficiency* scores, since the efficiency of each DMU is determined by means of an approximation of the indifference surface of an implicitly known value function at the MPS. The tangent cones define implicitly a range for acceptable weights, or prices, as the weight restriction approaches do. However, we argue that it is easier for the DM to articulate his/her preferences as a preferred unit than weight restrictions.

In Chap. 8 the value efficiency analysis is further developed. Whereas the original value efficiency scores are optimistic estimates of the true scores, this chapter presents an interactive procedure to determine true value efficiency scores. A procedure to test the assumptions of the value efficiency analysis is also presented.

References

Adler N, Friedman L, Sinuany-Stern Z (2002) Review of ranking methods in the data envelopment analysis context. Eur J Oper Res 140:249–265

Ali AI, Cook WD, Seiford LM (1991) Strict vs. weak ordinal relations for multipliers in data envelopment analysis. Manage Sci 37:733–738

Allen R, Athanassopoulos A, Dyson RG, Thanassoulis E (1997) Weights restrictions and value judgements in data envelopment analysis: evolution, development and future directions. Ann Oper Res 73:13–34

Andersen P, Petersen NC (1993) A procedure for ranking efficient units in data envelopment analysis. Manage Sci 39:1261–1264

Anderson TR, Hollingsworth K, Inman L (2002) The fixed weighting nature of a cross-evaluation model. J Prod Anal 17(3):249–255

Angulo-Meza L, Lins MP (2002) Review of methods for increasing discrimination in data envelopment analysis. Ann Oper Res 116:225–242

Belton V, Stewart T (1999) DEA and MCDA: competing or complementary approaches? In: Meskens N, Roubens M (eds) Advances in decision analysis. Kluwer Academic, Dordrecht, pp 87–104

Charnes A, Cooper WW, Golany B, Seiford LM, Stutz J (1985) Foundations of data envelopment analysis for Pareto-Koopmans efficient empirical production functions. J Econom 30(1/2):91–107

Charnes A, Cooper WW, Wei QL, Huang ZM (1989) Cone ratio data envelopment analysis and multi-objective programming. Int J Syst Sci 20:1099–1118

Charnes A, Cooper WW, Huang ZM, Sun DB (1990) Polyhedral cone- ratio DEA models with an illustrative application to large commercial banks. J Econom 46:73–91

Cook WD, Kress M, Seiford L (1992) Priorization models for Frontier decision making units in DEA. Eur J Oper Res 59:319–323

Cooper WW, Seiford LM, Tone K (2007) Data envelopment analysis: a comprehensive text with models, applications, references and DEA-Solver software, 2nd edn. Kluwer Academic, Boston

Doyle RH, Green JR (1994) Efficiency and cross-efficiency in DEA: derivations, meanings and uses. J Oper Res Soc 45:567–578

Dyson RG, Thanassoulis E (1988) Reducing weight flexibility in data envelopment analysis. J Oper Res Soc 6:563–576

Färe R, Lovell CAK (1978) Measuring the technical efficiency of production. J Econ Theory 19:150–162

Golany B (1988a) An interactive MOLP procedure for the extension of DEA to effectiveness analysis. J Oper Res Soc 39:725–734

Golany B (1988b) Note on including ordinal relations among multipliers in data envelopment analysis. Manage Sci 34:1029–1032

Golany B, Roll YA (1994) Incorporating standards via DEA. In: Charnes A, Cooper WW, Lewin AY, Seiford LM (eds) Data envelopment analysis: theory, methodology and applications. Kluwer Academic, Boston, pp 313–328

Golany B, Thore S (1997) Restricted best practice selection in DEA: an overview with a case study evaluating the socio-economic performance of nations. Ann Oper Res 73:117–140

Halme M, Korhonen P (2000) Restricting weights in value efficiency analysis. Eur J Oper Res 126 (1):175–188

Halme M, Joro T, Korhonen P, Salo S, Wallenius J (1999) A value efficiency approach to incorporating preference information in data envelopment analysis. Manage Sci 45(1):103–115

Halme M, Joro T, Koivu M (2002) Dealing with interval scale data in data envelopment analysis. Eur J Oper Res 137(1):22–27

Joro T, Viitala E-J (2004) Weight-restricted DEA in action: from expert opinions to mathematical models. J Oper Res Soc 55(8):814–821

Korhonen P (1987) VIG—a visual interactive support system for multiple criteria decision making. Belg J Oper Res Stat Comput Sci 27:3–15

Korhonen P (2001) Searching the efficient Frontier in data envelopment analysis. In: Bouyssou D, Jacquet-Lagrèze E, Perny P, Słowiński R, Vanderpooten D, Vincke P (eds) Aiding decisions with multiple criteria (essays in Honor of Bernard Roy). Kluwer Academic, Boston, pp 543–558

Korhonen P, Laakso J (1986) A visual interactive method for solving the multiple criteria problem. Eur J Oper Res 24:277–287

Korhonen P, Wallenius J (1988) A pareto race. Naval Res Log 35:615–623

Korhonen P, Wallenius J (1989) A careful look at efficiency and utility in multiple criteria decision making a tutorial. Asia Pac J Oper Res 6:46–62

Korhonen P, Silvennoinen K, Wallenius J, Öörni A (2013) Can a linear value function explain choices? An experimental study. Eur J Oper Res 219(2):360–367

Lovell CAK (1993) Production Frontiers and productive efficiency. In: Fried HO, Schmidt SS (eds) The measurement of productive efficiency: techniques and applications. Oxford University Press, Oxford, pp 3–67

Pedraja-Chaparro F, Salinas-Jimenez J, Smith P (1997) On the role of weight restrictions in data envelopment analysis. J Prod Anal 8:215–230

Podinovski V (1999) Side effects of absolute weight bounds in DEA models. Eur J Oper Res 115:583–595

Podinovski VV (2001a) DEA models for the explicit maximisation of relative efficiency. Eur J Oper Res 131(3):572–586

Podinovski VV (2001b) Validating absolute weight bounds in Data Envelopment Analysis (DEA) models. J Oper Res Soc 52(2):221–225

Podinovski VV (2004) Production trade-offs and weight restrictions in data envelopment analysis. J Oper Res Soc 55(12):1311–1322

Podinovski VV, Athanassopoulos AD (1998) Assessing the relative efficiency of decision making units using DEA models with weight restrictions. J Oper Res Soc 49:500–508

Roll Y, Golany B (1993) Alternate methods of treating factor weights in DEA. Omega 21:99–109

Roll Y, Cook WD, Golany B (1991) Controlling factor weights in data envelopment analysis. IIE Trans 23:2–9

Ruggiero J, Bretschneider S (1998) The weighted Russell measure of technical efficiency. Eur J Oper Res 108:438–451

Sárrico CS, Dyson RG (2004) Restricting virtual weights in data envelopment analysis. EJOR 159 (1):17–34

Sexton TR, Silkman RH, Hogan AJ (1986) Data envelopment analysis: critique and extensions. In: Silkman RH (ed) Measuring efficiency: an assessment of data envelopment analysis. Jossey-Bass, San Francisco, pp 73–105

Sinuany-Stern Z, Mehrez A, Barboy A (1994) Academic departments efficiency via data envelopment analysis. Comput Oper Res 21(5):543–556

Steuer RE (1986) Multiple criteria optimization: theory, computation and application. Wiley, New York

Steuer RE, Choo EU (1983) An interactive weighted Tchebycheff procedure for multiple objective programming. Math Program 26:326–344

Thanassoulis E, Allen R (1998) Simulating weight restrictions in data envelopment analysis by means of unobserved DMUs. Manag Sci 44:586–594

Thanassoulis E, Dyson RG (1992) Estimating preferred target input-output levels using data envelopment analysis. Eur J Oper Res 56:80–97

Thanassoulis E, Boussofiane A, Dyson RG (1995) Exploring output quality targets in the provision of perinatal care in England using data envelopment analysis. Eur J Oper Res 80:588–607

Thompson RG, Singleton FR Jr, Thrall RM, Smith BA (1986) Comparative site evaluation for locating a high-energy physics lab in Texas. Interfaces 16:35–49

Thompson RG, Langemeier LM, Lee C-T, Lee E, Thrall RM (1990) The role of multiplier bounds in efficiency analysis with application to Kansas farming. J Econ 46:93–108

Thompson RG, Lee E, Thrall RM (1992) DEA/AR efficiency of U.S. independent oil/gas producers over time. Comput Oper Res 19:377–392

Torgersen AM, Førsund FR, Kittelsen SAC (1996) Slack-adjusted efficiency measures and ranking of efficient units. J Prod Anal 7:379–398

Wei Q, Yu G (1997) Analyzing properties of K-cones in the generalized data envelopment analysis model. J Econom 80(1):63–84

Wierzbicki A (1986) On the completeness and constructiveness of parametric characterizations to vector optimization problems. OR Spektrum 8:73–87

Wilson P (1995) Detecting influential observations in data envelopment analysis. J Prod Anal 6:27–45

Wong Y-HB, Beasley JE (1990) Restricting weight flexibility in data envelopment analysis. J Oper Res Soc 41:829–835

Yu PL (1974) Cone convexity, cone extreme point, and nondominated solutions in decision problems with multi-objectives. J Optim Theory Appl 14:319–377

Zhu J (1996) Data envelopment analysis with preference structure. J Oper Res Soc 47:136–150

Chapter 7
Value Efficiency Analysis

Most Preferred Unit-Based Approach

7.1 Background

A basic assumption in multiple criteria decision-making research is that there is no objectively best solution for the problem. The best solution depends on a rational DM's preferences. The term "rational" means that the DM wants to choose the solution for which there is no other solution that is equally good on all given criteria and better at least on one criterion. As we have defined in Chap. 4, such solutions are called nondominated.

An original DEA problem (Charnes et al. 1978, 1979) is value free. If a unit is on the efficient frontier, it is regarded as good as other efficient units. If a unit is inefficient, it is projected onto the efficient frontier radially or using some other prespecified feature. Even the ranking of the units is based on the use of an "efficiency" measure such as an efficiency score.

When the DM is willing to insert his/her preference information into the analysis, the problem turns into a typical multiple criteria problem: there is a need not to consider efficient units equally good. A typical approach in DEA (see Chap. 6) is to use weights for inputs and/or outputs or to operate with target values.

The use of weights often is based on the intuitively appealing notion "the greater the importance, the larger the weight." Unfortunately, it does not always work. If the weights have a straightforward interpretation, such as prices, their definition and use is also straightforward. However, this is not always the case. When inputs are some raw materials and outputs produced goods, it is relatively easy to see the weights as prices. But when outputs are, for example, Ph.D. degrees and refereed publications or lives saved, it may be practically or politically impossible for the DM to give price estimates.

Identifying a target or ideal point is a natural way to give preference information, but a DM needs guidance to set up targets which are realistic and please him/her. Often the ultimate goal is to find the solution that the DM prefers most at the

© Springer Science+Business Media New York 2015
T. Joro, P.J. Korhonen, *Extension of Data Envelopment Analysis with Preference Information*, International Series in Operations Research & Management Science 218, DOI 10.1007/978-1-4899-7528-7_7

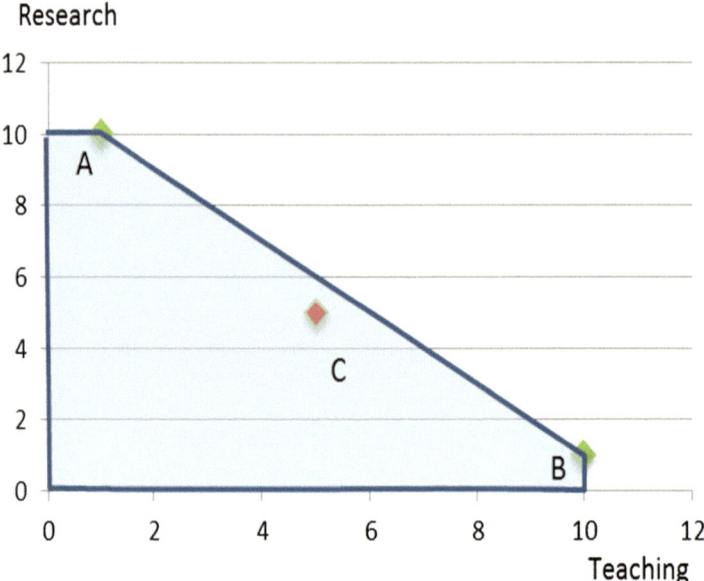

Fig. 7.1 Illustration on the use of weights and targets

moment of the final choice.[1] Such solution is called most preferred unit (MPU)/ most preferred solution (MPS).

When identifying targets, it is also important that the method provides a DM with a possibility to learn and to have a holistic view over possible solutions. Interactive approaches are suitable to fulfill these requirements.

The following example describes challenges of using weights and targets.

Example 7.1 Let us assume that three candidates have applied for a research assistant vacancy. We evaluate them with two criteria (outputs) on the scale from 1 to 10: competence in teaching and competence in research. We assume a constant input ($=1$). As we can see from Fig. 7.1, candidates A and B are efficient when the convex production possibility set is assumed.

Suppose we specify our preference expressing that research is slightly "more important" than teaching. If we interpret this expression as weights, it means that the weight of research is somewhat higher than that of teaching. The best candidate is A. Is this really the solution the DM is looking for? Perhaps not because he used the expression that research is only slightly "more important" and A is an excellent researcher, but a rather lousy teacher. The weights are an indirect way to find a candidate we are looking for, but sometimes the solution is quite poor.

---

[1] We use the expression "at the moment of the final choice," because we allow that the DM is learning and can change his/her mind during the search process.

Another way to find the candidate we are looking for is target setting. Freely given targets are very seldom on the efficient frontier—or not even feasible. That's why we need a method which has a good correspondence between a given target point and the efficient point approximating target values.

Consider a target setting approach proposed by Thanassoulis and Dyson (1992); see also Sect. 6.4.1. If a DM specifies point (10, 10) as a target and considers research slightly more important than teaching, using model (6.12), his/her solution is point A. Point A is efficient; thus model (6.13) does not change the solution. If he/she uses point C (reasonably good) as a target, model (6.12) does not change the situation, but model (6.13) gives either point (5.5, 6) or (6, 5.5) as a solution. (Any convex combination between those extreme values gives the same optimal solution.) In this case, the result is quite satisfactory.

In this chapter we present an approach where DM's preferences are incorporated into the efficiency analysis by first explicitly locating his/her MPS and then developing an efficiency measure which takes into account the preference information based on the choice of the MPS. The MPS is located using an interactive MOLP search procedure as described in Chap. 4. The search of MPS can be carried out by any MCDM procedure. The approach called *value efficiency analysis* is introduced in the theoretical production possibility set (T) framework. In practice, set T is replaced by the empirical production possibility set P.

Conceptually, an MPS can be defined as the point at which the DM's value function reaches its maximum when the search terminates. The value function is assumed to be pseudoconcave for outputs and for the negation of inputs.[2] Using the knowledge of the MPS, the indifference surface of a DM's (known only implicitly) value function at the MPS is approximated using the so-called tangent cones at the MPS. The efficiency of each DMU is then determined with respect to this tangent cone.

As a result we obtain scores that we call *value efficiency* scores, since the efficiency of each DMU is determined by means of an approximation of the indifference surface of an implicitly known value function at the MPS. The tangent cones implicitly defined a range for acceptable weights, or prices, as the weight restriction approaches do. However, we argue that it is easier for the DM to articulate his/her preferences as a preferred unit than weight restrictions.

In Chap. 8 the value efficiency analysis is further developed. Whereas the original value efficiency scores are optimistic estimates of the true scores, Chap. 8 presents an interactive procedure to determine true value efficiency scores. A procedure to test the assumptions of the value efficiency analysis is also presented. Some other points are also discussed in Chap. 8.

---

[2] The value function was defined strictly increasing to the criteria to be maximized.

7.2 Basic Concepts

In value efficiency analysis the purpose is to assist the DM to evaluate how much each vector $u = \begin{bmatrix} y \\ -x \end{bmatrix} \in T$ has to be improved to make it as preferable as the MPS. We are able to evaluate the value at $u \in \mathfrak{R}^{m+s}$ if we know the value function or it could be estimated. Unfortunately, generally in practice both assumptions are not realistic. That is why we use a different approach to incorporating a DM's preferences in the efficiency analysis. Our approach is based on the idea of using the DM's MPS as a way to have preference information.

The only assumption that we make about the DM's value function $v(u): \mathfrak{R}^{m+s} \to \mathfrak{R}$ is that it is pseudoconcave at the moment when the search for the MPS is terminated. When we have found the MPS, we approximate the indifference surface passing through the MPS. We first characterize the set of the tangent hyperplanes of the contours of all possible pseudoconcave value functions reaching the maximum at MPS. Then we evaluate the need to improve the current values of inputs and/or outputs in the spirit of DEA to reach the approximated indifference curve.

We assume a rational DM who prefers more of any output and less of any input. Thus the MPS is efficient. Our theoretical assumption is that the MPS is preferred by the DM to all other solutions. Unfortunately defining the MPS in this way provides no practical tool for efficiency analysis. It is not realistic to assume that the DM is generally able to compare all possible solutions to the final solution at the end of the search. In practice, the MPS is a solution at which the search process ends. It is difficult to know how good it is, because the DM will learn during the search process and even change his/her mind due to learning process. That's why we simply assume that the MPS is the solution at which the DM's value function $v(u): \mathfrak{R}^{m+s} \to \mathfrak{R}$ obtains its maximum over T. Note that we do not need to make any assumptions whatsoever concerning the value function during the search process. We only need the assumptions at the moment of termination in order to be able to say "something" about the quality of the final solution. The weaker these assumptions are, the better. We assume that the choice of the MPS was based on the DM's value function $v(u)$, $u = \begin{bmatrix} y \\ -x \end{bmatrix} \in \mathfrak{R}^{m+s}$, which is strictly increasing[3] (i.e., strictly increasing in y and in the negation of x) and with a (local) maximal value $v(u^*)$ over T, $u^* = \begin{bmatrix} y^* \\ -x^* \end{bmatrix} \in \mathfrak{R}^{m+s}$. Furthermore, we assume that v is pseudoconcave, because then its local optimum over a convex set is also global (Bazaraa et al. 1993, p. 570) and the optimality conditions can easily be verified. If the DM does not find a better solution in the environment of the currently best solution, it means that the current solution is locally optimal and further globally optimal, because v is assumed pseudoconcave.

---

[3] Function $f: \mathfrak{R}^k \to \mathfrak{R}$ is strictly increasing if $x_1 \geq x_2 \wedge x_1 \neq x_2 \Rightarrow f(x_1) > f(x_2)$.

Next we give some definitions.

Definition 7.1 Let S be a nonempty set in $\mathfrak{R}^k$, and let $f: \mathfrak{R}^k \to \mathfrak{R}$ be differentiable on S. The function f is said to be *pseudoconcave* if for each $x_1, x_2 \in S$ with $\nabla f(x)^T(x_2 - x_1) \leq 0 \Rightarrow f(x_2) \leq f(x_1)$.

Note that pseudoconcave functions are by definition differentiable and therefore continuous.

Definition 7.2 Assuming that $u^* \in T$ is the DM's most preferred solution, point $u \in \mathfrak{R}^{m+s}$ is *value efficient* iff $v(u) \geq v(u^*)$. If the point $u \in \mathfrak{R}^{m+s}$ is not *value efficient*, it is called *value inefficient*.

Definition 7.3 The *weighted true value efficiency score* γ for point u^0 is defined as $E_t^w(u^0) = \gamma^T$, where γ^T is the optimal value of the objective function of the following problem:

$$\sup \gamma$$
$$\text{s.t.} \tag{7.1}$$
$$u - \gamma w \geq u^0$$
$$u \in V = \left\{ u \mid v(u) \leq v(u^*) \right\}$$
$$w > 0$$

The function $v: \mathfrak{R}^k \to \mathfrak{R}$ is a pseudoconcave value function.

Lemma 7.1 Let $v: \mathfrak{R}^k \to \mathfrak{R}$ be a pseudoconcave value function. The following assertions are true:

1. $\gamma^T = 0$ iff $v(u^0) = v(u^*)$ (u^0 is *value efficient*).
2. $\gamma^T > 0$ iff $v(u^0) < v(u^*)$ (u^0 is *value inefficient*).
3. $\gamma^T < 0$ iff $v(u^0) > v(u^*)$ (u^0 is *value superefficient*).

Proof The result is proven for a general continuous strictly increasing function v in Soleimani-damaneh et al. (2014). □

In (7.1), if we set $w = u^0$, the model becomes radial in y and radial in x, and we may interpret γ^T as the percentage of improvement needed in both inputs and outputs to make u^0 value efficient.

Unfortunately, it is not realistic to assume that a DM's value function is known. Hence we only assume its form. Because all interactive algorithms stop in a finite number of steps, then instead of worrying about a convergence, it is more interesting to know how good the solution is, where the process terminates. If we assume that the value function is pseudoconcave, from hence it follows that the final solution is also globally best provided that one cannot find a feasible direction of improvement from the solution (see for more information Korhonen and Laakso 1986).

Performing the search for the MPS is discussed in Chap. 4. The MPS lies on the indifference contour of the DM's value function possessing the highest possible

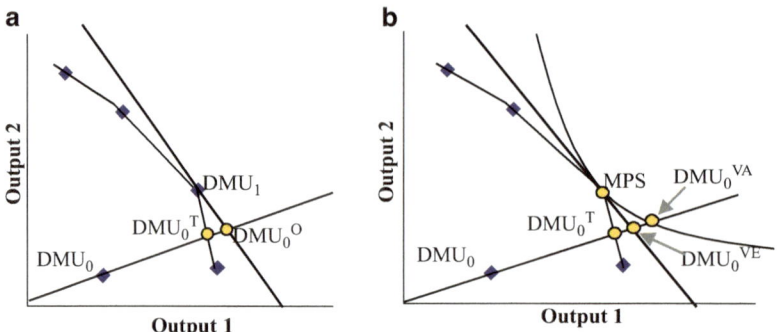

Fig. 7.2 (**a**, **b**) Overall efficiency and value efficiency

value among all feasible input/output vectors in T. Accordingly, the MPS has the highest possible *value efficiency* for the DM. Value inefficient DMUs should increase their performance to reach the contour on which the MPS lies in order to achieve the same value efficiency.

It is interesting to compare value efficiency to the concepts of classical efficiency: technical and overall efficiency (Farrell 1957). (See, e.g., Coelli et al. (2005) for a discussion of classical efficiency analysis and DEA.) Figure 7.2a, b illustrates different situations. Again, we assume that the DMUs consume the same amount of single input to produce two outputs.

Figure 7.2a illustrates the concept of classical efficiency. The downward sloping line through DMU_0^O represents the revenue equation, thus containing information about the prices. Only DMU_1 is overall efficient. For DMU_0 the ratio $\frac{O\text{-}DMU_0}{O\text{-}DMU_0^T}$ reflects technical efficiency and ratio $\frac{O\text{-}DMU_0}{O\text{-}DMU_0^O}$ overall efficiency ("O" refers to the origin).

Next, we seek to clarify the connection between classical overall efficiency and value efficiency. Classical overall efficiency is based on the idea of maximizing (minimizing) a known revenue (cost) function. In value efficiency analysis, this revenue function is replaced by a more general unknown pseudoconcave value function. Furthermore, we assume that the maximum of this function is known, but its precise form is unknown. Based on this information, in value efficiency analysis, we estimate "overall efficiency." More precisely, we postulate that the value function $\nu(\boldsymbol{u})$ is a pseudoconcave, which obtains its maximum over T at the MPS $\boldsymbol{u}^*$. The contours of a pseudoconcave function lie above their tangent hyperplanes. Hence we use the tangent hyperplane at the MPS as a linear approximation of $\nu(\boldsymbol{u})$. In Fig. 7.2b, the $\frac{O\text{-}DMU_0}{O\text{-}DMU_0^T}$ reflects technical efficiency. The ratio $\frac{O\text{-}DMU_0}{O\text{-}DMU_0^{VA}}$ reflects (true) value efficiency and the ratio $\frac{O\text{-}DMU_0}{O\text{-}DMU_0^{VE}}$ the approximated value efficiency score. For a value efficient unit, value efficiency score is zero. Unfortunately, we do not know the value function precisely. That's why we can neither specify its tangent precisely, but it is necessary to consider all possible tangents. It means that we cannot even use the approximation above. The requisite theory is developed in the next section. Our approximation of the value efficiency score is optimistic: it provides a lower bound for the true value efficiency score.   □

7.3   Mathematical Considerations

In this subsection we present the requisite mathematical theory to formulate an operational model for computing *value efficiency scores*.

Definition 7.4   A nonempty set G_x defined in an n-dimensional Euclidean space $\mathfrak{R}^n$ is called a *cone* with vertex x, if $x + y \in G_x \Rightarrow x + \lambda y \in G_x$ for all $\lambda \geq 0$. The cone with the origin as vertex is denoted by G.

Note that vertex $x \in G_x$. A singleton $\{x\}$ is also a cone with vertex x.

Definition 7.5   Let X be a nonempty polytope in $\mathfrak{R}^n$ and let $x \in X$. The cone $D(x)$ in $\mathfrak{R}^n$ is called the *cone of feasible directions* of X at x, if $D(x) = \{d \mid x + \lambda d \in X$ for all $\lambda \in (0, \delta)$ for some $\delta > 0\}$. Each $d \in D(x)$, $d \neq 0$, is called a feasible direction. The cone $G_x = \{y \mid y = x + d, d \in D(x)\}$ is called the *tangent cone* of X at x and the cone $W_x = \{s \mid s = y + z, y \in G_x, z \in \mathfrak{R}^n_-\}$ the *augmented tangent cone* of X at x.

Note that both G_x and W_x are closed and convex. For any $s \in W_x$ there is $y \in G_x$ such that $s \leq y$ and all points $z \leq s$ are in W_x.

We illustrate the tangent cone and the augmented tangent cone in Fig. 7.3. The area defines the polytope X. The tangent cone G_x at x is spanned by vectors d_1 and d_2, and the augmented tangent cone W_x by vectors d_1 and d_3.

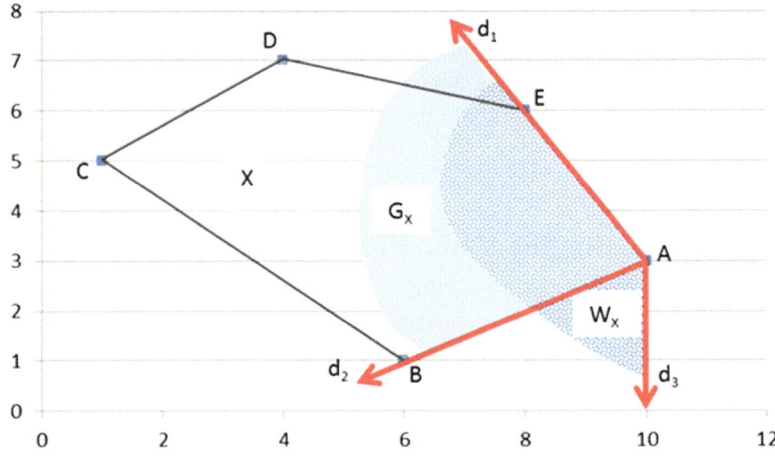

Fig. 7.3   Example illustrating the tangent and the augmented tangent cone

Lemma 7.2 Let $X = \{x|Ax = b, x \geq 0\}$ be a nonempty polytope, where $A \in \mathfrak{R}^{k \times n}$, $b \in \mathfrak{R}^k$, and $x^0 \in X$ an arbitrary point. Then $G_{x^0} = X^0$, where $X^0 = \{x|Ax = b, x_j \geq 0$ if $x_j^0 = 0$, and otherwise x_j is free, $j = 1, 2, \ldots, n\}$.

Proof Clearly the tangent cone of an affine set $X_a = \{x|Ax = b\}$ at x^0 is X_a itself. Moreover, the tangent cone of the closed half-space $H_j = \{x|x_j \geq 0\}$ at x^0 is $\mathfrak{R}^n$ if $x_j^0 > 0$ and H_j, if $x_j^0 = 0$, $j = 1, \ldots, n$. Because X is the intersection of X_a and the half-spaces H_j, $j = 1, \ldots, n$, the tangent cone of X at x^0 is the intersection of their tangent cones, respectively, i.e., set X^0. $\qquad\qquad\square$

Lemma 7.3 Let $U = \{u \in \mathfrak{R}^m | u = Bx, x \in X\}$, $B \in \mathfrak{R}^{m \times n}$ where $X = \{x|Ax = b, x \geq 0\}$, be a linear transformation of a nonempty polytope X and $u^0 \in U$ an arbitrary point. Let $x^0 \in X$ be any point such that $u^0 = Bx^0$. Then the tangent cone of U at u^0 is $G_{u^0} = BG_{x^0} = \{u|u = Bx, x \in G_{x^0}\}$.

Proof Any $u \in G_{u^0}$, $u \neq u^0$, defines a feasible direction $u - u^0$ for U at u^0, which must be generated by a feasible direction $x - x^0$ for X at x^0. Thus $G_{u^0} \subset BG_{x^0}$. Any $x \in G_{x^0}$, $x \neq x^0$, defines a feasible direction $x - x^0$ for X at x^0, which defines a feasible direction $u - u^0$ for U at u^0. Thus $G_{u^0} \supset BG_{x^0}$. $\qquad\qquad\square$

Let $X \subset \mathfrak{R}^n$ be a nonempty polytope and $x^* \in X$. Define $\Xi(x^*)$ as the set of strictly increasing pseudoconcave functions $\xi: \mathfrak{R}^n \to \mathfrak{R}$ which obtain their maximum in X at $x^* \in X$.

Lemma 7.4 Let $x^* \in X$ and $\Xi(x^*) \neq \varnothing$. Denote the *augmented tangent cone* of X at x^* by W_{x^*}. Then $x \in W_{x^*}$ iff $\xi(x) \leq \xi(x^*)$ for all $\xi \in \Xi(x^*)$.

Proof Let $x \in W_{x^*}$. Then there is $y \in G_{x^*}$ such that $x \leq y$. ξ is increasing $\Rightarrow \xi(x) \leq \xi(y)$. $y - x^* \in D(x^*)$ and ξ obtains its maximum in X at $x^* \Rightarrow \nabla\xi(x^*)^T(y - x^*) \leq 0$. Because ξ is pseudoconcave, $\xi(y) \leq \xi(x^*) \Rightarrow \xi(x) \leq \xi(x^*)$ for all $\xi \in \Xi(x^*)$. To prove the second part, let $x \in \mathfrak{R}^n$ for which $\xi(x) \leq \xi(x^*)$ for all $\xi \in \Xi(x^*)$. Assume $x \notin W_{x^*}$. Then, x can be strongly separated from W_{x^*}, i.e., $\exists p \in \mathfrak{R}^n$ such that $p^Tx > p^Ty$ for all $y \notin W_{x^*}$, i.e., for any $y = x^* + d + z$, where $d \in D(x^*)$, $z \leq 0$. Hence $p^Td \leq 0$ and $p^Tz \leq 0$ ($\Rightarrow p \geq 0$), because otherwise p^Td or p^Tz could be positive and arbitrarily large. Therefore a pseudoconcave increasing function $\xi(x) = p^Tx$ obtains its maximum in X at x^*, i.e., $\xi \in \Xi(x^*)$, and $\xi(x) > \xi(x^*)$ contrary to the assumption that $\xi(x) \leq \xi(x^*)$. $\qquad\square$

7.4 Approximating the Value Efficiency Scores

Now we are in a position to formulate and prove the requisite theorems for evaluating value efficiency. We make use of Lemmas 7.2–7.4 by substituting $\mathfrak{R}^{m+s}$ for $\mathfrak{R}^n$, set Λ for set X, set T for set U, and set $\Xi(u^*)$ for set $\Xi(x^*)$, where $\Xi(u^*)$ is the set of pseudoconcave strictly increasing functions $v(u)$, which obtain their maximum in T at u^*.

Lemma 7.4 is employed when approximating the set $V = \left\{ u = \begin{bmatrix} y \\ -x \end{bmatrix} \middle| v(u) \leq v(u^*) \right\}$ where v may be any function in $\Xi(u^*)$. This means that when the projections of inefficient units are restricted to the indifference contours of this set, the resulting efficiency scores are always surely better than the true ones.

Theorem 7.1 W_{u^*} is the largest cone with the property $W_{u^*} \subset V = \{u|v(u) \leq v(u^*)$, for any $v \in \Xi(u^*)\}$.

Proof Evident from Lemma 7.4. □

Thus V is approximated by the cone W_{u^*}, the tangent cone of T at u^* with all input/output points weakly dominated by T appended, which guarantees that the resulting scores are optimistic (not greater than the real ones). Without supplementary information this is the best approximation available for set V in the sense that it is the largest set contained in all the sets of input/output points which are not preferred by any pseudoconcave value function $v(u) \in \Xi(u^*)$.

Theorem 7.2 Let $u^* = \begin{bmatrix} y^* \\ -x^* \end{bmatrix} \in T$ be the DM's most preferred solution. Then $u \in \mathfrak{R}^{m+p}$, an arbitrary point in the input/output space, is value inefficient with respect to any strictly increasing pseudoconcave value function $v(u)$, $u = \begin{bmatrix} y \\ -x \end{bmatrix}$ with a maximum at point u^*, if the optimum value Z^* of the following problem is strictly positive:

$$\max Z = \sigma + \varepsilon \left(1^T s^+ + 1^T s^- \right)$$

$$\text{s.t.} \tag{7.2}$$

$$Y\lambda - \sigma\omega^y - s^+ = y_0$$
$$X\lambda + \sigma\omega^y + s^- = x_0$$
$$A\lambda + \delta = b$$
$$s^-, s^+ \geq 0$$
$$\varepsilon > 0$$
$$\lambda_j \geq 0, \quad \text{if } \lambda_j^* = 0, \quad j = 1, 2, \ldots, n$$
$$\delta_j \geq 0, \quad \text{if } \delta_j^* = 0, \quad j = 1, 2, \ldots, k$$

where $\lambda^* \in \Lambda$, δ^* correspond to the most preferred solutions,

$$y^* = Y\lambda^*$$
$$x^* = X\lambda^*$$

Proof By Lemmas 7.2 and 7.3 the tangent cone of T at $\boldsymbol{u}^*$ is the set $\left\{ \begin{bmatrix} \boldsymbol{v} \\ -\boldsymbol{z} \end{bmatrix} \middle| \boldsymbol{v}{=}\mathbf{Y}\boldsymbol{\lambda}, \boldsymbol{z}{=}\mathbf{X}\boldsymbol{\lambda}, \boldsymbol{\lambda} \in \mathbf{G}_{\lambda^*} \right\}$, where the tangent cone of Λ at $\boldsymbol{\lambda}^*$ is $G_{\lambda^*} = \left\{ \boldsymbol{\lambda} \middle| \mathbf{A}\boldsymbol{\lambda} + \boldsymbol{\mu} = \boldsymbol{b}, \lambda_j \geq 0 \text{ if } \lambda_j^* = 0, j = 1, 2, \ldots, n, \mu_j \geq 0 \text{ if } \mu_j^* = 0, j = 1, 2, \ldots, k \right\}$. The augmented tangent cone $W_{\boldsymbol{u}^*}$ of T at $\boldsymbol{u}^*$ is the set $\left\{ \begin{bmatrix} \boldsymbol{v} \\ -\boldsymbol{z} \end{bmatrix} \middle| \boldsymbol{v}{=}\mathbf{Y}\boldsymbol{\lambda} + \boldsymbol{d}^y, \boldsymbol{z}{=}\mathbf{X}\boldsymbol{\lambda} + \boldsymbol{d}^x, \boldsymbol{d}^y \leq \boldsymbol{0}, \boldsymbol{d}^x \geq \boldsymbol{0}, \boldsymbol{\lambda} \in \mathbf{G}_{\lambda^*} \right\}$. Therefore (7.2) has a solution with $\sigma \geq 0$ only if $\begin{bmatrix} \boldsymbol{y} \\ -\boldsymbol{x} \end{bmatrix} \in W_{\boldsymbol{u}^*}$. Now let $Z^*, \boldsymbol{\lambda}^s, \sigma^s, \boldsymbol{\mu}^s$ be a solution of (7.2). With $\varepsilon > 0$, $Z^* > 0$ only if either $\sigma^s > 0$ or $\sigma^s = 0$ and $(\boldsymbol{s}^-, \boldsymbol{s}^+) \neq (\boldsymbol{0}, \boldsymbol{0})$. In either case, $\begin{bmatrix} \boldsymbol{v}^s \\ -\boldsymbol{z}^s \end{bmatrix} \in W_{\boldsymbol{u}^*}$, $\boldsymbol{y}^s = \mathbf{Y}\boldsymbol{\lambda}^s \geq \boldsymbol{y}$, $\boldsymbol{x}^s = \mathbf{X}\boldsymbol{\lambda}^s \leq \boldsymbol{x}$, and $(\boldsymbol{y}, \boldsymbol{x}) \neq (\boldsymbol{y}^s, \boldsymbol{x}^s)$. Thus $v(\boldsymbol{y}, -\boldsymbol{x}) < v(\boldsymbol{y}^s, -\boldsymbol{x}^s) \leq v(\boldsymbol{y}^*, -\boldsymbol{x}^*)$, and by Theorem 7.1, $(\boldsymbol{y}, \boldsymbol{x})$ is value inefficient. □

Definition 7.6 The (*weighted*) *value efficiency score* for point $\boldsymbol{u}^0$ is defined as

$$E^{\mathrm{W}} \left(\boldsymbol{y}^0, -\boldsymbol{x}^0 \right) = \sigma^s$$

where σ^s is the value of σ at the optimal solution of problem (7.2).

Note that $\sigma^s > 0$ means that the point $\boldsymbol{u}^0$ is *value inefficient*. It is also *value inefficient* if $\sigma^s = 0$ and $\boldsymbol{1}^{\mathrm{T}}(\boldsymbol{s}^+ + \boldsymbol{s}^-) > 0$; otherwise $\sigma^s = 0$ means that the point is diagnosed *value efficient*. However, the point is not necessarily truly *value efficient*. Formulation (7.2) only guarantees that we use the largest possible set guaranteed not to include value efficient points except $\boldsymbol{u}^*$ to diagnose value inefficiency, but it is not the set consisting of all value inefficient points. If $\sigma^s < 0$, the point is diagnosed *value superefficient*. In that case the point does not belong to the production possibility set T.

Remark It is important to note that the most preferred solution $\boldsymbol{u}^* = \begin{bmatrix} \boldsymbol{y}^* \\ -\boldsymbol{x}^* \end{bmatrix}$ was assumed efficient in T. Then $D_{\boldsymbol{u}^*} = \{\boldsymbol{u} | \boldsymbol{u} = \boldsymbol{u}^* + \boldsymbol{w}, \boldsymbol{w} > \boldsymbol{0}\}$ is separated from T and also from $W_{\boldsymbol{u}^*}$. For any finite $\boldsymbol{w} > \boldsymbol{0}$ and $\boldsymbol{u}$, there is a finite σ so that $\boldsymbol{u} + \sigma\boldsymbol{w} > \boldsymbol{u}^* \Rightarrow \boldsymbol{u} + \sigma\boldsymbol{w} \in D_{\boldsymbol{u}^*} \Rightarrow \boldsymbol{u} + \sigma\boldsymbol{w} \notin W_{\boldsymbol{u}^*}$ and   a   finite σ so   that $\boldsymbol{u} + \sigma\boldsymbol{w} < \boldsymbol{u}^* \Rightarrow \boldsymbol{u} + \sigma\boldsymbol{w} \in W_{\boldsymbol{u}^*}$. Therefore for an efficient MPS, the solution of (7.2) is guaranteed to be bounded. If $\boldsymbol{u}^*$ is not efficient, e.g., an interior point of T, in which case $W_{\boldsymbol{u}^*} = \mathfrak{R}^{m+p}$ and (7.2) is guaranteed to be unbounded.

7.5 Value Efficiency Model

The models to evaluate value efficiency in envelopment and multiplier are given in Table 7.1.

Table 7.1 General value efficiency model in multiple and envelopment form

General value efficiency multiplier model	General value efficiency envelopment model
$\min \boldsymbol{\nu}^T \boldsymbol{g}^x - \boldsymbol{\mu}^T \boldsymbol{g}^y + \boldsymbol{\eta}^T \boldsymbol{b}$ s.t. $\quad -\boldsymbol{\mu}^T \mathbf{Y} + \boldsymbol{\nu}^T \mathbf{X} + \boldsymbol{\eta}^T \mathbf{A} - \boldsymbol{\gamma} = \mathbf{0}$ $\quad \boldsymbol{\mu}^T \boldsymbol{w}^y + \boldsymbol{\nu}^T \boldsymbol{w}^x = 1$ $\quad \boldsymbol{\mu}, \boldsymbol{\nu} \geq \varepsilon \mathbf{1}$ $\quad \varepsilon > 0$ $\gamma_j \begin{cases} \geq 0 & \text{if } \lambda_j^* = 0 \\ = 0 & \text{if } \lambda_j^* > 0 \end{cases}, \quad j = 1, 2, \ldots, n$ $\eta \begin{cases} \geq 0 & \text{if } \delta_j^* = 0 \\ = 0 & \text{if } \delta_j^* > 0 \end{cases}, \quad j = 1, 2, \ldots, k$ where $\boldsymbol{\lambda}^* \in \Lambda$, $\boldsymbol{\delta}^*$ correspond to the most preferred solution: $\quad\quad \boldsymbol{y}^* = \mathbf{Y}\boldsymbol{\lambda}^*$ $\quad\quad \boldsymbol{x}^* = \mathbf{X}\boldsymbol{\lambda}^*$	$\max \sigma + \varepsilon \left(\mathbf{1}^T \boldsymbol{s}^+ + \mathbf{1}^T \boldsymbol{s}^- \right)$ s.t. $\quad \mathbf{Y}\boldsymbol{\lambda} - \sigma \boldsymbol{w}^y - \boldsymbol{s}^+ = \boldsymbol{g}^y$ $\quad \mathbf{X}\boldsymbol{\lambda} + \sigma \boldsymbol{w}^x + \boldsymbol{s}^- = \boldsymbol{g}^x$ $\quad \mathbf{A}\boldsymbol{\lambda} + \boldsymbol{\delta} = \boldsymbol{b}$ $\quad \boldsymbol{s}^-, \boldsymbol{s}^+ \geq \mathbf{0}$ $\quad \varepsilon > 0$ $\lambda_j \begin{cases} \geq 0 & \text{if } \lambda_j^* = 0 \\ = \text{free} & \text{if } \lambda_j^* > 0 \end{cases}, \quad j = 1, 2, \ldots, n$ $\delta_j \begin{cases} \geq 0 & \text{if } \delta_j^* = 0 \\ = \text{free} & \text{if } \delta_j^* > 0 \end{cases}, \quad j = 1, 2, \ldots, k$ where $\boldsymbol{\lambda}^* \in \Lambda$, $\boldsymbol{\delta}^*$ correspond to the most preferred solution: $\quad\quad \boldsymbol{y}^* = \mathbf{Y}\boldsymbol{\lambda}^*$ $\quad\quad \boldsymbol{x}^* = \mathbf{X}\boldsymbol{\lambda}^*$

The only difference compared with standard primal DEA models is that some variables are allowed to have negative values. This simple modification of the DEA model makes it possible to take into account value judgments in the form of the MPS.

As we can see from Table 7.1, the tangent cone for the efficient frontier at the MPS can also be characterized by using the dual model. Then the problem can be seen as a special case of cone ratio DEA models by Charnes et al. (1989) (see also Charnes et al. (1990)). The cone is defined by restricting the values of input and output multipliers in such a way that they are located in the cone spanned by all normal vectors of the efficient facets meeting at the MPS (for more detailed discussion, see Sect. 9.2 and Halme and Korhonen (2000)). However, this approach requires far more computations than the approach by Halme et al. (1999).

7.6 An Illustrative Example

We illustrate the value efficiency analysis with a simple BCC model used in Chap. 6:[4]

---

[4] To improve readability, we have changed the order of input and output rows.

Table 7.2 The results of value efficiency analysis of DMU$_6$

MPS	α^* DMU$_3$ + $(1-\alpha)^*$ DMU$_4$, $\alpha \in (0, 1)$					
	DMU$_3$	DMU$_4$	DMU$_5$	σ	Input	Output
A:	1.966	−0.966		0.690	3.103	5.069
B:	−0.333	1.333		2.222	10	9.667
MPS	DMU$_4$					
	DMU$_3$	DMU$_4$	DMU$_5$	σ	Input	Output
C:	1.966	−0.966		0.690	3.103	5.069
D:		0.75	0.25	2.083	10	9.25

$$\max \sigma + \varepsilon(s^+ + s^-)$$
$$\text{s.t.} \tag{7.3}$$
$$3\lambda_1 + 4\lambda_2 + 6\lambda_3 + 9\lambda_4 + 13\lambda_5 + 10\lambda_6 + w^x\sigma + s^- = g^x$$
$$\lambda_1 + 4\lambda_2 + 7\lambda_3 + 9\lambda_4 + 10\lambda_5 + 3\lambda_6 - w^y\sigma - s^+ = g^y$$
$$\mathbf{1}^T\lambda = 1$$
$$\lambda \geq \mathbf{0}$$
$$s^-, s^+ \geq 0$$
$$\varepsilon > 0$$

Let's assume that we would like to analyze the value efficiency of DMU$_6$: $\begin{bmatrix} 10 \\ 3 \end{bmatrix}$.

We use two different orientations: (a) output orientation, $\begin{bmatrix} w^x \\ w^y \end{bmatrix} = \begin{bmatrix} 0 \\ 3 \end{bmatrix}$, and

(b) combined orientation, $\begin{bmatrix} w^x \\ w^y \end{bmatrix} = \begin{bmatrix} 10 \\ 3 \end{bmatrix}$. Furthermore, we use two different

MPSs: (I) α^* DMU$_3$ + $(1-\alpha)^*$DMU$_4$, $\alpha \in (0, 1)$ and (II) DMU$_4$. The results in case I are independent of the value of α as long as the MPS lies on the open line segment (DMU$_3$, DMU$_4$). When MPS = DMU$_4$, the only change in comparison to the standard DEA model is that λ_4 is free. Moreover, when MPS = α^* DMU$_3$ + $(1-\alpha)^*$DMU$_4$, $\alpha \in (0, 1)$, variables λ_3 and λ_4 are defined free. The results of the analyses are given in Table 7.2 and illustrated in Figs. 7.4 and 7.5.

The tangent cone in Fig. 7.4 is a (dotted) line passing through the points DMU$_3$ and DMU$_4$. The value efficiency of point is evaluated by projecting DMU$_6$ onto this line (=the tangent cone). The projection direction depends on the orientation we

use. When we use the combined model, the projection direction is $\begin{bmatrix} -10 \\ 3 \end{bmatrix}$, i.e., how

much we have to improve the current values (decrease input value and increase output value) proportionally, until we reach the surface of the tangent cone. The result is point A in Fig. 7.4. The inefficiency score σ is 69.0 % (row A in Table 7.1). The result tells how much the current values of DMU$_6$ have to be simultaneously improved, before the unit is value efficient. If we use the output orientation, the projection point is B. It means that we have to improve the current output value of DMU$_6$ with 222.2 % until the unit is value efficient.

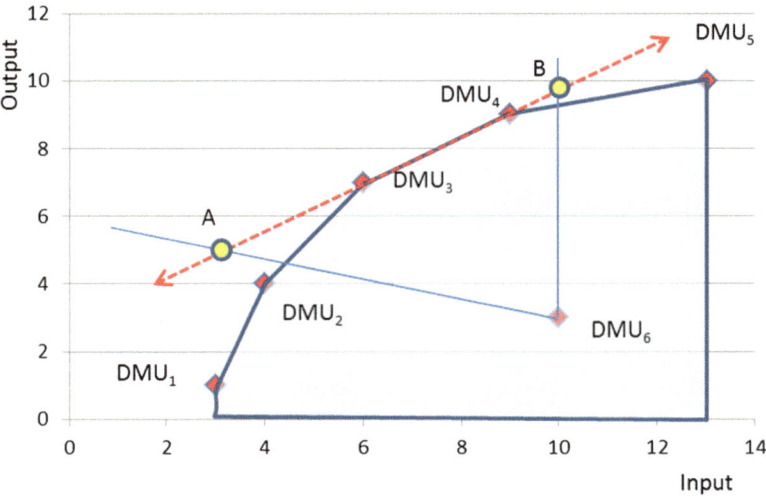

Fig. 7.4   Value efficiency of DMU_6, when MPS is on the open line segment (DMU_3, DMU_4)

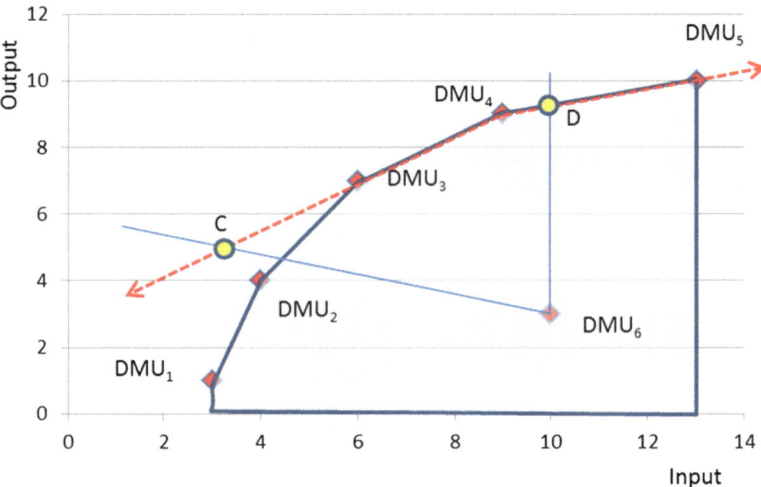

Fig. 7.5   Value efficiency of DMU_6, when MPS is DMU_4

If MPS is DMU_4, then the spanning directions of the tangent cone start from unit DMU_4 and pass through the adjacent units DMU_3 and DMU_5 (Fig. 7.5). The direction from DMU_4 through DMU_3 is the same as in the first case, and thus point A is equal to point C. The result of the output-oriented model will change a bit. Point D is on the line segment (DMU_4, DMU_5), and the result is the same with the standard output-oriented DEA model. The need of the improvement of the output value is now a bit less (208.3 %) than it was before. Usually, value efficiency decreases, when the distance from the MPS increases.

Note that an efficient unit is not generally value efficient. For instance, units DMU_1 and DMU_2 are efficient, but they are not value efficient. The value efficiency of point DMU_2 is better than that of DMU_1. In this case, this result is independent of the orientation we use, but generally this is not a case.

7.7 Practical Viewpoints

In this chapter we have developed an operational procedure and the requisite theory for incorporating DM's preference information into DEA-type efficiency analysis. Due to the well-known difficulties associated with the use of importance weights for inputs and outputs, we have taken a different route and modeled the DM's preferences via his/her MPS. Although also this approach leads to an implicitly defined set of acceptable weights, it is important to notice the fundamental difference in the preference elicitation: instead of thinking in terms of weights or in terms of their economic interpretations, prices, the DM is looking for the best solution.

The main difference between the value efficiency analysis and the target setting approaches found in DEA literature is that in value efficiency analysis, the best solution is explicitly sought on the efficient frontier, and this information is used to evaluate the need of improvement to reach the indifference surface of the unknown value function passing through the MPS.

Briefly, the DM is first supported by an interactive procedure in the search for the best input/output vector. Such a vector is a combination of the input/output vectors of the DMUs under consideration. Note that sensitivity analysis with respect to the choice of the MPS should be performed in each analysis. The DM is assumed to have a pseudoconcave value function at the moment he/she terminates the search, enabling us to use a linear approximation of the indifference contour of the value function at his/her MPS. When the linear approximation is not uniquely defined, our approximation will produce, in the spirit of DEA, the most optimistic efficiency score for each DMU. The formulation to calculate efficiency scores for each DMU, incorporating DM's preference information, reduces to a straightforward application of linear programming.

Our efficiency scores are most closely related to measuring classical overall efficiency. The model is immediately applicable and easily implemented for solving practical problems. In the next chapter, we will discuss some extensions and practical aspects (see, for more information, Korhonen et al. 2002, Halme and Korhonen 2000, and Korhonen and Syrjänen 2005).

References

Bazaraa M, Sherali HD, Shetty CM (1993) Nonlinear programming: theory and algorithms, 2nd edn. Wiley, New York

Charnes A, Cooper WW, Rhodes E (1978) Measuring efficiency of decision making units. Eur J Oper Res 2:429–444

Charnes A, Cooper WW, Rhodes E (1979) Short communication: measuring efficiency of decision making units. Eur J Oper Res 3:339

Charnes A, Cooper WW, Wei QL, Huang ZM (1989) Cone ratio data envelopment analysis and multi-objective programming. Int J Syst Sci 20:1099–1118

Charnes A, Cooper WW, Huang ZM, Sun DB (1990) Polyhedral cone-ratio DEA models with an illustrative application to large commercial banks. J Econ 46:73–91

Coelli TJ, Rao DSP, O'Donnell CJ, Battese GE (2005) An introduction to efficiency and productivity analysis, 2nd edn. Springer, New York

Farrell MJ (1957) The measurement of productivity efficiency. J R Stat Soc Ser A 120:253–290

Halme M, Joro T, Korhonen P, Salo S, Wallenius J (1999) A value efficiency approach to incorporating preference information in data envelopment analysis. Manage Sci 45(1):103–115

Halme M, Korhonen P (2000) Restricting weights in value efficiency analysis. Eur J Oper Res 126 (1):175–188

Korhonen P, Laakso J (1986) A visual interactive method for solving the multiple criteria problem. Eur J Oper Res 24:277–287

Korhonen P, Siljamäki A, Soismaa M (2002) On the use of value efficiency analysis and further developments. J Prod Anal 17(1/2):49–64

Korhonen P, Syrjänen M (2005) On the interpretation of value efficiency. J Prod Anal 24(2):197–201

Soleimani-damaneh M, Korhonen PJ, Wallenius J (2014) On value efficiency. Optimization, 63(4):617–631

Thanassoulis E, Dyson RG (1992) Estimating preferred target input-output levels using data envelopment analysis. Eur J Oper Res 56:80–97

Chapter 8
Value Efficiency Analysis in Practice

How to Use Value Efficiency Analysis in Practical Problems

8.1 Introduction

The value efficiency analysis (VEA) is an approach, in which the most preferred solution (MPS) plays a key role in the analysis as described in Chap. 7. For a rational DM any point on the efficient frontier of the production possibility[1] set is a possible and reasonable choice. If the production possibility set is convex, then the efficient given units are only a finite subset of the whole (uncountable) efficient frontier. In this case, the final choice of a DM is very seldom—if ever, a given efficient unit—if he/she freely searches for the MPS on the efficient frontier.

In multiple criteria decision making (MCDM), the aim is often just to find the MPS, because a DM is looking for the best (efficient) decision. In DEA, he/she is interested to diagnose the efficient (given) units and to measure how close to the efficient frontier the other (given) decision-making units (DMUs) are. In MCDM, the focus is in preference information and in DEA in the measuring of efficiency. VEA synthesizes these two different purposes.

At the conceptual level, the MPS can be defined as the solution maximizing a DM's value function. According to one of the basic properties (Definition 4.4), the minimum requirement is that the value function is strictly increasing for outputs and strictly decreasing for inputs assuming the outputs are maximized and the inputs are minimized. If not more is assumed, the assumption is too weak for helping a DM to find the MPS and to have any information about the "value" of the other given units. On the other hand, it is possible to make a very strong assumption that the value function is fully known. However, the problem is to find such a function. A more realistic assumption lies between these extreme cases. A typical approach and much used in MCDM is to assume that the form of the value function is known.

---

[1] In this chapter, we use the term "production possibility set" without making a difference between empirical and theoretical sets. Mostly, we operate with an empirical PPS.

© Springer Science+Business Media New York 2015
T. Joro, P.J. Korhonen, *Extension of Data Envelopment Analysis with Preference Information*, International Series in Operations Research & Management Science 218, DOI 10.1007/978-1-4899-7528-7_8

If the value function is known, it is easy to compute the value of all DMUs. No further value analysis is needed. Unfortunately, the assumption that the value function is known is not realistic. Usually, we have not even precise information about the form of the value function. Although its form is known, it is not even easy to estimate the parameters of the value function because often the information the DM is able to provide is not very reliable or accurate.

In this chapter, we explore background assumptions and practical aspects of VEA:

1. Using pseudoconcavity assumption for value function
2. Illustrating the measurement of value analysis
3. Locating the MPS
4. Dealing with practical situations in the choice of the MPS:

    (a) Choice of several alternative MPSs
    (b) Choice of an inefficient (nondominated) MPS
    (c) Choice from among the set of given DMUs
    (d) Choice in conflict with the value function assumption

8.2 Pseudoconcave Value Function

At the conceptual level, a DM is assumed to have an unknown value function, and the purpose is to find the point maximizing it. However, in practice the situation is the other way round. The DM helped to find a point at which the search process ends in a finite number of steps and to "prove" that the point is really the most preferred one. It is quite natural to assume that the value function has several properties:

1. The value function has a higher value at a dominating point A than at B dominated by A (strictly increasing for outputs and strictly decreasing for inputs in the area the value function is used).
2. The value function can reach unique maximum value at any efficient point.
3. The local MPS is also global.
4. The value function is as general as possible and meets the requirement of the behavioral realism.
5. The value function provides a theoretically solid (and practical) base to evaluate units.

The first property is the basic one. If we would like to afford the DM a possibility to choose any point on the efficient frontier as the MPS, then it is natural to assume that the value function can reach a unique maximum at this MPS.

If we do not impose the requirement three, it makes the search very difficult, because the search of the environment of the currently best point does not guarantee that the point found is really most preferred in the whole production possibility set. This property is sometimes problematic in practice because the DM may find several good candidates which emphasize different feature, and he/she is not able to decide which of those candidates is really most preferred.

Property four means that the value function does not set unnecessary restrictions and describes a DM's behavior in a realistic way. For instance, it is very natural to assume that the value difference is not very big between two close neighbor alternatives. Of course, there are exceptions. (For instance, to a student it is a big difference if the grade is over or under the passing grade.)

Requirement five emphasizes the need to use the properties of the value function to evaluate other units.

A widely used assumption for the form of a value function is linear. However, the linear function has some drawbacks. If the production possibility set is a polytope, then the value function has no unique values at non-extreme points. Instead, for the extreme points of the polytope, it is easy to check if the current solution is locally best, and if yes, then solution is also globally best. It is not true for non-extreme points. If the production possibility set is not convex, then the linear function cannot generally reach the optimal solution at all efficient points. Let's reconsider Example 7.1, in which we evaluated three candidates with two criteria (research and teaching). Into the replica of Fig. 7.1, an area with a dotted line is marked off.

Let us assume that the value function $v(u) = w_R u_1 + w_T u_2$ is linear with: $w_R = 0.5 + \varepsilon$ and $w_T = 0.5 - \varepsilon$, where u_1 and u_2 refer to research and teaching, $\varepsilon > 0$ is a small number, and w_R and w_T are the weights for research and teaching in the linear function. When research has a bit higher weight as specified in the original example, the solution is A. If $\varepsilon < 0$, then the solution is B. If $w_R = w_T$, then any efficient solution is an optimal solution. Perhaps, DM means that he/she prefers the solution which is fairly good on both criteria. Unfortunately, the linear value function cannot pick up such a unique optimal solution.

When a DM is looking for the MPS by freely searching the efficient frontier by using a suitable decision support system (DSS), it is unlikely that he/she will choose the efficient extreme solution (=a given DMU).

Assume that a DM articulates his/her desire to search for the MPS from among the set of the given DMUs. It means that the convex production possibility is unlikely convex, because the DM may choose the unit, which is efficient among the set of given DMUs, but do not lie on the frontier of the convex production possibility set. Figure 8.1 illustrates the non-convex set which is marked off with the dotted line (=the free disposal hull), and in this set point C is efficient. If the DM would like to find the candidate who is reasonably good in research and teaching and even a bit better researcher than a teacher, he/she will likely choose alternative C. The choice cannot be modeled by a linear function. Thus the linear value function violates the important property two.

The linear form of the value function is popular and widely applied. People are used to think that the importance of criteria and the magnitude of the weights go hand in hand. Unfortunately, it is not true. A simple example (Table 8.1) provides a counter example.

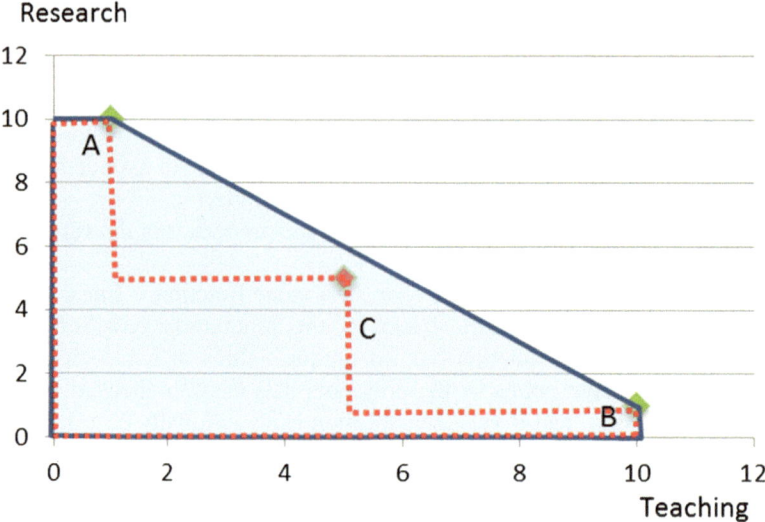

Fig. 8.1 Illustration of using a linear value function

Table 8.1 Finding the best place for holiday

	Price	Outing	Surfing	Hiking	Fishing	Swimming	
Weights	−5	1	1	1	1	1	Sum
Cheap	4	4	3	6	5	6	4
Fair	8	7	6	9	7	7	−4
Expensive	12	12	13	14	14	12	5

Example 8.1 Assume a family is looking for the best place for spending holiday. Family members have ended up with three options (cheap, fair, and expensive place) which are evaluated on six criteria (price and five various activity opportunities: outing, surfing, hiking, fishing, and swimming). The high numbers for activities mean excellent possibilities, and for the price a high number means it is expensive. The parents agree that the price as a criterion is five times more important than any of the activities. The absolute value of the weight for price is 5 and the weights for activities are ones. In the proposal of the analysis in column "sum," choose the most "expensive" one, for which the value is highest! (Even if the weights are varied, the "fair place" is never chosen.) Perhaps, the solution is not quite the parents had in their minds!

The pseudoconcavity of the value function is the assumption used in the VEA. It fulfills all requirements, except not fully the last one. In the spirit of DEA, we can approximate how much inputs and/or outputs must be improved to make a DMU under consideration as preferred by the MPS, but we cannot measure its value. For that purpose, we need stronger assumptions.

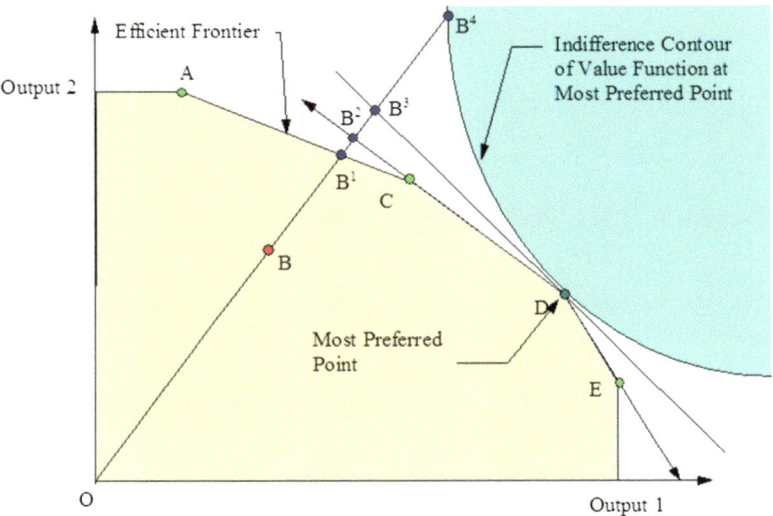

Fig. 8.2 Approximating the indifference contour of value function

Because the indifference surface is unknown, we use a tangent cone to the approximation. This cone characterizes the region consisting of the points surely less or equally preferred to the most preferred point. The efficiency of each DMU is then determined with respect to this tangent cone. As a result we obtain scores that we call *value efficiency scores*, because the efficiency of each DMU is determined by means of an approximation of the indifference surface of an implicitly known value function at the MPS. The approximation of the score is always more optimistic than the true one.

The basic idea of VEA is illustrated in Fig. 8.2. We have five units (A, B, C, D, E), which produce two outputs and use the same amount of one input. In Fig. 8.2, the problem has been described in the output space. Clearly all units but unit B are efficient. The technical efficiency measure for unit B in standard DEA is the ratio $\frac{OB}{OB^1}$. In VEA, we would like to evaluate the ratio $\frac{OB}{OB^4}$, where point B^4 lies on the indifference contour of the pseudoconcave value function at point D, which is assumed to be MPS. Because the value function is unknown, we are not able to compute the ratio because only the form of the value function is known, not the function. If we could approximate the indifference contour by a tangent, then we could use the ratio $\frac{OB}{OB^3}$. However, we cannot even make an assumption that the tangent is known. That's why we have to consider all possible tangents of the contour. This idea leads to the use of the ratio $\frac{OB}{OB^2}$ as an approximation to the (true) value efficiency score. Because this approximation is the best we can get, we will call this ratio simply as value efficiency score.

The resulting value efficiency scores are always optimistic approximations of the true scores.

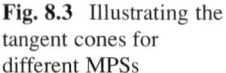

Fig. 8.3 Illustrating the
tangent cones for
different MPSs

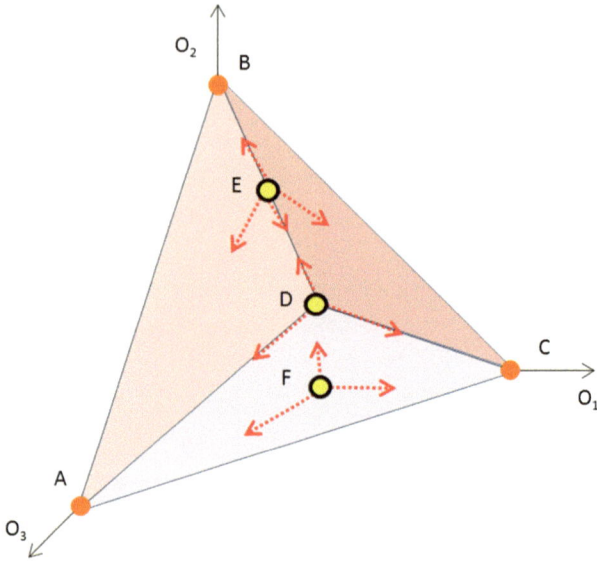

The spanning directions of three possible types of tangent cones are illustrated in
Fig. 8.3. The model to carry out the VEA is explained in Chap. 7 and illustrated in
Fig. 7.2. More illustrations are given in Sect. 8.3.

Figure 8.3 illustrates an important property of a pseudoconcave function which
makes it possible to check if the "best" point found so far is true MPS. Using the
spanning directions of a tangent cone, it is possible first to check if the "best" point
is a local MPS. If a DM does not like any of the changes the spanning directions
propose, then the "best" point is a local MPS, and then based on the property of a
pseudoconcave function, it is also the global MPS (see Korhonen and Laakso
1986). The method is the extension of the idea proposed by Zionts and Wallenius
(1976) to use adjacent efficient extreme points to check if the current efficient
extreme solution is the MPS.

In Fig. 8.3, we have four DMUs (A, B, C, and D), which characterize the
efficient frontier (all full facets, Fig. 8.3). If the DM chooses point D as the best
one, then to be sure that is the (global) MPS, it is enough to check those three
directions from D (D to A, D to B, and D to C). If none of those directions is the
direction of improvement, then D is the MPS. Correspondingly, in case E, we have
to check four directions, and finally in case F only three directions are needed. For
example, a quasiconcave function do not have this property, because it is not
differentiable.

8.3 Illustrating the Use of Value Efficiency Analysis

In this subsection, we illustrate the use of VEA with a simple example. We begin the considerations by formulating a general DEA model and discuss how various special models can be introduced from this presentation. Moreover, we illustrate how the VEA models for various classical DEA models are formulated. In Table 8.2 a unifying formulation is presented for general envelopment and multiplier models (for short, GEN). From this general formulation, the standard models (CRS, VRS, NIRS, and NDRS) are introduction. In addition to those standard models, our general formulation allows the use of a general projection vector: $w = \begin{bmatrix} w^y \\ w^x \end{bmatrix} \in \mathfrak{R}_+^{s+m}$ where $w \neq 0$. If $w_i^y > 0$, $i = 1, 2, \ldots, s$, and $w_j^x = 0$, $j = 1, 2, \ldots, m$, then the model is output oriented; if $w_i^y = 0$, $i = 1, 2, \ldots, s$, and $w_j^x > 0$, $j = 1, 2, \ldots, m$, then the model is input oriented; and if $w_i^y > 0$, $i = 1, 2, \ldots, s$, and $w_j^x > 0$, $j = 1, 2, \ldots, m$, then the model is combined. One more feature in the formulation is that the point $g = \begin{bmatrix} g^y \\ g^x \end{bmatrix} \in \mathfrak{R}^{s+m}$ to be projected onto the efficient frontier does not necessarily belong to the production possibility set. Note that depending on the values of vectors g and w, the solution may be infeasible.

Example 8.2 Suppose that we have six DMUs which are evaluated with one input and one output (Table 8.3).

Which units are efficient depends on the returns to scale assumption. We use two assumptions: (a) RTS is VRS and (b) RTS is NIRS. In both cases, units A, B, and C

Table 8.2 The general DEA models

General envelopment DEA model (GEN-E)	General multiplier DEA model (GEN-M)
$\max Z = \sigma + \varepsilon(\mathbf{1}^\mathsf{T} s^+ + \mathbf{1}^\mathsf{T} s^-)$ s.t. $Y\lambda - \sigma w^y - s^+ = g^y$ $X\lambda + \sigma w^x + s^- = g^x$ $\mathbf{1}^\mathsf{T}\lambda + \tau = 1$ $s^-, s^+ \geq 0$ $\varepsilon > 0$ (Non‑Archimedean) $\tau \begin{cases} = 0, & \text{if RTS is VRS} \\ = \text{free}, & \text{if RTS is CRS} \\ \geq 0, & \text{if RTS is NIRS} \\ \leq 0, & \text{if RTS is NDRS} \end{cases}$	$\min W = \nu^\mathsf{T} g^x - \mu^\mathsf{T} g^y + \xi$ s.t. $-\mu^\mathsf{T}Y + \nu^\mathsf{T}X + \xi\mathbf{1} \geq \mathbf{0}^\mathsf{T}$ $\mu^\mathsf{T}w^y + \nu^\mathsf{T}w^x = 1$ $\mu, \nu \geq \varepsilon\mathbf{1}$ $\varepsilon > 0$ $\xi \begin{cases} = 0, & \text{if RTS is CRS} \\ = \text{free}, & \text{if RTS is VRS} \\ \geq 0, & \text{if RTS is NIRS} \\ \leq 0, & \text{if RTS is NDRS} \end{cases}$

Table 8.3 The data set of Example 8.2

Units	A	B	C	D	E	F
Input	1	3	5	1.5	3	5
Output	2	5	5.5	1.5	3	4

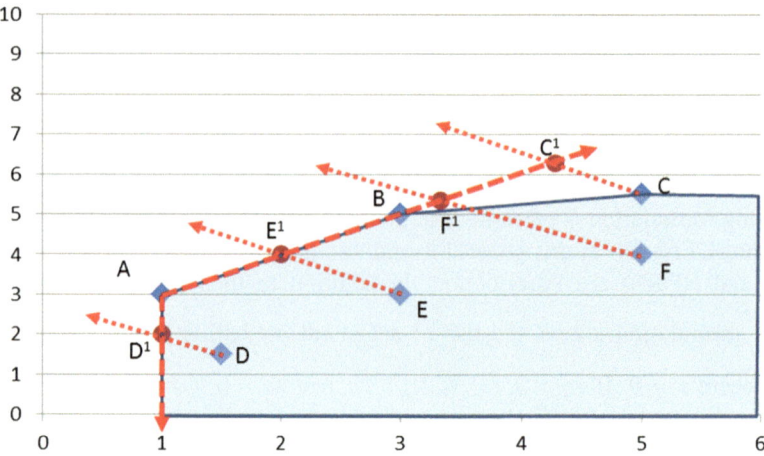

Fig. 8.4 The combined orientation using VRS assumption, when A is MPS (Case 1)

are (technically) efficient and D, E, and F inefficient (see, e.g., Fig. 8.4). The formulation of the model is as follows:

$$\max \sigma + \varepsilon(s^+ + s^-)$$
$$\text{s.t.} \tag{8.1}$$

$$\lambda_1 + 3\lambda_2 + 5\lambda_3 + 1.5\lambda_4 + 3\lambda_5 + 5\lambda_6 + w^x\sigma + s^- = g^x$$
$$3\lambda_1 + 5\lambda_2 + 5.5\lambda_3 + 1.5\lambda_4 + 3\lambda_5 + 4\lambda_6 - w^y\sigma - s^+ = g^y$$
$$\lambda_1 + \lambda_2 + \lambda_3 + \lambda_4 + \lambda_5 + \lambda_6 + \mu = 1$$
$$\lambda_2, \lambda_3, \lambda_4, \lambda_5, \lambda_6, s^- \geq 0$$
$$\varepsilon > 0$$
$$\mu \begin{cases} = 0, & \text{if RTS} = \text{VRS} \\ \geq 0, & \text{if RTS} = \text{NIRS} \end{cases}$$

λ_1 is free in all models below, because efficient unit A is assumed to be involved in all specifications of MPS.

First, we assume that RTS $=$ VRS and use the combined orientation. Let's suppose that DM states that unit A (without any additional information) is his/her MPS. Thus λ_1 is free, $\mu = 0$, and $s^+ \geq 0$, and other variables are nonnegative as specified in the model (Case 1). These definitions specify the tangent cone with two spanning vectors: one down from A and another one from A passing through B.

The value efficient is now defined for each unit by computing how much (proportionally) the outputs have to be increased (improved) and the inputs to be decreased (improved) until the surface of the tangent cone is reached. We see from

Table 8.4 The value efficiency scores, when RTS = VRS (Cases 1 and 2)

| Unit | λ_1 Free | | λ_1 and s^+ are free | |
	Reference unit	Inefficiency score	Reference unit	Inefficiency score
B	B^1	0.000	B^2	0.667
C	C^1	0.143	C^2	0.800
D	D^1	0.333	D^2	0.333
E	E^1	0.333	E^2	0.667
F	F^1	0.333	F^2	0.800

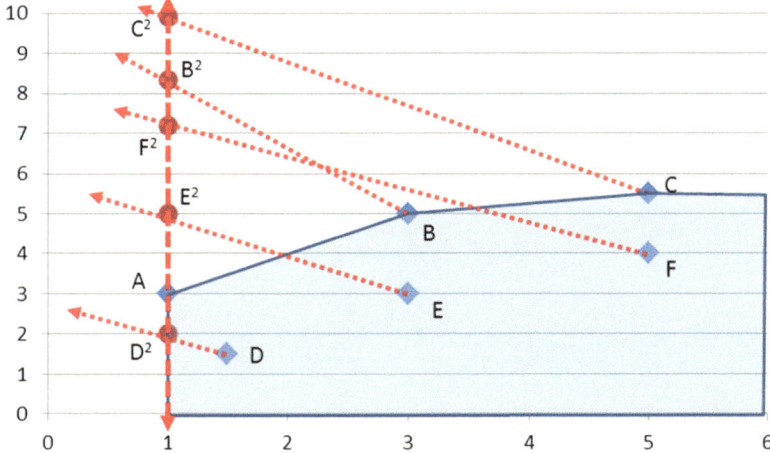

Fig. 8.5 The combined orientation using VRS assumption, when A is MPS and the solutions from A down are "almost" equally preferred to A (Case 2)

Table 8.4 that all units except unit B are value inefficient. Units D, E, and F are inefficient; that's why they are also value inefficient. Unit B is efficient and also value efficient. Instead, unit C is efficient, but it is not value efficient. Figure 8.4 illustrates the results of the analysis.

After seeing the result, assume that the DM does not like the result that according to the analysis B was equally preferred to A, because its value (in)efficiency score is 0. He/she may think that all solutions on the line segment from A to B are less preferred than on the line segment from A down. We may use this additional information by specifying that s^+ is free instead of requiring that it is nonnegative (Case 2). In theory, it means that any solutions (see Fig. 8.5) on the line segment from A down are equally preferred to A. It is not a rational decision because all other solutions except A are only weakly efficient, i.e., A is dominating those solutions. However, it may define the better approximation to the true tangent of the value function. That's why the DM may be willing to use it.

The value efficiency scores are given in Table 8.4 and illustrated in Fig. 8.5. Unit D is the only unit which has the same value efficiency score as before.

Table 8.5 The value efficiency scores, when RTS = NIRS (Cases 3 and 4)

	A free		A and μ are free	
	Reference unit	Inefficiency score	Reference unit	Inefficiency score
B	B^3	0.000	B^4	0.444
C	C^3	0.300	C^4	0.633
D	D^3	0.667	D^4	0.667
E	E^3	0.667	E^4	0.667
F	F^3	0.600	F^4	0.733

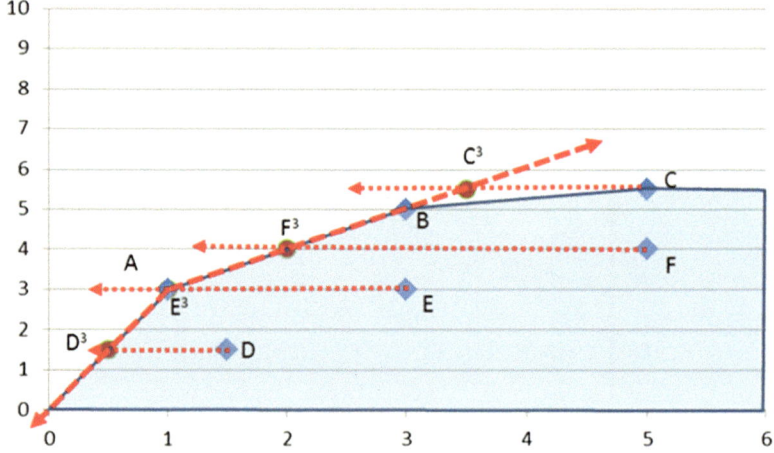

Fig. 8.6 The input orientation using NIRS assumption, when A is MPS (Case 3)

Figure 8.5 tells why. Now unit B is not any more value efficient. Its score is even worse than that of unit D.

Next, we assume that RTS = NIRS and use the input orientation. As before, we assume that unit A is MPS. Thus λ_1 is still free, $\mu \geq 0$, and $s^+ \geq 0$ (Case 3). The other variables are nonnegative as specified in the model. These definitions specify the tangent cone spanning vectors from A to the origin and from A passing through B. The results are given in Table 8.5 and illustrated in Fig. 8.6.

The profile of the results is quite similar as before. The score of C is the best one and the other scores are almost equal as they were before. If we assume as before that the DM cannot accept B to be equally preferred to A, consider that the "true" MPS is somewhere between the origin and A.

The best solution is the one at which $\mu > 0$. We modify the model such that μ is defined now as free (Case 4). The new tangent cone is spanned by the vector starting from the origin and passing through A as illustrated in Fig. 8.7. Unit B is now value efficient, but not so much as the other value inefficient units. The score of unit D is the same as before.

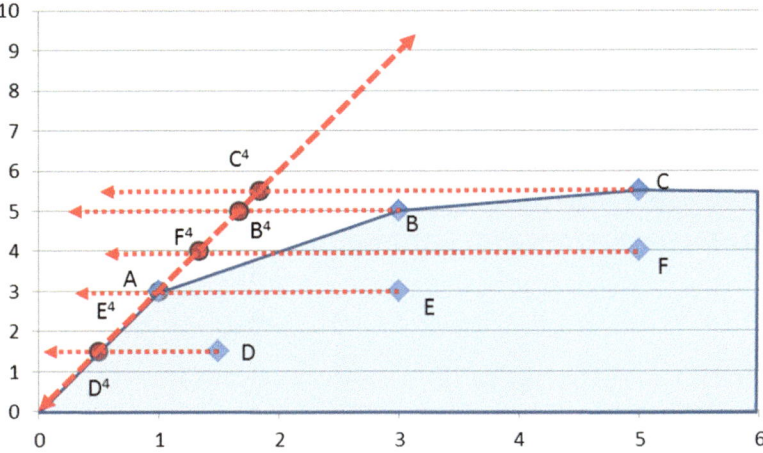

Fig. 8.7 The input orientation using NIRS assumption, when the MPS is between the origin and A (Case 4)

8.4 Applying Value Efficiency Analysis

In this subsection, we will discuss how the VEA can be used in practical applications. VEA enhances the usability of the efficiency analysis by helping analyze the effects of a DM's preference information. At minimum, VEA will require a very little amount of extra effort. Computationally VEA is as easy to perform as a technical efficiency analysis.

Throughout this subsection, we consider a data set consisting of 25 firms (hypermarkets) situated in Finland belonging to the same group. The data set was already represented in Sect. 5.4 (Table 5.4). The original application consisted of more variables, but in our illustrative example only two outputs and two inputs are used. The outputs are "sales" (in money units) and "net profit" (in money units). The inputs are "man hours" (10^3 h) and floor space (10^3 m^2). "Man hours" refer to labor force available within a certain period and "floor space" is the total area of the firm. The original application consisted of three output variables (sales, gross profit, and net profit) and seven input variables (personnel costs, other expenses, rents, machinery and equipment costs, current assets, TT, and floor space). We would like to emphasize that these variables were chosen by the management—not by us.

To make considerations more illustrative, we will consider BCC models, i.e.,

$$\Lambda = \left\{ \lambda \middle| \lambda \in \mathfrak{R}_+^n \ \text{ and } \ \mathbf{1}^T \lambda = 1 \right\}$$

and calculations are made assuming output orientation.

The first task in VEA is to locate MPS. It means that a DM has to solve the following multiple objective linear programming problem (MOLP):

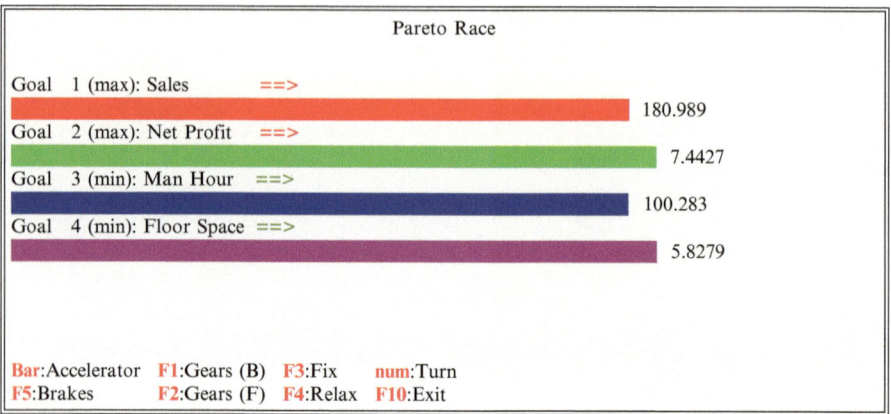

Fig. 8.8 Searching for the most preferred values for inputs and outputs

$$
\begin{aligned}
\text{Max} \quad & \mathbf{Y}\lambda \\
\text{Min} \quad & \mathbf{X}\lambda \\
\text{s.t.} \quad & \\
& \mathbf{1}^{\mathrm{T}}\lambda = 1
\end{aligned}
$$

(8.2)

After finding a solution on the efficient frontier for MOLP model (8.2), the rest of the analysis is very straightforward provided we accept the assumption that the solution is the unit maximizing a DM's implicitly known pseudoconcave value function.

To solve model (8.2), any available interactive MOLP system can be used. We use the VIG software (Korhonen 1987). VIG implements Pareto Race (Korhonen and Wallenius 1988), which provides an interactive procedure for dynamic and visual free search on the efficient frontier of the MOLP problem. (To have more information about other multiple objective linear programming methods, see, e.g., Steuer 1986.)

Pareto Race enables a DM to freely search any part of the efficient frontier by controlling the speed and direction of motion (see Fig. 8.8). The objective function values are represented in numerical form and as bar graphs on the computer screen (see, for more details, Korhonen and Wallenius 1988). It is important to remember that the efficient frontier depends on the underlying scale assumption. For instance, if we use the BCC model for technical efficiency, the same model has to be used for VEA as well. The orientation has no effect on the efficient frontier.

Let us assume that the DM regards the values of input and output variables in Fig. 8.8 as the most preferred ones. The values are obtained by using the λ values: $\lambda_{\text{Firm3}} = 0.286$ and $\lambda_{\text{Firm10}} = 0.714$. It means that the MPS is a convex combination of firms 3 and 10. Pareto Race guarantees that the convex combination is efficient. The value efficiency scores (see, Table 8.6) are computed by using a standard BCC model with one exception: nonnegativity constraints of the λ variables of firms 3 and 10 are relaxed. The results are given in column "firms #3 and 10." The technical efficient firms 3, 4, 10, and 25 are also value efficient. The rest of the

Table 8.6 Efficiency and value efficiency scores

	Efficiency	Value efficiency score				
		Firm # 3	Firm # 8	Firm # 10	Firms # 3 and 10	Firms # 3 and 8 ⇒ # 8 and 10 and 25
Firm1	0.821	0.794	0.768	0.821	0.794	0.720
Firm2	0.772	0.663	0.772	0.772	0.663	0.758
Firm3	1.000	1.000	0.931	1.000	1.000	0.931
Firm4	1.000	1.000	0.661	1.000	1.000	0.661
Firm5	0.769	0.689	0.769	0.769	0.689	0.757
Firm6	0.806	0.780	0.805	0.806	0.780	0.805
Firm7	1.000	0.815	1.000	1.000	0.815	0.953
Firm8	1.000	0.731	1.000	1.000	0.731	1.000
Firm9	1.000	0.743	1.000	1.000	0.743	1.000
Firm10	1.000	1.000	1.000	1.000	1.000	1.000
Firm11	1.000	0.749	0.913	0.966	0.749	0.913
Firm12	0.824	0.824	0.613	0.824	0.824	0.592
Firm13	0.673	0.673	0.588	0.673	0.673	0.558
Firm14	0.736	0.596	0.736	0.736	0.596	0.722
Firm15	0.803	0.625	0.803	0.803	0.625	0.802
Firm16	0.978	0.858	0.948	0.978	0.858	0.881
Firm17	0.930	0.884	0.914	0.930	0.884	0.887
Firm18	0.817	0.767	0.613	0.807	0.767	0.605
Firm19	0.969	0.716	0.969	0.959	0.716	0.915
Firm20	0.804	0.681	0.774	0.804	0.681	0.703
Firm21	0.858	0.793	0.600	0.846	0.793	0.600
Firm22	0.876	0.854	0.724	0.876	0.854	0.716
Firm23	1.000	0.960	0.973	1.000	0.960	0.973
Firm24	0.973	0.787	0.838	0.907	0.787	0.819
Firm25	1.000	1.000	1.000	1.000	1.000	1.000

technical efficient firms 7, 8, 9, 11, and 23 are value inefficient. It means that the structure of those input and output values deviates too much from the values of a convex combination of firms 3 and 10. Note that the value efficiency scores are never higher than the technical efficiency scores!

In practice, a DM is not necessarily willing to use any MOLP method to locate the MPS. He/she often feels him/herself comfortable to name one of the existing units as the MPS. The last two columns in Table 8.6 are standing for the value efficiency scores when the MPSs were firm 3 and firm 8. Both firms are technical efficient. Firms 3, 4, 10, and 25 are value efficient, when the MPS is firm 3. Correspondingly, firms 7, 8, 9, 10, and 25 are value efficient, when the MPS is firm 8. Firms 10 and 25 are value efficient in both cases. Let us consider more closely firm 4. It is technical efficient, and it is also value efficient when the MPS is firm 3. If the MPS were firm 8, then the value efficiency score of firm 4 is only 0.661. The structure of the input and output values of firm 4 is "closer" to firm 3 than 8. The fact is easy to see from Table 5.4.

It is necessary that the unit the DM will point as the MPS is efficient. In case the number of efficient units is large—let us say few thousands or millions—the DM may need a help in finding the most preferred (existing) unit as well. There exist decision support systems which provide him with the tool which helps him/her to find the "best" alternative from among a huge set of given alternatives. An example of such a system is VIMDA (Korhonen 1988). VIMDA is developed to help a DM to choose the most preferred alternative from a large set of alternatives. An improved version of the algorithm is published in Korhonen and Karaivanova (1999).

Above, we compared the results obtained from using alternatively two units as the most preferred units. Actually, in practical applications the DM often seems to be willing to specify more than one MPS. If he/she will pick several units, there is a problem: how to interpret his/her choice? By pointing several example units, the DM may think that from some point of view, they all are "good." On the other hand, he/she may think that the best unit is a kind of combination of the named units.

If the units are on the same efficient facet, we just relax the nonnegativity constraints of the corresponding λ variables in the output-oriented BCC model and obtain the value efficiency scores. In practice, it is very likely that the units are not on the same efficient facets, if the DM will make his/her choice without any support. In that case, relaxing the nonnegativity constraints of the λ variables leads to an unbounded solution of the value efficiency model.

In this case, the line connected to these two units is not efficient—except the end points. It means that pseudoconcavity assumption is wrong, or the DM has made a mistake. In these situations, it is best to figure out what the reason is.

Technically, we may overcome the problem, for instance, by taking the average of the values of the input and output values of the units specified by the DM and projecting the point onto the efficient frontier. However, this is not a satisfactory trick unless we are sure that the DM is really looking for a kind of combination of those units, but is unable to express it. He/she may also mean that some units are "good examples" for certain types of units and some other units are "good examples" for another kind of units. In this case, we may use different units as the MPSs at a time and ask the DM to associate each unit with one of the alternative MPSs.

If we assume that the first interpretation is true, we may "correct" the evaluation of the DM by computing the average of the values of those two units (142.4, 5.85, 85.74, 5.30) and projecting the point onto the efficient frontier by using the output-oriented BCC model. We obtain the following information: the efficiency score of the point (142.4, 5.85, 85.74, 5.30) is 0.943, and the units belonging to the reference set for the point are firms 8 ($\lambda_{Firm8} = 0.033$), 10 ($\lambda_{Firm10} = 0.876$), and 25 ($\lambda_{Firm25} = 0.090$). It means that those three units specify an efficient facet, and the VEA can be carried out by relaxing the nonnegativity constraints of those three λ variables. Value efficiency scores are in Table 8.6, in the column "firms #3 and 8 $\Rightarrow$ # 8 and 10 and 25." The approach means that we "corrected" the DM's evaluation: instead of the accepted conflicting information that firms 3 and 8 are equally preferred, we "corrected" it into the form: firms 8, 10, and 25 that are equally preferred.

Assume now that interpretation (2) is true. The DM might mean that firm 3 is a "good example" for large units with big sales and firm 8 is good for small units.

Then we will carry out two different analyses. First, we use firm 3 as the most preferred unit and then firm 8. Table 8.6 shows the results. This kind of situation may also appear, when we have many decision makers in choosing the MPS; then, it is natural to assume that they do not generally choose the same MPS. It is not necessary to try to find out the compromise solution. The situation can easily be solved by computing value efficiency scores for all different MPSs separately.

The DM is free to choose how to use the results, but we give the following recommendation: VEA is performed for all different MPSs named by the DM. Each unit is associated with each MPS a priori or a posteriori. A priori association means that we select in advance the MPS for each unit. The selection can be made according to some specific values of input and output variables or some uncontrollable characteristics of the units. A posteriori association means that the classification of units is made afterward. Each unit is associated with the MPS having the highest value efficiency score. For instance, firm 5 is associated with firm 8 because the value efficiency scores were 0.689 and 0.769 for firms 3 and 8, correspondingly. Thus firm 8 is a better "example" to firm 5 than firm 3.

We may further develop the idea by finding for each unit its own MPS. For instance, for a given level of input values, we may first search the most preferred output values and then compute the value efficiency score of the unit under consideration with respect to the specific MPS. In practice, the approach may be too time-consuming. It is more realistic to assume that a DM is more willing first to group the units and to search the MPS for each group.

8.5 Concluding Remarks

In this paper, we have considered the use of VEA in practice. A key issue for VEA is to locate the MPS or the most preferred unit on the efficient frontier. In practice, the decision maker often seems to be more willing just to pick out his/her MPS or most preferred unit without trying to find it using an interactive multiple objective linear programming technique. In this paper, we have proposed different ways to deal with this kind of an approach.

We have illustrated the use of VEA with the data set that was extracted from a real application. In the numerical considerations we have consistently employed the output-oriented BCC model. It is of course possible to perform a general VEA and use any of data envelopment analysis models.

VEA gives a response to many practical problems. Here we have considered a few and showed how to use VEA in those problems. VEA provides a possibility to understand more deeply the nature of performance at the units under considerations. In addition, VEA is as easy to carry out as DEA. It does not need any special models. The only difference to a DEA model is the relaxation of the nonnegativity constraints of the strictly positive variables determining the MPS. People working in practice have found efficiency analysis in general and value efficient analysis in particular useful.

References

Korhonen P (1988) A visual reference direction approach to solving discrete multiple criteria problems. Eur J Oper Res 34(2):152–159

Korhonen P (1987) VIG—a visual interactive support system for multiple criteria decision making. Belgian J Oper Res Stat Comput Sci 27:3–15

Korhonen P, Karaivanova J (1999) An algorithm for projecting a reference direction onto the nondominated set of given points. IEEE Trans Syst Man Cybern Part A Syst Hum 29 (5):429–435

Korhonen P, Laakso J (1986) A visual interactive method for solving the multiple criteria problem. Eur J Oper Res 24:277–287

Korhonen P, Wallenius J (1988) A pareto race. Naval Res Logist 35:615–623

Steuer RE (1986) Multiple criteria optimization: theory, computation and application. Wiley, New York

Zionts S, Wallenius J (1976) An interactive programming method for solving the multiple criteria problem. Manag Sci 22:652–663

Chapter 9
Extensions to Value Efficiency Analysis

Implementing New Features to Value Efficiency Analysis

9.1   Topics

In this chapter, we provide an overview on possibilities to extend value efficiency analysis. First, we describe how to incorporate additional preference information into the analysis by using the "price" information of inputs and outputs. The extension is made in the spirit of cone ratio approach.

As we have emphasized, the computation of value efficiency scores is based on an approximation, because a DM's value function and thus the indifference contour passing through to the MPS are unknown. The approximation of the scores is optimistic, in the sense that the true value efficiency is always worse than the approximation provided. To find the true score, there is no need to estimate the whole indifference curve. It is enough to find the point at which the line standing for the proportional improvement of inputs and/or outputs meets the indifference curve. This point can be found by means of an interactive approach.

The third extension deals with the assumptions of the value function needed for enabling the value efficiency analysis to provide information on the value difference between the unit under considerations and the MPS. Generally, the value efficiency score only provides ordinal information. We will discuss two sets of additional assumptions that enable the value (in)efficiency score to provide a value difference/ratio interpretation.

9.2   Weight Restrictions and Value Efficiency Analysis

Originally, it was considered an advantage of DEA that no preference information is needed; i.e., weights apart from nonnegativity were not restricted. However, many value judgment schemes have been proposed for several reasons. The first weight restrictions in DEA were put forward by Thompson et al. (1986). Weight

© Springer Science+Business Media New York 2015
127
T. Joro, P.J. Korhonen, *Extension of Data Envelopment Analysis with Preference
Information*, International Series in Operations Research & Management
Science 218, DOI 10.1007/978-1-4899-7528-7_9

restrictions are the most straightforward and commonly used way in economic analysis to incorporate preference information into the DEA analysis as discussed in Chap. 6. It is often the case that some information on the relative importance or relative prices of the inputs and outputs is available. It would not be reasonable to exclude that from the analysis. The weights do not always have an interpretation as prices. Outside of weight restrictions, preference information can be incorporated into DEA by target setting (see Chap. 6 for review).

VEA is an approach to incorporate value judgments into DEA via the most preferred solution (MPS), which is the input–output vector on the efficient frontier preferred by the DM to all other possible input–output vectors. To insert this information into efficiency analysis, a modification of the original model is required. The modification may interpret as the change of the efficient frontier. In that sense, VEA is analogous to weight restrictions models. In VEA, the DM does not explicitly consider the weights. He/she only chooses the MPS from among all the efficient (virtual) units.

In this subsection we combine two kinds of preference information: the most preferred input–output vector and information on weights of inputs and/or outputs, when it is reasonable. Weight restrictions may be applied before or after VEA. The use of weight restrictions as the component of VEA can be interpreted as an aim to improve the precision of the approximation of value efficiency scores.

To illustrate the approach, we describe as an example the analysis of municipal dental units in Finland, where among others there are two kinds of labor inputs: better paid dentists and less paid other staff (in man years). The outputs are divided into two parts: patients under 18 years of age and other patients (that have been taken care of). The treatment of the latter group is more expensive. We demonstrate that we get very interesting results by combining the two different ways to incorporate preference information.

9.2.1   DEA Model with Weight Restrictions

The demands of real-life applications probably are the origin of the incorporation of preference information in DEA (see, for further discussion, Allen et al. 1997). A natural incentive is some a priori knowledge on prices or the relative importance of outputs but also the need to have more realistic efficiency scores as well as the need to rank the efficient units. Because in the DEA literature, so far, only linear weight restrictions have been encountered, we may present the absolute and relative weight restrictions in the following form (see, e.g., Halme and Korhonen 2000):

$$\boldsymbol{\mu}^{\mathrm{T}}\mathbf{R}^{y} - \boldsymbol{\nu}^{\mathrm{T}}\mathbf{R}^{x} \leq \boldsymbol{c} \tag{9.1}$$

where $\mathbf{R}^{y} \in \mathfrak{R}^{s \times k}$, $\mathbf{R}^{x} \in \mathfrak{R}^{m \times k}$ $(k > 0)$, and $\boldsymbol{c} \in \mathfrak{R}^{k}$ (row vector). We denote $\mathbf{R} = \begin{bmatrix} \mathbf{R}^{y} \\ \mathbf{R}^{x} \end{bmatrix} \in \mathfrak{R}^{(s+m) \times k}$. With the help of vector $\boldsymbol{c}$, it is possible to present both

Table 9.1 The general weight-restricted DEA models

General envelopment DEA model with weight restrictions (GEN-WR-E)	General multiplier DEA model with weight restrictions (GEN-WR-M)
$\max \ Z \ = \ \sigma \ + \ \varepsilon(\mathbf{1}^T s^+ + \mathbf{1}^T s^-) \ + \ c^T \theta$ s.t. $\quad \mathbf{Y}\lambda \ - \ \sigma w^y - s^+ + \mathbf{R}^y \theta \ = \ g^y$ $\quad \mathbf{X}\lambda \ + \ \sigma w^x + s^- + \mathbf{R}^x \theta \ = \ g^x$ $\quad \mathbf{1}^T \lambda \ + \ \tau \ = \ 1$ $\quad s^-, s^+, \ \boldsymbol{\theta} \geq 0$ $\quad \varepsilon \ > \ 0 \text{(non-Archimedean)}$ $\tau \begin{cases} = 0 & \text{if RTS is VRS} \\ = \text{free} & \text{if RTS is CRS} \\ \geq 0 & \text{if RTS is NIRS} \\ \leq 0 & \text{if RTS is NDRS} \end{cases}$	$\min \ W \ = \ \nu^T g^x - \mu^T g^y + \xi$ s.t. $\quad -\mu^T \mathbf{Y} + \nu^T \mathbf{X} + \xi \mathbf{1} \geq \mathbf{0}$ $\quad \mu^T w^y + \nu^T w^x = 1$ $\quad -\mu^T \mathbf{R}^y + \nu^T \mathbf{R}^x \geq c$ $\quad \mu, \nu \ \geq \ \varepsilon \mathbf{1}$ $\quad \varepsilon \ > \ 0 \text{(non-Archimedean)}$ $\xi \begin{cases} = \text{free} & \text{if RTS is VRS} \\ = 0 & \text{if RTS is CRS} \\ \geq 0 & \text{if RTS is NIRS} \\ \leq 0 & \text{if RTS is NDRS} \end{cases}$

the absolute $(c \neq 0)$ and relative $(c = 0)$ weight restrictions (see Chap. 6). In Table 9.1, we present how these constraints are incorporated into traditional DEA models. We present the models in the general framework in which there is a general projection vector used: $w = \begin{bmatrix} w^y \\ w^x \end{bmatrix} \in \mathfrak{R}_+^{s+m}$ where $w \geq 0$, $w \neq 0$. If $w_i^y > 0$, $i = 1$, $2, \ldots, s$, and $w_j^x = 0$, $j = 1, 2, \ldots, m$, then the model is output oriented; if $w_i^y = 0$, $i = 1, 2, \ldots, s$, and $w_j^x > 0$, $j = 1, 2, \ldots, m$, then the model is input oriented; and if $w_i^y > 0$, $i = 1, 2, \ldots, s$, and $w_j^x > 0$, $j = 1, 2, \ldots, m$, then the model is combined. One more feature in the formulation is that the point $g = \begin{bmatrix} g^y \\ g^x \end{bmatrix} \in \mathfrak{R}^{s+m}$ to be projected onto the efficient frontier does not necessarily belong to the production possibility set (PPS).

Note that we may interpret that the weight restrictions modify PPS. As we can see from the envelopment model, we may interpret $\mathbf{R} = \begin{bmatrix} \mathbf{R}^y \\ \mathbf{R}^x \end{bmatrix}$ as the matrix consisting of the input and output values of k artificial units. Actually, the interpretation is not quite right because we do not require that $\mathbf{R}^y \geq 0$, $\mathbf{R}^y \neq 0$ and $\mathbf{R}^x \geq 0$, $\mathbf{R}^x \neq 0$.

We define set $T = \{u \mid u = \mathbf{U}\lambda, \lambda \in \Lambda\}$, which have one-to-one connection to the PPS. In this chapter, we refer to this set as a PPS as well. Set $\Lambda = \{\lambda \mid \mathbf{1}^T \lambda + \tau = 1\}$, where τ is defined as in Table 9.1. The original efficient frontier clearly changes after the incorporation of weight restrictions. The resulting new feasible set is $T^w = \{u \mid u = \mathbf{U}\lambda + \mathbf{V}\theta, \ \lambda \in \Lambda, \ \boldsymbol{\theta} \geq 0\}$, where $\mathbf{U} = \begin{bmatrix} \mathbf{Y} \\ -\mathbf{X} \end{bmatrix}$ and $\mathbf{V} = \begin{bmatrix} \mathbf{R}^y \\ -\mathbf{R}^x \end{bmatrix}$. Clearly $T \subseteq T^w$. Thus the units originally efficient in set T are not necessarily efficient in T^w.

When the absolute weight restriction method is used, it is possible that the multiplier model has no feasible solution and the envelopment model has an unbounded solution. It may, of course, happen in case of relative weights as well. Then the weight restrictions are in conflict with one another.

9.2.2 Restricted Weights in Value Efficiency Analysis

In some cases, there may be a need to impose additional weight restrictions, absolute or relative, to fine-tune preference information we would like to incorporate into VEA.

The reason for this might be the knowledge of relative prices or relative weights of some of the input/output variables. Also there might arise a need to check if the additional weight restrictions are in harmony with the MPS chosen. Thus information on the absolute or relative weights may be used as a supplement to VEA and thus to improve value efficiency score estimates. Also, it may happen that the DM is unable to locate a unique MPS. Then the weight restrictions may be used to choose among the MPS candidates; particularly some of them can be rejected owing to the conflict with the new information.

To impose weight restrictions in value efficiency analysis, we supplement the multiplier model with linear constraints, $-\boldsymbol{\mu}^{\mathrm{T}}\mathbf{R}^y + \boldsymbol{\nu}^{\mathrm{T}}\mathbf{R}^x \geq \boldsymbol{c}$, $\mathbf{R}^y \in \mathfrak{R}^{s \times k}$, and $\mathbf{R}^x \in \mathfrak{R}^{m \times k}$ ($k > 0$), in the same way as weight restrictions were added in the standard DEA model in Chap. 6. In Table 9.2, we present the dual model with

Table 9.2 The general weight-restricted VEA models

General envelopment VEA model with weight restrictions (GEN-WR-VEA-E)	General multiplier VEA model with weight restrictions (GEN-WR-VEA-M)
max $Z = \sigma + \varepsilon(\boldsymbol{1}^{\mathrm{T}}\boldsymbol{s}^+ + \boldsymbol{1}^{\mathrm{T}}\boldsymbol{s}^-) + \boldsymbol{c}^{\mathrm{T}}\boldsymbol{\theta}$ s.t.	min $W = \boldsymbol{\nu}^{\mathrm{T}}\boldsymbol{g}^x - \boldsymbol{\mu}^{\mathrm{T}}\boldsymbol{g}^y + \xi$ s.t.
$\mathbf{Y}\boldsymbol{\lambda} - \sigma \boldsymbol{w}^y - \boldsymbol{s}^+ + \mathbf{R}^y\boldsymbol{\theta} = \boldsymbol{g}^y$ $\mathbf{X}\boldsymbol{\lambda} + \sigma \boldsymbol{w}^x + \boldsymbol{s}^- + \mathbf{R}^x\boldsymbol{\theta} = \boldsymbol{g}^x$ $\boldsymbol{1}^{\mathrm{T}}\boldsymbol{\lambda} + \tau = 1$ $\boldsymbol{s}^-, \boldsymbol{s}^+ \geq 0$ $\varepsilon > 0$ (non-Archimedean)	$-\boldsymbol{\mu}^{\mathrm{T}}\mathbf{Y} + \boldsymbol{\nu}^{\mathrm{T}}\mathbf{X} + \xi\boldsymbol{1} - \boldsymbol{\gamma} = \boldsymbol{0}^{\mathrm{T}}$ $\boldsymbol{\mu}^{\mathrm{T}}\boldsymbol{w}^y + \boldsymbol{\nu}^{\mathrm{T}}\boldsymbol{w}^x = 1$ $-\boldsymbol{\mu}^{\mathrm{T}}\mathbf{R}^y + \boldsymbol{\nu}^{\mathrm{T}}\mathbf{R}^x - \boldsymbol{\eta} = \boldsymbol{c}$ $\boldsymbol{\mu}, \boldsymbol{\nu} \geq \varepsilon\boldsymbol{1}$ $\varepsilon > 0$ (non-Archimedean)
$\lambda_j \begin{cases} \geq 0 & \text{if } \lambda_j^* = 0 \\ = \text{free} & \text{if } \lambda_j^* > 0 \end{cases}, \ j = 1, 2, \ldots, n$	$\gamma_j \begin{cases} \geq 0 & \text{if } \lambda_j^* = 0 \\ = 0 & \text{if } \lambda_j^* > 0 \end{cases}, \ j = 1, 2, \ldots, n$
$\theta_j \begin{cases} \geq 0 & \text{if } \theta_j^* = 0 \\ = \text{free} & \text{if } \theta_j^* > 0 \end{cases}, \ j = 1, 2, \ldots, k$	$\eta_j \begin{cases} \geq 0 & \text{if } \theta_j^* = 0 \\ = 0 & \text{if } \theta_j^* > 0 \end{cases}, \ j = 1, 2, \ldots, k$
where $\boldsymbol{\lambda}^*, \boldsymbol{\theta}^*$ correspond to the MPS: $\boldsymbol{y}^* = \mathbf{Y}\boldsymbol{\lambda}^* + \mathbf{R}^y\boldsymbol{\theta}^*$ $\boldsymbol{x}^* = \mathbf{X}\boldsymbol{\lambda}^* + \mathbf{R}^x\boldsymbol{\theta}^*$	where $\boldsymbol{\lambda}^*, \boldsymbol{\theta}^*$ correspond to the MPS: $\boldsymbol{y}^* = \mathbf{Y}\boldsymbol{\lambda}^* + \mathbf{R}^y\boldsymbol{\theta}^*$ $\boldsymbol{x}^* = \mathbf{X}\boldsymbol{\lambda}^* + \mathbf{R}^x\boldsymbol{\theta}^*$
The original DEA model: $\tau \begin{cases} = 0 & \text{if RTS is VRS} \\ = \text{free} & \text{if RTS is CRS} \\ \geq 0 & \text{if RTS is NIRS} \\ \leq 0 & \text{if RTS is NDRS} \end{cases}$	The original DEA model: $\xi \begin{cases} = \text{free} & \text{if RTS is VRS} \\ = 0 & \text{if RTS is CRS} \\ \geq 0 & \text{if RTS is NIRS} \\ \leq 0 & \text{if RTS is NDRS} \end{cases}$
In the VEA model: VRS: $\tau = 0$ always CRS: $\tau = $ free always	In the VEA model: VRS: $\xi = $ free always CRS: $\xi = 0$ always
NIRS : $\tau \begin{cases} \geq 0 & \text{if } \tau^* = 0 \\ = \text{free} & \text{if } \tau^* > 0 \end{cases}$	NIRS : $\xi \begin{cases} \geq 0 & \text{if } \tau^* = 0 \\ = 0 & \text{if } \tau^* > 0 \end{cases}$
NDRS : $\tau \begin{cases} \leq 0 & \text{if } \tau^* = 0 \\ = \text{free} & \text{if } \tau^* < 0 \end{cases}$	NDRS : $\xi \begin{cases} \leq 0 & \text{if } \tau^* = 0 \\ = 0 & \text{if } \tau^* < 0 \end{cases}$

weight restrictions and the corresponding primal model with additional columns corresponding to the new restrictions.

When weight restriction approach and VEA are combined, there is a reason to be careful. There is a high risk to make two kinds of errors:

1. Weight restrictions are defined in such a way that the envelopment model has unbounded solution, i.e., the multiplier model has no feasible solution.
2. The MPS is found without restrictions and then the restrictions make it inefficient.

The second problem is easy to avoid, when the MPS is searched with the model which includes the weight restrictions. The first problem requires a deeper analysis for finding a reason why there exist no feasible weights. In that case we have to ask the DM to reconsider the weight restrictions.

If the DM is willing to first find the MPS and carry out VEA and insert the weight restrictions afterward—if needed—then problems may appear.

9.2.3 An Example: Municipal Dental Units

We have adopted the data set from Halme and Korhonen (2000).

The data from year 1995 consists of 21 Finnish municipal dental units located in different cities. The units are evaluated with three input variables: material costs (1,000 FIM[1]), dentists (working years), and other staff (working years). The two output variables are the number of patients treated which are divided into two categories: less than 18 years and more than or equal to 18 years old (Table 9.3).

Assume the DM considers VEA with and without weight restrictions to fit to his/her problem. He/she decides to use the nonincreasing returns to scale (NIRS) assumption and a combined model in the analysis. First, he/she computes the inefficiency DEA scores for those 21 municipal dental units. They are given in the first column of Table 9.4. Let's suppose that after seeing the results, he/she would like to name the unit in Espoo the most preferred unit without using any support system.

Furthermore, we will impose the following additional weight restrictions into the model:

$$\nu_2 \geq 1.5\nu_3 \Rightarrow -\nu_2 + 1.5\nu_3 \leq 0 \text{ and}$$
$$\mu_1 \leq \mu_2 \Rightarrow \mu_1 - \mu_2 \leq 0$$

Setting those restrictions is based on the requirement that the weight (the annual costs) of dentists should be at least 150 % of that of the other staff. Moreover the weight (cost) of younger patients should be less or equal to that of the older patients. If this restriction is not set, units might manipulate efficiency by favoring

---

[1]FIM = Finnish Mark, which is nowadays replaced by Euro: 1€ = 5,95 FIM

Table 9.3 The dental units' input–output data

Dental units	Inputs			Outputs	
	Material	Dentists	O staff		
	1,000 FIM	Years	Years	Patients <18	Patients ≥18
Helsinki	5,648	132	212	73,158	54,154
Espoo	2,396	54.5	83	33,098	25,357
Tampere	2,789	40.5	52	28,486	17,157
Vantaa	2,231	59.5	85	29,580	10,624
Turku	2,061	53.5	52	24,139	17,291
Oulu	1,689	36.5	61.5	20,223	11,293
Lahti	1,001	27	43	20,565	14,251
Kuopio	898	29.5	37.5	14,049	9,348
Pori	1,393	26.5	33	13,785	7,415
Jyväskylä	973	23	34.5	12,106	11,945
Hämeenlinna	1,511	27.5	40.5	13,247	9,958
Lappeenranta	799	15.5	21	10,737	4,164
Kotka	523	16	27	10,021	4,480
Vaasa	1,341	21.5	29	10,534	6,200
Mikkeli	758	21	25.5	10,526	5,298
Porvoo	1,046	19.5	30.5	9,687	5,349
Joensuu	1,296	22	29	8,958	6,575
Seinäjoki	767	18	24	10,161	9,207
Rauma	960	23	29.5	9,452	8,245
Kokkola	972	17	22	9,520	2,753
Kouvola	550	17	20.5	8,238	5,647

the treatments of younger, easier patients. The restrictions in the matrix form are as follows:

$$[\mu_1, \mu_2, \nu_1, \nu_2, \nu_3] \begin{bmatrix} 1 & 0 \\ -1 & 0 \\ 0 & 0 \\ 0 & -1 \\ 0 & 1.5 \end{bmatrix} \leq 0$$

where $\mathbf{R}^y = \begin{bmatrix} 1 & 0 \\ -1 & 0 \end{bmatrix}$ and $\mathbf{R}^x = -\begin{bmatrix} 0 & 0 \\ 0 & -1 \\ 0 & 1.5 \end{bmatrix} = \begin{bmatrix} 0 & 0 \\ 0 & 1 \\ 0 & -1.5 \end{bmatrix}$ because we defined

$$[\boldsymbol{\mu}, \boldsymbol{\nu}] \begin{bmatrix} \mathbf{R}^y \\ -\mathbf{R}^x \end{bmatrix} \leq \mathbf{0}$$

The weight restrictions are based on information about relative prices. Note that each relative weight restriction corresponds to inputs/outputs measured in the same units.

Table 9.4 The inefficiency score for DEA and VEA models without and with weight restrictions

Dental units	DEA inefficiency scores		VEA inefficiency scores	
	Weight restrictions		Weight restrictions	
	Without	With	Without	With
Helsinki	0	0	0	0
Espoo	0	0	0	0
Tampere	0	0	0	0
Vantaa	0.077	0.226	0.167	0.227
Turku	0	0.099	0	0.099
Oulu	0.139	0.183	0.192	0.192
Lahti	0	0	0	0
Kuopio	0.123	0.143	0.177	0.227
Pori	0.111	0.177	0.251	0.270
Jyväskylä	0.002	0.003	0.002	0.015
Hämeenlinna	0.173	0.176	0.176	0.192
Lappeenranta	0.001	0.106	0.313	0.336
Kotka	0.035	0.113	0.373	0.382
Vaasa	0.187	0.208	0.307	0.340
Mikkeli	0.089	0.201	0.328	0.364
Porvoo	0.207	0.247	0.400	0.407
Joensuu	0.222	0.24	0.275	0.315
Seinäjoki	0	0	0	0.037
Rauma	0.149	0.164	0.152	0.197
Kokkola	0.097	0.235	0.463	0.498
Kouvola	0.094	0.159	0.226	0.291

The combined model, which also includes the weight restrictions, is formulated now for unit in Kouvola:

max σ

s.t.

	Helsinki		Espoo		Kouvola	RI		RO		σ		Kouvola
Material:	$5{,}648\lambda_1$	+	$2{,}396\lambda_2$	+...	$+550\lambda_{21}$				+	550σ	$\leq$	550
Dentists:	$132\lambda_1$	+	$54.5\lambda_2$	+...	$+17\lambda_{21}$	+	θ_1		+	17σ	$\leq$	17
Other staff:	$212\lambda_1$	+	$83\lambda_2$	+...	$+20.5\lambda_{21}$	−	$1.5\theta_1$		+	20.5σ	$\leq$	20.5
Patients <18:	$73{,}158\lambda_1$	+	$33{,}098\lambda_2$	+...	$+ 8238\lambda_{21}$			+	θ_2	−	$8{,}238\sigma$	$\geq$	8,238
Patients >18:	$54{,}154\lambda_1$	+	$25{,}357\lambda_2$	+...	$+5{,}647\lambda_{21}$			−	θ_2	−	$5{,}647\sigma$	$\geq$	5647

$$\sum\nolimits_{i=1}^{21} \lambda_i \leq 1 \quad (NIRS)$$

$\lambda_i \geq 0, i = 1, 3, \ldots, 21, \theta \geq 0, \lambda_2$ is free (because Espoo is MPS)

As a solution, we get inefficiency scores for each unit. Inefficiency score tells how much the unit has to improve proportionally the inputs and outputs in order to become efficient. Improving for inputs means decreasing and for outputs increasing. For instance, a score of 0.183 (for Oulu, Table 9.4) means that inputs have to be decreased with 18.3 % and the outputs to be increased with 18.3 % so that the unit reaches the (weakly) efficient frontier. It is possible that the projection of the point is on the weakly efficient frontier, but it has no impact on (in)efficiency scores.

From Table 9.4, we see that the standard DEA model gives the smallest inefficiency scores, and the VEA model with weight restrictions provides the largest ones. That is consistent with theory. Instead, the values in the middle columns "DEA inefficiency scores with weight restrictions" and "VEA model without weight restrictions" have no natural rank order. In our problem, all but four in the column "DEA inefficiency scores *with* weight restrictions" are smaller than in the column "VEA model *without* weight restrictions." The only exceptions are the units in Turku, Jyväskylä, and Rauma. The scores are equal to the unit in Hämeenlinna.

We may now ask what kind of operational improvements the different DEA scores would cause, e.g., for the city of Turku. In the basic DEA model, Turku is efficient. However, when the weight restrictions are imposed into the model, inefficiency is revealed—it turns out that all inputs could be reduced by roughly 10 % and all outputs increased by the same figure. However, when Espoo is used as the MPS and no weight restrictions are imposed, Turku remains efficient. In this case it seems that the use of additional weight restrictions was very much motivated.

Consider next the scores for the unit Kotka. In the basic DEA model, Kotka is almost efficient; its score is only 0.035, but the weight restrictions change the score to 0.113 indicating 11.3 % inefficiency. Including preference information into the model, the VEA scores reveal higher inefficiency. The inefficiency scores are 0.373 and 0.379 without and with weight restrictions. The values mean that there is a need for additional analyses for figuring out the reason for the impact of preference information on inefficiency.

Finally, we would like to emphasize that even if the data is real, there is no DM in making decisions based on the analysis.

9.3   Estimating the True VEA Scores with an Interactive Procedure

9.3.1   Illustration of the Problem

In VEA, the preference information is incorporated into the analysis by assuming that a DM evaluates DMUs using a value function. Because the value function is unknown, the reasoning is based on the MPS and the indifference contour passing

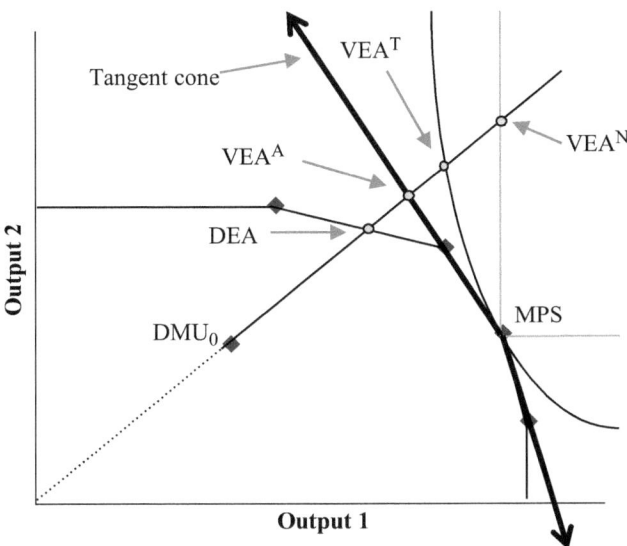

Fig. 9.1 Illustration of value efficiency analysis

through the MPS (see Fig. 9.1). Thus when evaluating DMU_0, we would like to calculate the ratio $\frac{VEA^T - DMU_0}{DMU_0 - O}$ (=true inefficiency score for DMU_0), but since the value function is unknown, we have no information on VEA^T.

For each value function strictly increasing in outputs and decreasing in inputs, we may calculate the range for unit DMU_0 $\left[\frac{DEA - DMU_0}{DMU_0 - O}, \frac{VEA^N - DMU_0}{DMU_0 - O}\right]$, because each point VEA^T at the intersection of the ray from the origin through point DMU_0 and the value function contour through MPS holds that $DEA \leq VEA^T \leq VEA^N$. To prove the above, assume $VEA^T < DEA$. Because $MPS \approx VEA^T \Rightarrow MPS$ should be less preferred than DEA^2. On the other hand, if we should assume that $VEA^T > VEA^N$, then $MPS \approx VEA^T \Rightarrow VEA^N$ is less preferred than MPS, although $VEA^N \geq MPS$. Unfortunately, the above bounds are too loose in most cases.

However, if we assume that the value function is pseudoconcave and increasing in outputs and in the additive inverse of inputs, it is possible to introduce a tighter lower bound; see Chap. 7 and Halme et al. (1999) for required theory. The idea is based on the use of the tangent cone at MPS defined by the binding constraints at the MPS. This cone consists of solutions surely less preferred than MPS. The intersection of the ray from the origin through point DMU_0 and the cone defines the point VEA^A which is at least as preferred as point DEA. Thus a tighter lower bound for the value efficiency is $\frac{VEA^A - DMU_0}{DMU_0 - O}$, and the revised bounds are $\left[\frac{VEA - DMU_0}{DMU_0 - O}, \frac{VEA^N - DMU_0}{DMU_0 - O}\right]$.

---

[2]Symbol "$\approx$" means equally preferred.

9.3.2   Theoretical Considerations

To be able to calculate the true value inefficiency scores, one must know the value function. That assumption was not made in Chap. 7, or in Halme et al. (1999). Instead it was assumed that the DM is able to determine an MPS, i.e., a (virtual or existing) DMU based on his/her underlying value function $v(\boldsymbol{u})$,

$\boldsymbol{u} = \begin{bmatrix} \boldsymbol{y} \\ -\boldsymbol{x} \end{bmatrix} \in \mathfrak{R}^{m+s}$, which is strictly increasing (i.e., strictly increasing in $\boldsymbol{y}$ and

strictly decreasing in $\boldsymbol{x}$) and with a (local) maximal value $v(\boldsymbol{u}^*)$ over T,

$\boldsymbol{u}^* = \begin{bmatrix} \boldsymbol{y}^* \\ -\boldsymbol{x}^* \end{bmatrix} \in \mathfrak{R}^{m+s}$. Furthermore, v is assumed to be pseudoconcave, because

its local optimum over a convex set is also global (Bazaraa et al. 1993, p. 570) and the optimality conditions can easily be verified.

Unfortunately, knowing the MPS is not sufficient to specify the contour of an unknown pseudoconcave value function and not even its tangent at the MPS. However, it is possible to define the region consisting of all points surely not more preferred than the MPS. This region is an (augmented) tangent cone W_{u*} at the MPS (see Theorem 7.1 and Halme et al. 1999). Thus $W_{u*} \subseteq V =$

$\left\{ \boldsymbol{u} = \begin{bmatrix} \boldsymbol{y} \\ -\boldsymbol{x} \end{bmatrix} \middle| v(\boldsymbol{u}) \leq v(\boldsymbol{u}^*) \right\}$ which is true for any pseudoconcave value function

with a maximum at $\boldsymbol{u}^*$ (see Fig. 7.3 for illustration). This means that in the projections of inefficient units restricted to the cone W_{u*}, the resulting efficiency scores are always surely not worse than the true ones (cf. the points VEA^A and VEA^T in Fig. 9.1).

Mathematically this reduces to a straightforward application of linear programming resulting in the (approximated) value efficiency scores. Value efficiency is studied using model (7.2). The value of σ at the optimum of model (7.2) is the (approximated) value inefficiency score and it is denoted by σ^A.[3]

As said, since $W_{u*} \subseteq V$, the approximated value (in)efficiency score σ^A is a lower bound for the true value (in)efficiency score σ^T, i.e., $\sigma^A \leq \sigma^T$. The upper bound for σ^T is easy to compute, even the pseudoconcavity is not needed. The result follows from Lemma 9.1.

Lemma 9.1 If function $v(\boldsymbol{u})$, $\boldsymbol{u} \in \mathfrak{R}^{m+s}$, is continuous and strictly increasing, then $\{\boldsymbol{u}|\ v(\boldsymbol{u}) \leq v(\boldsymbol{u}^*)\} \cap \{\boldsymbol{u}\ |\ \boldsymbol{u}^* < \boldsymbol{u}\} = \varnothing$.

---

[3]Note that the only difference to measure inefficiency instead of efficiency is that in measuring inefficiency the current values of the controllable variables are also on the right-hand side in the VEA model (7.2).

Proof Straightforward

Thus we can easily obtain an upper bound as a solution to the following model:

$\max \sigma$

s.t.

$u - \sigma u_0 \geq u_0$

$u \in K = \{u | u^* < u\}^C,$

where superscript "C" refers to the complement of set $\{u | u^* < u\}$. The solution is called the "naïve" value efficiency score and denoted by σ^N. Thus for true scores we have $\sigma^A \leq \sigma^T \leq \sigma^N$.

We may also easily show that the DEA scores σ^E determine a lower bound for the approximated VEA scores.   □

Lemma 9.2 $\sigma^E \leq \sigma^A$.

Proof The result follows from the fact that $T \subseteq W_{u^*}$.

Thus we have the following inequalities: $0 \leq \sigma^E \leq \sigma^A \leq \sigma^T \leq \sigma^N$, which we proceed to consider in the following section.

If the approximated and the "naïve" scores (σ^A and σ^N) are very close to each other, there may be no need to locate the true value efficiency scores. However, if the scores are far apart, the DM may want to more accurately estimate the score. In the next subsection, we propose an approach for finding the true value efficiency score.

Finally, we prove the following lemmas, which we will use in the approach presented in the following section.   □

Lemma 9.3 If function $f: \mathfrak{R}^n \to \mathfrak{R}$ is *pseudoconcave* on a convex set S, then all x_1, $x_2 \in S$, $f(\lambda x_1 + (1 - \lambda) x_2) \geq \min\{f(x_1), f(x_2)\}$ for all $\lambda \in [0, 1]$.

Proof See, e.g., Bazaraa et al. (1993).   □

Lemma 9.4 Assume that v is a (strictly) increasing pseudoconcave (value) function defined in $\mathfrak{R}^{m+s}$, and let σ^A be the solution (7.2) corresponding to value efficiency analysis of unit u_0 and with an assumption that u^* is the MPS. If $\exists \sigma^s$, $0 \leq \sigma^s < \sigma^A$ and $u^s = u_0 + \sigma^s u_0$, such that the DM is indifferent between u^s and u^* ($u^s \approx u^*$), then $\exists u^m \in T$ such that $v(u^m) > v(u^*)$.

Proof Assume that v has its maximum at u^*, i.e., $v(u^*) \geq v(u), u \in T$. Let $W(u^*)$ be the augmented tangent cone of T at u^*. By Lemma 7.4 (see also Halme et al. 1999), $u \in W(u^*) \Rightarrow v(u^*) \geq v(u)$. By Theorem 7.2 (see also Halme et al. 1999), where $u^A \in W(u^*)$, $u^A = u_0 + \sigma^A u_0$. By assumption $u^s \approx u^* \Rightarrow v(u^*) = v(u^s)$. Because v is increasing, $v(u^s) < v(u^A)$, which is a conflict. Thus v has no maximum at u^* in set $T \Rightarrow \exists u^m \in T$, $v(u^*) < v(u^m)$, which is a contradiction with the assumption.   □

9.3.3 An Approach to Find the True Value Efficiency Score

To determine the true value inefficiency score, we present an interactive approach developed by Joro et al. (2003), which enables the DM to make a simple line search on the ray u_0 starting from u_0 (denoted by DMU_0 in figures), i.e., on the ray $u_0 + \sigma u_0$, $\sigma \in [0, \sigma^N]$. In this section, we describe the approach and illustrate it using a simple numerical example illustrated in Figs. 9.2 and 9.3. Our theoretical considerations were presented in a general form. A prototype of our approach is implemented using macros in Excel.

	DMU_0	VEA^T	MPS
Output 1	0.6888	1.4121	1.6408
Output 2	0.0169	0.0347	0.0180

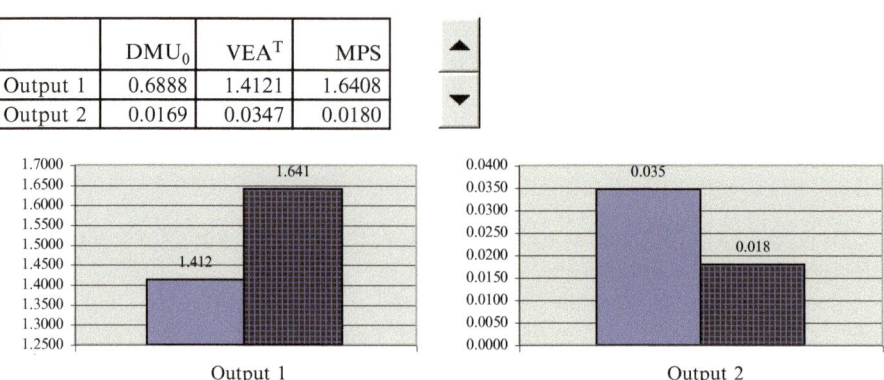

Fig. 9.2 The interface for the search of the indifferent point

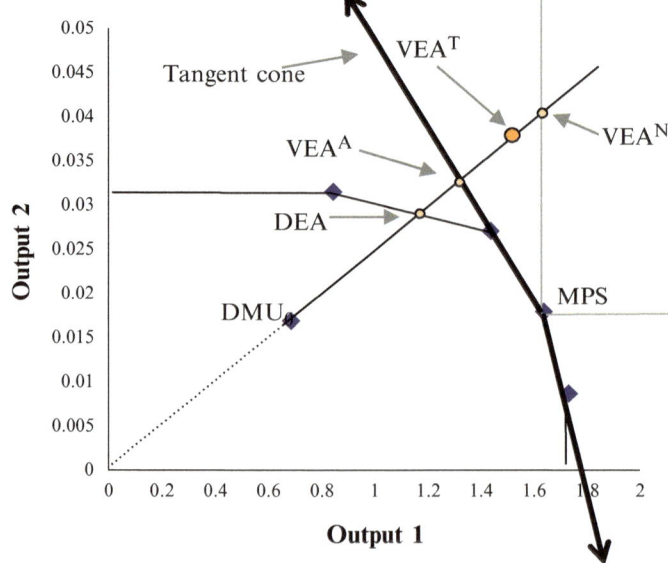

Fig. 9.3 A possible stop of the search

Approach

Step 0: *Most preferred solution*
Assist the DM in finding his/her MPS u^* on the efficient frontier $u^* \in T$.

Step 1: *Value efficiency of point u_0*
If the DM is willing to choose unit (existing or virtual) $u \in T$ for consideration, denote it as u_0; otherwise, **stop**. Define a ray $r = (1 + \sigma)u_0$, $\sigma > 0$, and determine the specific values: σ^E and σ^N. The value σ^A with model (7.2) is determined only if the pseudoconcavity assumption of the value function is tested and holds. Otherwise, set σ^E to σ^A.

Step 2: *An indifferent point to u^* on the ray r*
By varying the values of σ, $\sigma \in [0,\sigma^N]$, find the point u for which $u \approx u^*$. (The DM is indifferent between u and u^*, i.e., $v(u) \approx v(u^*)$ for an unknown value function.) Let the corresponding parameter value be σ^I.

For this purpose, we use the following interface (Fig. 9.2):

We present each input/output variable (here only output variables) in its own graph. In each graph, the DM compares the values (right histograms) of the MPS to the values in the left histograms, a trial value for VEA^T which the DM chooses by moving back and forth on the ray r with parameter $\sigma \in [0, \sigma^N]$. When the values are equally preferred, the DM will stop the search. He/she should get the same information in numerical and graphical forms.

Step 3: Rationality checking

$$\text{If } \sigma^I \in \begin{cases} [\sigma^0, \sigma^E), & \text{then go to } \textbf{Step 4} \\ [\sigma^E, \sigma^A), & \text{then go to } \textbf{Step 5} \\ [\sigma^A, \sigma^N), & \text{then use } \sigma^I \text{ as a true VEA score } \sigma^T \text{ for } u_0; \text{ go to } \textbf{Step 1}. \end{cases}$$

The last option is illustrated in Fig. 9.3.
For simplicity, we assume that $u_0 + \sigma^E u_0$ is efficient. If the DM chooses $\sigma^I < \sigma^E$, the choice is not rational. Then we have to provide the DM with those two options in **Step 4**.

Step 4: No rational choice
The DM has chosen $\sigma^I < \sigma^E$. It means that the point $u_0 + \sigma^I u_0$ is dominated by $u_0 + \sigma^E u_0 \in T$. Because the (unknown) value function was assumed to be strictly increasing in u, $v(u_0 + \sigma^E u_0) > v(u_0 + \sigma^I u_0) = v(u^*)$. It implies that the DM has chosen the MPS that is less preferred than a feasible solution.

We may provide the DM with two options:

1. He/she can return to Step 2 to correct his/her evaluation.
2. He/she can choose a new MPS. It may be found through a new search (go to **Step 0**), or the solution on the efficient frontier for point u_0 may be chosen as the most preferred one. If it is acceptable, denote it by u^* and return to **Step 2**.

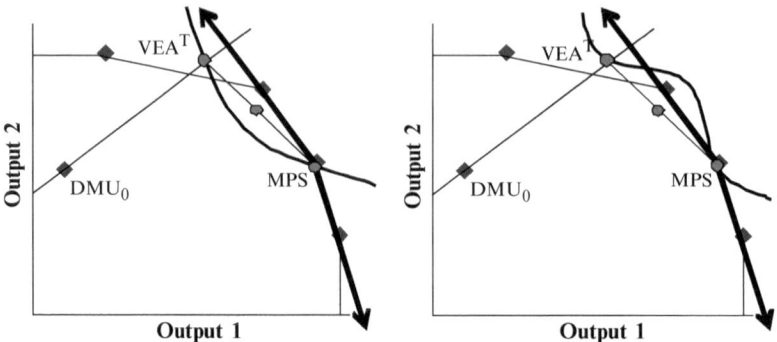

Fig. 9.4 Illustration of explanations for conflicting choice in Step 4

In Fig. 9.3, the choice is made on the ray (starting from the origin and passing through DMU_0) from the interval (DMU_0, DEA).

Step 5: *Conflicting choice*

If the DM chooses $\sigma^E \leq \sigma^I < \sigma^A$, it means that:

1. He/she has made an irrational choice.
2. His/her choice is rational, but the pseudoconcavity assumption of the value function is not valid.

These choices are illustrated in Fig. 9.4a, b. Consider the convex combination $u(\mu) = \mu u^I + (1 - \mu)u^*$, $\mu \in [0,1]$, where $u^I = (1 + \sigma^I)u_0$. (The end points u^I and u^* in figures are denoted by VEA^T and MPS, correspondingly.)

If the DM is able to point out at least one solution on the line $u(\lambda^1)$, $\lambda^1 \in (0,1)$, which is strictly less preferred than u^*, then we have to reject the pseudoconcavity assumption (Lemma 9.3). In this case, the current solution u^I is acceptable. Further considerations based on the pseudoconcavity assumption are not necessary, unless it is not specifically desired by the DM. Go to **Step 2**.

In case we do not find any evidence to reject the pseudoconcavity assumption, we assume it to be true. By Lemma 9.3, then there exists at least one point $u^D \in T$, which is strictly preferred to u^*. To search such a point, we may use the following procedure (Figs. 9.5 and 9.6). We restrict the search on the line $u(\mu)$ into the part $\mu \in [0, \mu_0]$, for which $u(\mu) \in T$, and project this line onto the efficient frontier as explained, e.g., by Korhonen and Laakso (1986). (This part is existing because the direction $u^I - u^*$ is feasible by the definition of the augmented tangent cone W_{u*}.) When the DM will vary the value of μ, he/she will see on the screen the values on this efficient curve—not on the original line. Then the DM is asked to search the MPS on this curve. If he/she is not able or willing to do it, assist him/her to make the search on the whole efficient frontier. Go to **Step 2**.

The left- and rightmost histograms in both figures correspond to points u^I and u^*. The central histogram is a convex combination of those two points.

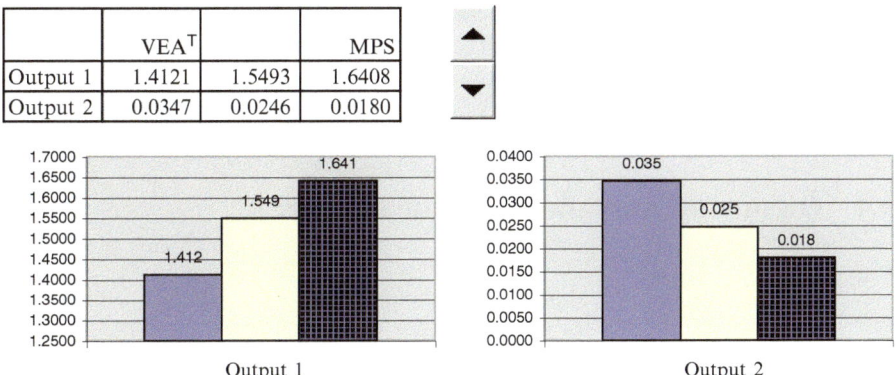

	VEA^T		MPS
Output 1	1.4121	1.5493	1.6408
Output 2	0.0347	0.0246	0.0180

Fig. 9.5 The interface for the search on line MPS–VEA^T

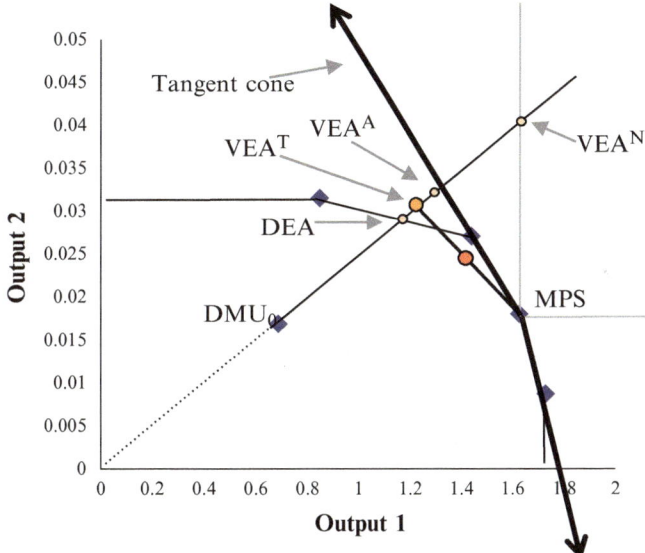

Fig. 9.6 Illustrating the search

9.3.4 Practical Considerations

The analysis proposed in this chapter provides the DM with the possibility to have more precise preference information than the (approximative) value efficiency analysis proposed in the previous chapter and in Halme et al. (1999). However, the analysis may be quite time consuming, especially in case of large data sets, and it may be difficult to the DM to specify indifferent points to the MPS, if the number of input and output variables is not small (let's say 7 ± 2). Therefore in practical applications, the approach presented in this subsection is a refinement and improvement to the value efficiency analysis.

9.4 On the Interpretation of Value Efficiency

9.4.1 Background

The basic idea in value efficiency analysis is to measure efficiency as a distance to an approximated indifference contour of a DM's value function. The distance is measured to the contour that passes through the MPS in the PPS. Although the value function is not explicitly specified, the DM is assumed to be able to identify the MPS, which maximizes the unknown value function over the PPS.

Generally, a value function and especially its approximation include only ordinal information, and thus a value efficiency score does not provide information on the value of a decision-making unit (DMU) to the DM (except that the maximal value is achieved at the MPS). Hence, the score only describes the improvements in the input/output values that are needed in order to reach the contour at which the DMU is as preferred as the MPS. However, by making more restrictive assumptions about the value function, value efficiency scores can be interpreted to give value information as well. Our aim is to discuss those additional assumptions.

Let us assume that we have n DMUs each consuming m inputs and producing s outputs. $\mathbf{X} \in \mathfrak{R}_+^{m \times n}$ and $\mathbf{Y} \in \mathfrak{R}_+^{s \times n}$ are matrices representing the observed input and output measures for the DMUs. Vector $y \in \mathfrak{R}_+^s$ refers to outputs and $x \in \mathfrak{R}_+^m$ to inputs. In the DEA context, the PPS is defined as a set $T = \{(y, x) | y$ that can be produced from $x\} = \{(y, x) | x \geq \mathbf{X}\lambda, y \leq \mathbf{Y}\lambda, \lambda \in \Lambda\}$. In the case of the CCR model (Charnes et al. 1978), $\Lambda = \mathfrak{R}_+^n$, and in the case of the BCC model (Banker et al. 1984), $\Lambda = \{\lambda | \mathbf{1}^T\lambda = 1, \lambda \in \mathfrak{R}_+^n\}$.

Because the value function and thus also the indifference contour are generally unknown, Halme et al. (1999) developed the requisite theory and the procedure to approximate the indifference curve of the unknown value function by the tangent cone at the MPS. The value function $v(y, x)$ is assumed to be strictly increasing in y and strictly decreasing in x, and function $u(y, -x)$ $(=v(y, x))$ is assumed to be pseudoconcave. In this case, there is a unique MPS $(y^*, x^*) \in T$ at which the value function $v(y, x)$ of the DM has a maximum value $v(y^*, x^*)$. The value efficiency analysis provides the scores, which are lower bounds for true value inefficiency scores. For more theoretical considerations, see Halme et al. (1999). The use of value efficiency in practice is discussed in Korhonen et al. (2002).

In this subsection, we consider the interpretation of the value efficiency score at a conceptual level without discussing the approximation of the value function. Because v is continuous and strictly increasing, for each existing unit $(y^0, x^0) \in T$ and for any $(w^y, w^x) \geq \mathbf{0}$, $(w^y, w^x) \neq \mathbf{0}$, there exists such a parameter $\gamma \geq 0$ that

$$v\left(y^0 + \gamma w^y, x^0 - \gamma w^x\right) = v(y^*, x^*) \tag{9.2}$$

Parameter γ is called the *weighted true value inefficiency score* γ for point (y^0, x^0). Vector (w^y, w^x) determines the preassigned direction to the (weakly) efficient boundary of T. When the weighting vector or direction (w^y, w^x) for the unit under consideration is $(y^0, \mathbf{0})$, the model is output oriented. Correspondingly, when the vector is $(\mathbf{0}, x^0)$, the model is input oriented. These projections are called radial in the DEA literature. We may use the so-called combined orientation by letting the weighting vector be (y^0, x^0). For general discussion on the use of directional distance functions, see Chambers et al. (1998).

The true value inefficiency score tells how much a DMU has to improve its current output and input values (y^0, x^0) in the direction (w^y, w^x) in order to be as preferred as the MPS. It is evident that $\gamma > 0$ iff the point (y^0, x^0) is value inefficient.

Without additional assumptions, the value inefficiency score represents just the (minimum) change in inputs and/or outputs (in the direction of (w^y, w^x)) required for achieving the value equal to the value at the MPS. Continuity, monotonicity, and pseudoconcavity assumptions alone do not provide enough information for evaluating the change in value. The assumptions are not even sufficient for ranking the units on the basis of their value inefficiency scores.

Even if we assume that the value function has a cardinal interpretation, we have to make more specific assumptions concerning the functional form of the value function. However, some quite general assumptions enable us to have information about value changes as well.

Next we consider assumptions concerning the functional form of the value function and demonstrate that in those cases value inefficiency score provides a possibility to evaluate value changes. The representation is based on the paper by Korhonen and Syrjänen (2005).

Homogeneity assumptions that are widely used in economic analysis play an important role in the following considerations. An additional reason to use a homogeneity assumption is that the traditional Farrell efficiency measure is homogeneous of degree 1 (Färe and Lovell 1978).

Assumption 1 Assume that the value function v can be separated so that $v(y, x) = f$ $(y)/g(x)$ for all $(y, x) \in$ T. Function f is assumed to be continuous, strictly increasing, and homogeneous of degree $r > 0$, and g is assumed to be continuous, strictly increasing, and homogeneous of degree $q > 0$. Note that the assumption implies that v is homogeneous of degree $r-s$.

Let us first consider a combined-oriented model, i.e., $(w^y, w^x) = (y^0, x^0)$. Equation (9.1) can now be written as $v(y^0 + \gamma y^0, x^0 - \gamma x^0) = f(y^0 + \gamma y^0)/g(x^0 - \gamma x^0) = f((1+\gamma)$ $y^0)/g((1-\gamma)x^0) = (1+\gamma)^r f(y^0)/[(1-\gamma)^q g(x^0)] = v(y^*, x^*)$. Thus, we may calculate the ratio of the value at the current point to the value at the MPS: $v(y^0, x^0)/ v(y^*, x^*) = f(y^0)/g(x^0) / [(1+\gamma)^r f(y^0)/[(1-\gamma)^q g(x^0)]] = (1-\gamma)^q/(1+\gamma)^r$.

Consider next an output-oriented model, i.e., $(w^y, w^x) = (y^0, \mathbf{0})$. Equation (9.1) can now be written as $v(y^0 + \gamma y^0, x^0) = f(y^0 + \gamma y^0)/g(x^0) = f((1+\gamma)y^0)/g(x^0) = (1+\gamma)^r f(y^0)/g(x^0) = v(y^*, x^*)$. In this case, the ratio can be written as follows: $v(y^0, x^0)/ v(y^*, x^*) = f(y^0)/g(x^0)/[(1+\gamma)^r f(y^0)/g(x^0)] = 1/(1+\gamma)^r$. Note that in the output-oriented case, we do not need to make assumptions about the homogeneity of g.

Correspondingly, in the case of an input-oriented model, $v(y^0, x^0)/v(y^*, x^*) = f(y^0)/g(x^0)/[f(y^0)/[(1-\gamma)^q g(x^0)]] = (1-\gamma)^q$. (Note that $\gamma < 1$.) In this case, we do not need the homogeneity assumptions about f.

Assumption 1 enables us to measure the proportional difference in value as a function of the inefficiency score. The result is valid only if efficiency measurement is based on radial projection as is usually the case in standard DEA models. The ratios calculated above are always possible, but the interpretation only makes sense if we may assume that $v(\mathbf{0}, \mathbf{0}) = 0$, i.e., value is zero in case no inputs are used and no outputs are produced.

If the projection is made using any given direction (w^y, w^x) or if we like to measure the change in an absolute value, Assumption 1 is not generally sufficient. Then we need a stronger assumption that separates the current value and the change.

Assumption 2 Assume that the value function v is linear.

This assumption means that v is homogeneous of degree 1 and $v(y_1+y_2, x_1+x_2) = v(y_1, x_1) + v(y_2, x_2)$. (Note that, e.g., the value function $v(x, y) = a + bx + cy$, $a \neq 0$, does not have these properties.) It is easy to see that the assumption implies that $v(\mathbf{0}, \mathbf{0}) = 0$.

Suppose now that we would like to evaluate the change in value, when the projection vector $(w^y, w^x) \geq 0$, $(w^y, w^x) \neq \mathbf{0}$ is given. From Assumption 2, it follows that we can write $v(y^0+\gamma w^y, x^0-\gamma w^x) = v(y^0, x^0) + v(\gamma w^y, -\gamma w^x) = v(y^0, x^0) + \gamma v(w^y, -w^x)$. Furthermore we can measure the difference between the value at the current point and the value at the MPS in the following way: $[v(y^*, x^*) - v(y^0, x^0)]/v(w^y, -w^x) = \gamma v(w^y, -w^x)/v(w^y, -w^x) = \gamma$. In this case, the change in value is related to the value of the weighting vector or direction (w^y, w^x), which serves as a common benchmark.

As we see, Assumption 2 leads to a simple interpretation and is valid for any (w^y, w^x). If the linearity assumption of the value function is acceptable, then this is a valid approach in practical application. In practical DEA applications, radial projection is often used. In this case, we can use a more general assumption for a value function (Assumption 1).

9.4.2 Illustrations

A specific function commonly used in economic analysis is the Cobb–Douglas function. Let us define $v(y, x) = A \prod_{i=1}^{s} \prod_{j=1}^{m} y_i^{\alpha_i} x_j^{\beta_j}$, where $A > 0$, $\alpha_i > 0$ and $\beta_j < 0$ are constants. Clearly, the function v can be separated:

$$v(y, x) = \prod_{i=1}^{s} \prod_{j=1}^{m} y_i^{\alpha_i} x_j^{\beta_j} = \prod_{i=1}^{s} y_i^{\alpha_i} \left(\prod_{j=1}^{m} x_j^{\beta_j}\right)^{-1} = f(y)/g(x), \text{ where } f(y) \text{ is a strictly}$$

increasing homogeneous function of degree $\sum_{i=1}^{s} \alpha_i$ and $g(x)$ is strictly increasing

homogeneous function of degree $\sum_{j=1}^{m} -\beta_j$. Function v thus fulfills Assumption 1. If

the inefficiency score for the output-oriented model is γ, the proportional value will

be $1/(1+\gamma)^{\omega}$, where $\omega = \sum_{i=1}^{s} \alpha_i > 0$. Correspondingly, the proportional value for

the input-oriented model is $(1-\gamma)^{\delta}$, where $\delta = \sum_{j=1}^{m} -\beta_j > 0$.

For instance, if we may assume that the value function is a Cobb–Douglas function of its functional form, we do not need to specify it explicitly. If we assume

that $\delta = \sum_{j=1}^{m} -\beta_j = 1$, then in the input-oriented case, we may say that inefficiency

score also stands for value change.

Suppose next that the value function is of the form $v(y, x) = a'y - b'x$, where $a \in \mathfrak{R}_+^s$ and $b \in \mathfrak{R}_+^m$. Assumption 2 is fulfilled, and the inefficiency score γ describes the value change relative to the change in direction vector used in the projection. If $(w^y, w^x) \geq 0$, $(w^y, w^x) \neq 0$, the proportional value change is γ, when the current point is projected onto the efficient frontier in the direction (w^y, w^x).

9.5 Final Remarks

In this chapter, we considered three different ways to extend the use of VEA:

1. To add restrictions to weights if more flexibility is needed to specify preference information into DEA. The restrictions can be given in an absolute and relative form.
2. To use interactive methods to find true value efficiency scores and to test if the DM behaves rationally and if the assumption that the value function is pseudoconcave are reasonable.
3. To set additional assumptions to value function for enabling to value efficiency score to provide cardinal information as well.

References

Allen R, Athanassopoulos A, Dyson RG, Thanassoulis E (1997) Weights restrictions and value judgements in data envelopment analysis: evolution, development and future directions. Ann Oper Res 73:13–34

Banker RD, Charnes A, Cooper WW (1984) Some models for estimating technical and scale inefficiencies in data envelopment analysis. Manage Sci 30:1078–1092

Bazaraa M, Sherali HD, Shetty CM (1993) Nonlinear programming: theory and algorithms, 2nd edn. Wiley, New York

Charnes A, Cooper WW, Rhodes E (1978) Measuring efficiency of decision making units. Eur J Oper Res 2:429–444

Chambers RG, Chung Y, Färe R (1998) Profit, directional distance functions, and Nerlovian efficiency. J Optim Theory Appl 98(2):351–364

Färe R, Lovell CAK (1978) Measuring the technical efficiency of production. J Econ Theory 19:150–162

Halme M, Joro T, Korhonen P, Salo S, Wallenius J (1999) A value efficiency approach to incorporating preference information in data envelopment analysis. Manage Sci 45 (1):103–115

Halme M, Korhonen P (2000) Restricting weights in value efficiency analysis. Eur J Oper Res 126:175–188

Joro T, Korhonen P, Zionts S (2003) An interactive approach to improve estimates of value efficiency in data envelopment analysis. Eur J Oper Res 149:688–699

Korhonen P, Laakso J (1986) A visual interactive method for solving the multiple criteria problem. Eur J Oper Res 24:277–287

Korhonen P, Siljamäki A, Soismaa M (2002) On the use of value efficiency analysis and further developments. J Prod Anal 17(1/2):49–64

Korhonen P, Syrjänen M (2005) On the interpretation of value efficiency. J Prod Anal 24(2):197–201

Thompson RG, Singleton FR Jr, Thrall RM, Smith BA (1986) Comparative site evaluation for locating a high-energy physics lab in Texas. Interfaces 16:35–49

Chapter 10
Non-convex Value Efficiency Analysis

Value Efficiency Analysis and FDH

10.1 Why Is a Convex Relaxation Needed?

As we have discussed and demonstrated in Chaps. 7–9, the value efficiency analysis can be applied to input-, output-, and combined-oriented models. It is also applicable to various returns to scale assumptions (CRS, VRS, NIRS, and NDRS). However, the convex property of a production possibility set is required. Unfortunately, the extension to non-convex PPS is not straightforward. Not only the extension is theoretically interesting, it has an important practical meaning in some situations.

During our experience of VEA applications, we have repeatedly encountered the phenomenon that DMs are more reluctant to evaluate virtual units belonging to an empirical PPS than real (observed) DMUs. As Bogetoft et al. (2000) pointed out: *Fictitious production possibilities, generated as convex combinations of those actually observed units are usually less convincing as benchmarks or reference DMUs than actually observed ones.*

Because the empirical PPSs (P_{VRS}, P_{NIRS}, P_{NDRS}, and P_{CRS}) are based on the sample $S_0 = \{(y_i, x_i) \mid i = 1, 2, \ldots, n\}$ (see Chap. 3) and are convex, a subset of those points are the efficient extreme points of a polytope. If a DM names any of such points as the most preferred solution, it means that his/her value function has a maximum at the extreme point of the polytope. If a DM constantly selects an extreme DMU as his/her MPS, a plausible explanation is that the value function is linear.

However, the linearity assumption is in conflict with the observation that the DM will often pick up a virtual unit from the efficient frontier of a convex PPS, when he/she has freedom to search the efficient frontier. This kind of choice behavior is an indicator that the DM's value function is not linear and/or PPS is not convex. In the next subsection, we demonstrate the bias caused by a wrong choice of the most preferred solution.

© Springer Science+Business Media New York 2015
T. Joro, P.J. Korhonen, *Extension of Data Envelopment Analysis with Preference Information*, International Series in Operations Research & Management Science 218, DOI 10.1007/978-1-4899-7528-7_10

There is one choice, which is definitely in conflict with the convex assumption of PPS: the MPU chosen by the DM is not on the efficient frontier of the convex PPS. Actually it happens in practice. For instance, in our Parish application (Chap. 11), we assumed the convex PPS, but the DM wanted to use an inefficient unit to characterize the virtual MPS.[1] The unit was not dominated by any other observed unit. However, the choice is not rational if the PPS is convex.

There is an obvious need for the value efficient analysis, which does not require the convex assumption of the PPS. Halme et al. (2014) quite recently developed a value efficiency approach to a non-convex environment. The approach is based on quasiconcave (quasiconvex) value function and convex cones (Korhonen et al. 1984). The value function is quasiconcave for outputs and quasiconvex for inputs. In the sequel, for a value efficiency analysis with convex PPS set, we use the term convex VEA, and with a non-convex PPS, we call it non-convex VEA.

10.2   Consequences of Using a Wrong Convexity Assumption

Consider the sample data set in Table 10.1, also used in Example (3.5). Assume that the DM thinks that an NIRS model sounds quite reasonable and will name unit B as his/her MPU.[2] Let's assume further that making the free search on the efficient frontier, he/she will end up at the point denoted by MPS in Fig. 10.1. If we assume as before that DM's value function is pseudoconcave for outputs and pseudoconvex for inputs, so the indifference contour passing through point MPS might be such as drawn in Fig. 10.1. On the other hand, the indifference contour of that value function passing through B might be as drawn in Fig. 10.1. Thus we assume that the value function reaches the maximum at B among the set of observed points. However, there are many points in the convex PPS more preferred than B. Hence B is not the most preferred in the whole convex PPS. We have drawn the contour in such a way that the inefficient unit A is almost on the contour, i.e., almost equally preferred to B (Fig. 10.1).

Consider the difference between the value efficiency of unit C, when B or MPS is used as the most preferred unit. When B is used, then the spanning directions of the tangent cone are from B down to origin and from B up to D. The value inefficiency score of C is 0.27 (point C^B), when a combined orientation is used. It is the same as the technical inefficiency score. Instead if we use the "true" MPS, the value inefficiency score is 0.47 (point C^{MPS}). Because we do not know explicitly the true value function—only its functional form is assumed—the use of point C^{MPS} gives an optimistic score for value (in)efficiency, but the use of point C^B leads to an

---

[1] To overcome the problem, we used the trick described in Chap. 8.
[2] When an observed unit is the most preferred one, we use abbreviation MPU to refer to it. For a virtual most preferred point, we use MPS.

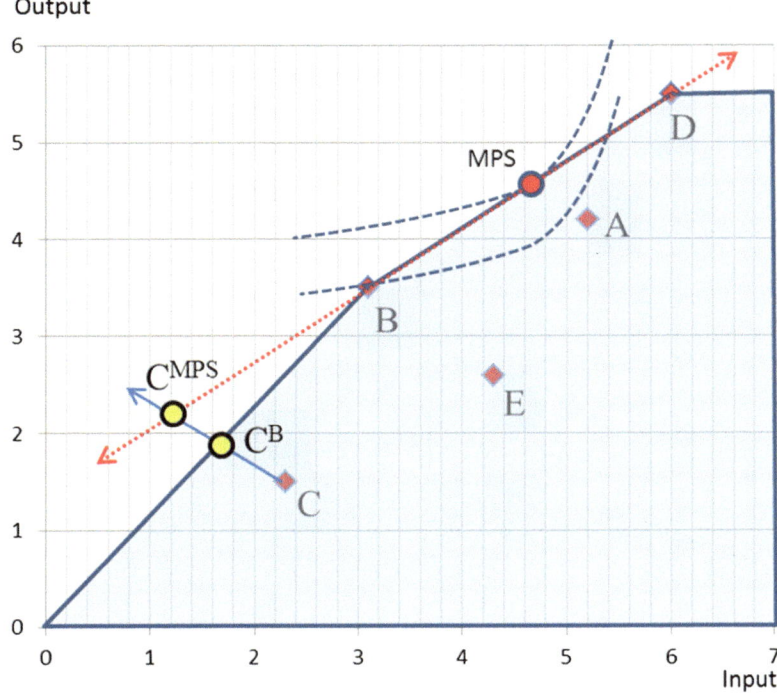

Fig. 10.1 Effect of erroneous choice of the given DMU as an MPS

Table 10.1 The data sets used in illustrations

DMUs	Input	Output
A	5.2	4.2
B	3.1	3.5
C	2.3	1.5
D	6	5.5
E	4.3	2.6

overoptimistic score. If the value function is quasiconcave to outputs and quasiconvex to inputs, and point MPS is the true most preferred point, then the indifference contour at MPS cannot pass through point C^B. The approximation of the most preferred point by the efficient extreme point may lead to a very biased value efficiency measurement.[3]

Actually, without any additional information it is difficult to claim an error in the choice of unit B as the MPU is erroneous, because B lies on the efficient frontier. Instead, choosing units A and C is rational only if the PPS is not assumed to be

---

[3] Note that the most preferred virtual unit can also be defined by articulating that B and D are equally good, or to say that B and D belong to the facet where MPU lies.

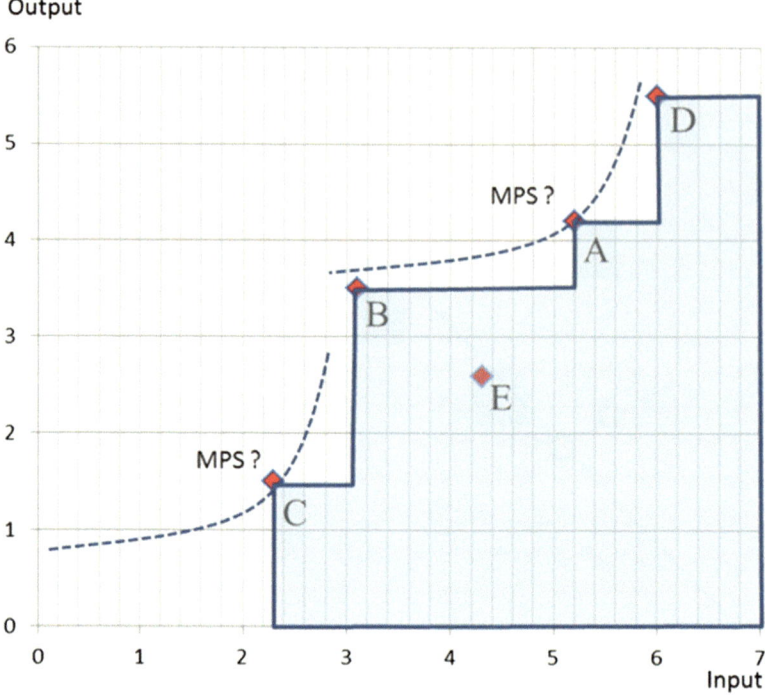

Fig. 10.2 Possible choice of units A and C as a potential MPS

convex, because they are not dominated by any observed unit. In this case, it is justifiable to propose to the DM the use of a non-convex PPS. Instead, the choice E is never rational, because unit B dominates it (Fig. 10.1).

Points such as A and C are called convex dominated, in which concept is formally defined as follows (see Zionts and Wallenius 1980):

Definition 10.1 Let S be a set in a p-dimensional Euclidean space $\mathfrak{R}^p$. Then point $z^* \in S \in \mathfrak{R}^p$ is *convex dominated* iff there does not exist $z = \sum_{i=1}^{p} \lambda_i z_i$, $\lambda_i \geq 0$, $\sum_{i=1}^{p} \lambda_i = 1$, $z_i \in S$, $i = 1, 2, \ldots, p$, such that $z \geq z^*$ and $z \neq z^*$.

Note that the convex-dominated point may be efficient. The efficient, but convex dominated, points are also called nonsupported efficient points, because no linear function can reach the maximum at such a point. It means that in the non-convex value efficiency, we cannot assume the value function to be linear because such a value function cannot reach a unique optimum at all efficient points (Fig. 10.2).

In the value efficiency analysis in a convex production possibility set, we assume that the value function is pseudoconcave for outputs and pseudoconvex for inputs. We could use the same assumption, but we do not need a so strong assumption because we do not take advantage of differentiability of the value function. In a non-convex value efficiency analysis, we assume that PPS is a free disposal hull (see Deprins et al. 1984). It means that the efficient set is a subset of observed units, and preference comparisons are made between those points. The evaluation of value efficiency is based on those preference comparisons as we show in Sect. 10.4. For our purpose, it is sufficient to assume that the value function is quasiconcave for outputs and quasiconvex for inputs (see next subsection).

The main purpose—as in the original value efficiency analysis—is to approximate the distance of each unit from the indifference contour of the value function passing through the most preferred unit. The approximation is never worse than true value efficiency. The idea is based on the so-called convex cones developed by Korhonen et al. (1984) and briefly reviewed in the next subsection.

Measuring value efficiency in the case of a non-convex production possibility set is based on *convex cones*, which are further based on the assumption that the value function is quasiconcave for outputs and for the additive inverse of inputs. The pseudoconcave function is quasiconcave, but not the other way around.

Because the value function is quasiconvex for inputs, in order to unify our formulations, we replace the input values with their additive inverses to make them behave as outputs. To simplify notation we write $u = \begin{bmatrix} y \\ -x \end{bmatrix}$ and call $v(u)$ a value function, because it carries the same information as $v(y, x)$.

Definition 10.2 Function $f: \mathfrak{R}^p \to \mathfrak{R}$ is said to be *quasiconcave* if for each z_1, $z_2 \in \mathfrak{R}^p$ the following inequality is true:

$$f(\lambda z_1 + (1 - \lambda)z_2) \geq \min\{f(z_1), f(z_2)\} \text{ for each } \lambda \in (0, 1)$$

Function f is said to be *quasiconvex* if $-f$ is quasiconcave.

Consider r (distinct) points $u_1, u_2, \ldots, u_r \in \mathfrak{R}^{s+m}$ such that $u_i \succeq u_k$ for $i = 1, \ldots,$ r, $i \neq k$, $r \leq n$. Based on this information, we construct convex cone $C(u_1, \ldots, u_r; u_k)$, where point u_k is the vertex:

$$C(u_1, \ldots, u_r, u_k) = \left\{ u \,\Big|\, u = u_k + \sum_{\substack{i=1 \\ i \neq k}}^{r} \mu_i(u_k - u_i), \mu_i \geq 0, \ i = 1, \ldots, r, \ i \neq k \right\}$$

(10.1)

If the determination of cone C includes only one point in addition to the vertex, we call it a *two-point cone*, and in the case $r > 1$, it is called an *r-point cone*.

Because $v: \mathfrak{R}^{s+m} \to \mathfrak{R}$ is a value function (Definition 4.4), then $v(u_k) \leq v(u_i)$, $i = 1, \ldots, r$. Moreover, for any $u_0 \in C(u_1, \ldots, u_r; u_k)$, the inequalities $v(u_i) \geq v(u_k) \geq v(u_0)$ hold for $i = 1, \ldots, r$, $i \neq k$ based on the quasiconcavity assumption of a value function (Korhonen et al. 1984, Lemma 2). We employ Theorem 1 in Korhonen et al. (1984) to diagnose whether $u_0 \in \mathfrak{R}^{s+m}$ is dominated by points in the cone (10.1). Consider the following LP problem:

$$\max \ \varepsilon$$

$$\text{s.t.} \tag{10.2}$$

$$u_k + \sum_{\substack{i = 1 \\ i=k}}^{r} \mu_i(u_k - u_i) - \varepsilon \geq u_0$$

$$\mu_i \geq 0, \quad i = 1, 2, \ldots, r$$

If at the optimum $\varepsilon \geq 0$, there exists at least one vector $u^* \in C(u_1, \ldots, u_m; u_k)$ with $u^* \geq u_0$ and $v(u_i) \geq v(u_k) \geq v(u^*) \geq v(u_0)$, $i = 1, \ldots, r$. If $\varepsilon > 0$ in the optimum, then $u^* > u_0 \Rightarrow v(u_i) \geq v(u_k) \geq v(u^*) > v(u_0)$.

Definition 10.3 Point $u_0 \in \mathfrak{R}^{s+m}$ is *dominated by cone* $C(u_1, \ldots, u_r; u_k)$ if there exists a point $u^* \in C(u_1, \ldots, u_r; u_k)$, $u^* \geq u$, $u^* \neq u_0$.

Definition 10.4 Point $u_0 \in \mathfrak{R}^{s+m}$ is *strongly dominated by cone* $C(u_1, \ldots, u_r; u_k)$ if there exists a point $u^* \in C(u_1, \ldots, u_r; u_k)$, $u^* > u_0$.

If problem (10.2) has an optimal solution with $\varepsilon > 0$, vector u_0 is strongly dominated by cone $C(u_1, \ldots, u_r; u_k)$. Solution $\varepsilon = 0$ in the optimum has two interpretations: (1) $u_0 \in C(u_1, \ldots, u_r; u_k)$ and u_0 is not dominated by cone $C(u_1, \ldots, u_r; u_k) \Rightarrow v(u_k) \geq v(u_0)$ or (2) u_0 is dominated by cone $C(u_1, \ldots, u_r; u_k)$, but not strongly $\Rightarrow v(u_k) > v(u_0)$, because v is a value function (Definition 4.4).

Consider next a slightly modified problem[4]:

$$\max \ \varepsilon$$

$$\text{s.t.} \tag{10.3}$$

$$u_k + \sum_{\substack{i = 1 \\ i=k}}^{r} \mu_i(u_k - u_i) - \varepsilon w \geq u_0$$

$$\mu_i \geq 0, \quad i = 1, 2, \ldots, r; \quad w \in \mathfrak{R}^{s+m}, \quad w \geq 0, \quad w \neq 0$$

Lemma 10.1 If at the optimum of problem (10.3) for some $w \in \mathfrak{R}^{s+m}$, $w \geq 0$, $w \neq 0$, $\varepsilon^* > 0$ or $\varepsilon^* = 0$ and at least one slack is positive, then u is dominated by cone C $(u_1, \ldots, u_r; u_k)$.

Proof If $\varepsilon^* \geq 0 \Rightarrow u_k + \sum_{\substack{i=1 \\ i=k}}^{r} \mu_i(u_k - u_i) \geq u_0 \Rightarrow$ if $\varepsilon^* > 0$ or $\varepsilon^* = 0$ and at least one slack is positive, i.e., for one component, an inequality is strict. The result follows about the definition of the cone dominance.   □

Remark If model (10.2) has the optimal solution $\varepsilon^* = 0$, but u_0 is dominated by the cone $C(u_1, \ldots, u_m; u_k)$, then $v(u_k) > v(u_0)$, because the value function is strictly increasing.

---

[4] Note that if in the optimum of (10.2) $\varepsilon^* > 0$, all the elements of z can be increased, which is not the case in (10.3).

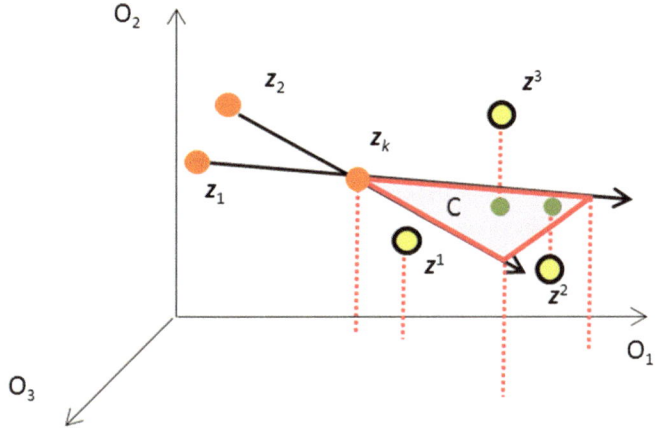

Fig. 10.3 Illustration of convex cone in three dimensions

Lemma 10.2 If $\exists\, w \in \mathfrak{R}^{s+m}$, $w \geq 0$, $w \neq 0$ such that at the optimum of (10.3), ε^* is unbounded, then the preference information $u_i \succeq u_k$ for $i = 1, \ldots, r$, $i \neq k$ is not consistent with the quasiconcavity assumption of the value function $v \colon \mathfrak{R}^{s+m} \to \mathfrak{R}$.

Proof Assume that the optimal solution ε^* of model (10.3) is unbounded for some $w \in \mathfrak{R}^{s+m}$, $w \geq 0$, $w \neq 0$. Then $\exists\, \mu^* \geq 0$, $\mu_i^* \neq 0$, for some $i = 1, 2, \ldots, r$ such that $\sum_{\substack{i=1 \\ i=k}}^{r} \mu_i^*(u_k - u_i) \geq 0$, $\sum_{\substack{i=1 \\ i=k}}^{r} \mu_i^*(u_k - u_i) \neq 0$, and $\sum_{\substack{i=1 \\ i=k}}^{r} \mu_i^*(u_k - u_i) > 0$ for the elements of $w \in \mathfrak{R}^{s+m}$ with $w_j > 0$, $j = 1, \ldots, s+m$. This implies $u_k + \sum_{\substack{i=1 \\ i=k}}^{r} \mu_i^*(u_k - u_i) \geq u_k, u_k + \sum_{\substack{i=1 \\ i=k}}^{r} \mu_i^*(u_k - u_i) \neq u_k$. Because the value function is strictly increasing in all its arguments, this, in turn, implies that $v\left(u_k + \sum_{\substack{i=1 \\ i=k}}^{r} \mu_i^*(u_k - u_i)\right) > v(u_k)$. However, as Korhonen et al. (1984, Lemma 2) state, owing to the quasiconcavity of v, $v(u_k) \geq v\left(u_k + \sum_{\substack{i=1 \\ i=k}}^{r} \mu_i^*(u_k - u_i)\right)$. Hence it follows that the preference information $u_i \succeq u_k$ for $i = 1, \ldots, r$, $i \neq k$ is not consistent with the quasiconcavity assumption of the value function $v \colon \mathfrak{R}^{s+m} \to \mathfrak{R}$.

Figure 10.3 demonstrates a convex cone in three dimensions. We may think that we have one constant input and three outputs, from which we may control only output O_2. Let's assume further that $z_1 \succeq z_k$ and $z_2 \succeq z_k$. Thus we may generate a three-point cone with two spanning direction vectors: $z_k - z_1$ and $z_k - z_2$ with vertex z_k: $z = z_k + \lambda_1(z_k - z_1) + \lambda_2(z_k - z_2)$, $\lambda_1 \geq 0$ and $\lambda_2 \geq 0$. The cone dominates the points z^1 and z^2, but not point z^3. On the basis of Fig. 10.3, we may conclude that the two-point cone alone with spanning vector $z_k - z_2$ dominates point z^2. It means that there is at least one point on the line $\lambda(z_k - z_2)$, $\lambda \colon 0 \to \infty$, dominating z^2.

The dominance in this example is considered in relation to output O_2, which was assumed to be the only controllable output. $\square$

10.3   Development of the Approach

10.3.1   Basic Method

The purpose to measure value efficiency is to find a solution to the same problem as in (7.1):

$$
\begin{aligned}
&\sup \; \gamma \\
&\text{s.t.} \\
&\quad \boldsymbol{u} - \gamma \boldsymbol{w} \geq \boldsymbol{u}_0 \\
&\quad \boldsymbol{u} \in \mathrm{V} = \left\{ \boldsymbol{u} \middle| v(\boldsymbol{u}) \leq v(\boldsymbol{u}^*) \right\} \\
&\quad \boldsymbol{w} > \boldsymbol{0}
\end{aligned}
\tag{10.4}
$$

where $\boldsymbol{u}_0$ refer to the unit under the considerations, $\boldsymbol{u}$ the projection point on the efficient frontier, $\boldsymbol{u}^*$ the most preferred point, and $\boldsymbol{w}$ the projection direction vector. Problem (10.4) is not possible to solve because the value function is unknown. However, the purpose is to find the "best possible" $\boldsymbol{u}$ by improving the input and output values in the direction $\boldsymbol{w}$ as much as possible, but to maintain that the inequality $v(\boldsymbol{u}) \leq v(\boldsymbol{u}^*)$ is true even if the value function is known only of its functional form. In the convex value efficiency analysis, we assumed that the value function is pseudoconcave.

In the non-convex value efficiency analysis, the same principle is used. The value function is assumed to be quasiconcave, which makes it possible to use convex cones in the same way as tangent cone was used in convex value efficiency analysis. The main difference is that in convex VEA one tangent cone is used to compute the approximation of value inefficiency score. Instead, in the non-convex VEA, there are many convex cones used for approximation. For each convex cone C_i, $i = 1, 2, \ldots, d$, where d is the number of cones and vector $\boldsymbol{w} \in \mathfrak{R}^{s+m}$, $\boldsymbol{w} \geq \boldsymbol{0}$, $\boldsymbol{w} \neq \boldsymbol{0}$ is a projection direction, it is computed how much it is possible to improve the inputs and/or outputs of point $\boldsymbol{u}_0$ until point $\boldsymbol{u}_i = \boldsymbol{u}_0 + \gamma_i \boldsymbol{w}$ is not anymore dominated by cone C_i provided $\boldsymbol{u}_0$ is dominated by C_i. If we denote by $\boldsymbol{u}_{i_k}$ the vertex of cone C_i, then

$$
v(\boldsymbol{u}^*) \geq v(\boldsymbol{u}_{i_k}) \geq v(\boldsymbol{u}_0 + \gamma_i \boldsymbol{w}), \quad i = 1, 2, \ldots, d \Rightarrow v(\boldsymbol{u}^*) \geq v(\boldsymbol{u}_0 + \gamma_{\max} \boldsymbol{w}),
$$
$$
\gamma_{\max} = \max\left\{ \gamma_i \middle| i = 1, 2, \ldots, d \right\}
$$

The value $\gamma_{\max}$ is the best approximation $\gamma_{\max} \leq \gamma_{\text{true}}$ for the true value (in)efficiency score γ_{true} based on the information available.

Now we are ready to present a basic version of the approach for computing a value inefficiency score (Halme et al. 2014). Some variations and comments are given in the next subsection.

Approach

Step 0: Find the most preferred existing unit u^* from among set $S_u = \{u_i \mid i = 1, 2, \ldots, n\}$. If needed, use a multiple criteria approach developed for a multiple criteria evaluation problem. An example of such an approach is VIMDA (Korhonen 1988; Korhonen and Karaivanova 1999). Let subscript h refer to the MPS, i.e., u^* and u_h refer to the same unit.

Step 1: Set $i \leftarrow 0$. Recognize two-point convex cones $C_k(u^*, u_k; u_k)$, $k = 1, 2, \ldots, n$, $h \neq k$ ($u^* = u_h$). Those cones are possible to generate on the basis of the information that u^* is most preferred.
   While $i \leq n$, repeat **Steps 2–3**.

Step 2: Set $i \leftarrow i + 1$ and find γ_k, $k = 1, 2, \ldots, n$, $k \neq h$. $k \neq i$, by solving the following LP problems, which are simplified versions of model (10.3):

$$\max \gamma_k$$
$$\text{s.t.} \tag{10.5}$$
$$u_k + \mu(u_k - u^*) - \gamma_k w \geq u_i$$
$$\mu \geq 0; w \in \mathfrak{R}^{s+m}, w \geq 0, w \neq 0$$

Depending on the choice of the values of w, we can deal with output-, input-, and combined-oriented or general VEA models.

Step 3: Compute $\gamma_{\max} = \max \{\gamma_k \mid k = 1, 2, \ldots, n, \ k \neq h, \ k \neq i\}$ and mark $\max \{\gamma_{\max}, \gamma_T\} \to \sigma_i$, where γ_T is the technical (in)efficiency score of unit u_i. (σ_i is the best approximation for the true value (in)efficiency score on the basis of the preference information available.)

Step 4: Report σ_i, $i = 1, 2, \ldots, n$ as value (in)efficiency scores.
   In Table 10.2, we present the cone problem of (10.5) in the envelopment and multiplier form by using symbols y and x for outputs and inputs. In Table 10.2, we have given the models using a general projection vector $w = \begin{bmatrix} w^y \\ w^x \end{bmatrix} \in \mathfrak{R}^{s+m}$,

Table 10.2 A unified model for a two-point cone in the envelopment and multiplier form

Envelopment model for a two-point cone	Multiplier model for a two-point cone
$\max \gamma$ s.t. $\qquad\qquad\qquad\qquad$ (10.6a) $\quad y_k + \mu(y_k - y^*) - \gamma w^y \geq y_0$ $\quad x_k + \mu(x_k - x^*) + \gamma w^x \leq x_0$ $\quad \mu \geq 0$ $\quad w = \begin{bmatrix} w^y \\ w^x \end{bmatrix} \in \mathfrak{R}^{s+m}, \quad w \geq 0, \ w \neq 0$	$\min -\mu^T y_k + v^T x_k$ s.t. $\qquad\qquad\qquad\qquad$ (10.6b) $\quad -\mu^T y_k + v^T x_k \geq 0$ $\quad -\mu^T(y_k - y^*) + v^T(x_k - x^*) \geq 0$ $\quad \mu^T w^y + v^T w^x = 1$ $\quad w = \begin{bmatrix} w^y \\ w^x \end{bmatrix} \in \mathfrak{R}^{s+m}, \quad w \geq 0, \ w \neq 0$

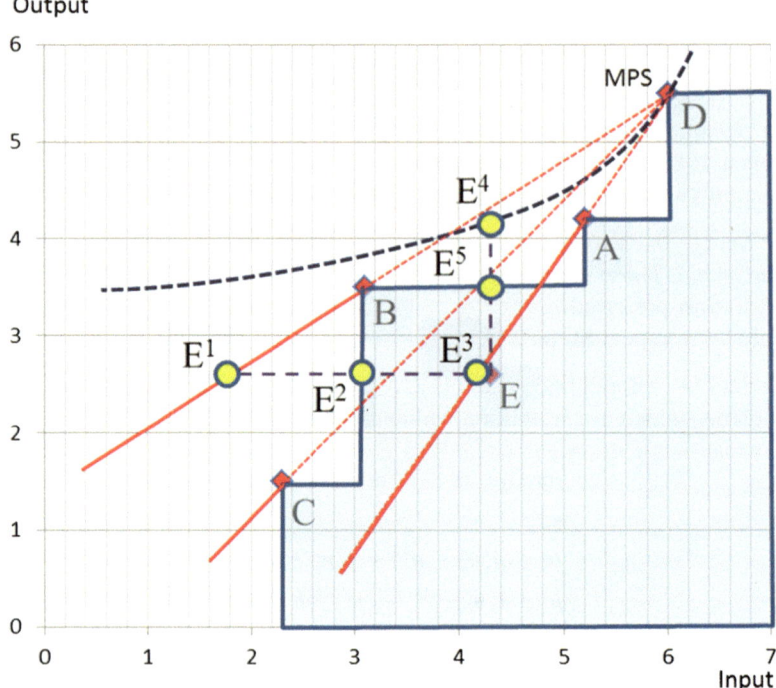

Fig. 10.4 Measuring value efficient when PPS is not convex

$w \geq 0$, $w \neq 0$. Input, output, and combined models can be given by using $w = \begin{bmatrix} 0 \\ x_0 \end{bmatrix}$

(for input orientation), $w = \begin{bmatrix} y_0 \\ 0 \end{bmatrix}$ (for output orientation), and $w = \begin{bmatrix} y_0 \\ x_0 \end{bmatrix}$ (for combined orientation).

10.3.2   Illustration

Let's consider Fig. 10.4. Assume that the most preferred unit is D (In this problem no support tool is needed.). Hence we may generate two-point cones C(D, A; A), C (D, B; B), C(D, C; C), and C(D, E; E). We have marked three two-point cones with solid lines. Cone C(D, E; E) is dominated by cone C(D, A; A), and that's why it does not provide any additional information.

Let's assume that we are interested in value efficiency of unit E. If the DM has been willing to use an input-oriented model, then the maximal decrease in input is reached at point E^1 defined by means of cone C(D, B; B). Point E^3 based on cone C (D, A; A) provides a very poor approximation because its use leads to the worse (too optimistic) approximation of value efficiency than point E^2, which is used for measuring technical efficiency. The usefulness of cone C(D, A; A) is very marginal. The only interesting part, which an impact on value efficiency has in some cases, is the line from unit A down to point (4.8, 3.5). Below this point, the cone C(D, A; A) is inside of the production possibility set and does not provide additional information. Cone C(D, C; C) does not contribute to the evaluation of value efficiency of point E.

Point E^1 gives value inefficiency score ($\sigma_D = 0.58$) (value efficiency score is 0.42). Correspondingly, technical inefficiency score $\sigma_{E(i)} = 0.28$ at point E^2 and value inefficiency score $\sigma_A = 0.02$ at E^3. Because $\sigma_A < \sigma_E$, we know that σ_A is too optimistic provided quasiconcavity assumption is valid. We use inefficiency scores because they are applicable in combined models as well, and they have a clear interpretation: how much do you have to improve proportionally the inputs and/or outputs (decrease inputs and increase outputs) for reaching the efficient frontier?

If we apply an output-oriented model, we cannot obtain a better approximation for value efficiency than the technical (in)efficiency score $\sigma_{E(o)} = 0.35$ at point E^5. Point E^4 demonstrates why we cannot use line from D to B to measure value efficiency on the interval (D, B). The evaluation would be too pessimistic: point E^4 on the indifference contour passing through the most preferred point D lies below the line from D to B.

10.3.3   Modifications

To recognize the most preferred point is not the only way to gather preference information. We can freely make pairwise comparisons, or even to gather this information by ranking units, and use all this information to form convex cones—not only two-point cones. We know on the basis of the properties of quasiconcave functions that the value function at the vertex of any convex cone has a higher value than at the point the cone dominates. Thus if we choose the greatest inefficiency score, it is based on the vertex of a cone at which the value is not higher or equal than at the most preferred unit.

On the other hand, when the number of comparisons increases, the computational burden is increasing as well. For each cone, we have to solve an LP problem. A two-point cone problem is simple and that's why it is easy to solve.

If desired it is possible to incorporate all the preference information of different cones into one model. Assume that we have r cones $C_j = C\left(\boldsymbol{u}_{j_1}, \ldots, \boldsymbol{u}_{j_{n_j}}; \boldsymbol{u}_{j_k}\right), j = 1,$ $2, \ldots, r, j_k \in \left\{j_1, j_2, \ldots, j_{n_j}\right\}$. For each cone we introduce a binary variable $t_j, j = 1,$ $2, \ldots, r$, with the coefficient "big M," and require that the sum of the binary variables is $r - 1$. To calculate the value (in)efficiency score, we solve the problem (Halme et al. 2014):

max σ

s.t.   (10.7)

$$\boldsymbol{u}_{j_k} + \sum_{\substack{i=1 \\ i=k}}^{n_j} \mu_{j_i}\left(\boldsymbol{u}_{j_k} - \boldsymbol{u}_{j_i}\right) - \sigma w + M t_i \geq \boldsymbol{u}_0, j = 1, 2, \ldots, r$$

$$\sum_{j=1}^{r} t_j = r - 1$$

$$t_j = 0, 1, j = 1, 2, \ldots, r$$

$$\mu_{j_i} \geq 0, i = 1, 2, \ldots, n_j, w \in \Re^{s+m}, w \geq 0, w \neq 0, j = 1, 2, \ldots, r$$

Note that in formulation, we make only one cone relevant because we force for $t_j = 1$, for all r cones except for one which maximizes σ. The optimal value for σ is hence the best approximation; we can find the value inefficiency score when we use all preference information available.

Model (10.7) demonstrates that for the value (in)efficiency score, the best approximation can be found by solving one LP problem. However, binary variable (t_j) of model (10.7) makes it harder to solve than a regular LP in the original value efficiency problem formulation.

10.4   Concluding Remarks

We presented model (10.7) to demonstrate that the approach is flexible to different variations to gather preference information, and all this information can be taken into account in one model. To use model (10.7), we may face challenges.

If we gather a lot of preference information from DM, there is a high risk to have conflicting information, which may lead to an unbounded solution (Lemma 10.2). That's why we recommend to keep a preference information gathering process as simple as possible. To find the most preferred unit using a multiple criteria decision support system is a safe approach.

DMs seem to be often willing to characterize the MPS by applying "on the one hand–on the other" principle (see our hypermarket example in Chap. 8 and Parish application in Chap. 11). If a DM characterizes the MPS by naming many existing units, this approach may also lead easily to conflicting information and cause an unbounded solution. A rescue from this problem is to use all those candidates as independent MPSs and associate each unit to the MPS with the best value (in) efficiency score. This is also an approach to automatically cluster the units.

To find a true (in)efficiency score, it is possible to use the idea described in Sect. 9.3 with an aim to find a true score in the convex VEA environment (Joro et al. 2003).

References

Bogetoft P, Tama JM, Tind J (2000) Convex input and output projections of nonconvex production possibility sets. Manage Sci 46(6):858–869

Deprins D, Simar L, Tulkens H (1984) Measuring labour efficiency in post offices. In: Marchand M, Pestieau P, Tulkens H (eds) The performance of public enterprises: concepts and measurement. North-Holland, Amsterdam, pp 243–267

Halme M, Korhonen P, Eskelinen J (2014) Non-convex value efficiency analysis and its application to bank branch sales evaluation. Omega 48:10–18

Joro T, Korhonen P, Zionts S (2003) An interactive approach to improve estimates of value efficiency in data envelopment analysis. Eur J Oper Res 149:688–699

Korhonen P (1988) A visual reference direction approach to solving discrete multiple criteria problems. Eur J Oper Res 34(2):152–159

Korhonen P, Karaivanova J (1999) An algorithm for projecting a reference direction onto the nondominated set of given points. IEEE Trans Syst Man Cybernet Part A 29(5):429–435

Korhonen P, Wallenius J, Zionts S (1984) Solving the discrete multiple criteria problem using convex cones. Manage Sci 30:1336–1345

Zionts S, Wallenius J (1980) Identifying efficient vectors: some theory and computational results. Oper Res 28:785–793

Chapter 11
Applications of Value Efficiency Analysis

How Value Efficiency Analysis Is Applied in Practice

11.1 Topics

In this chapter we report three real-life applications of value efficiency analysis. The first one looks into the efficiency of academic research (Korhonen et al. 2001), the second one discusses benchmarking and applies value efficiency analysis into efficiency of parishes (Halme and Korhonen 2013), and the last one investigates the efficiency of bank branches using non-convex value efficiency analysis (Halme et al. 2014). Please note that the scores reported are efficiency scores—this is possible given that the combined orientation has not been used.

11.2 Value Efficiency Analysis of Academic Research

11.2.1 Introduction

As Korhonen et al. (2001) report, in the early 1990s, the Ministry of Education in Finland signaled that in future years government research funding would to a larger extent than previously be allocated to universities and schools demonstrating a track record of high-quality research. This led the Research Development Group (TUTKE) at the Helsinki School of Economics,[1] chaired by the rector, to establish a two-person team[2] with the goal of developing an approach to evaluating research performance and to helping the administration allocate research resources in the "best" possible way.

Korhonen et al. (2001) view here academic research as analogous to production process in economics, having inputs and outputs. The analogy between research and

---

[1] Currently Aalto University School of Business.

[2] Professor Korhonen was a member of the team.

© Springer Science+Business Media New York 2015
T. Joro, P.J. Korhonen, *Extension of Data Envelopment Analysis with Preference Information*, International Series in Operations Research & Management Science 218, DOI 10.1007/978-1-4899-7528-7_11

production processes is not novel, and some other authors have—in the same spirit—also proposed the use of DEA to evaluating research performance. Indeed, the presence of multiple outputs and their intangible nature that makes pricing them difficult makes this problem very well suited to DEA. However, at the same it is obvious that not all outputs have the same importance, and this calls for incorporation of preference information in some form.

The same intangible nature that makes pricing the outputs impractical makes weight restrictions difficult to define as they have the interpretation of implicit prices. On the other hand, the idea of an ideal, or most preferred, research unit is intuitively appealing, and thus the problem lends itself as an excellent VEA application.

11.2.2 Characterization of an Ideal Type of Research Unit

The first step in the study was to characterize an ideal type of research unit in a concise manner, which can serve as an example to other units, using general terms so that a broad unanimity can easily be reached. The purpose of the characterization is to help identify relevant criteria.

A research unit whose members continuously produce high quality, innovative and internationally recognized research, and who actively supervise doctoral students and actively take part in various activities of the scientific community.

Korhonen et al. (2001) point out that it is not difficult to reach unanimity about such a characterization of an ideal type of research unit, provided that the discussion is kept at a rather high level of abstraction as above. It is also important to use a large enough set of attributes in the characterization. In the authors' experience, it even seems possible to specify some jointly agreed upon aspiration levels for the attributes, as long as a discussion concerning the importance of achieving such aspiration levels is not engaged. The aspiration levels are needed for making the discussion more concrete regarding abstract expressions such as: "high quality" or "continuously produce."

At the Helsinki School of Economics, the following characterization was found acceptable. When aspiration levels were specified for different attributes at the school, they are being mentioned in parenthesis.

The research problems investigated are relevant from the point of view of the school's mission. The quality of research is internationally recognized, i.e. research results are accepted for publication in refereed journals (1–2 articles/year/ researcher), and they have impact on the development of the research field (1–2 citations/year/researcher). Research is active (1–2 working papers/year/ researcher) and interdisciplinary. Each professor has a number of active doctoral students (2–6) on his/her responsibility with whom joint publications are written. The research unit has established international research contacts, and well known foreign researchers visit the research unit, providing supervision and advice to doctoral students. The researchers are invited to foreign universities to give invited and key-note presentations in international seminars and conferences. The researchers enjoy a certain position in the scientific community. They are board members of professional associations, editors or members of editorial boards in professional journals and members of program and organizing committees of scientific conferences. Their expertise is solicited to review journal articles and the qualifications of colleagues applying for various scientific positions. The research results have a real impact on teaching, keeping it timely and of high quality. Furthermore, private and public organizations have an interest in applying the research results in practice.[3]

11.2.3   Evaluation Criteria and Indicators

Next Korhonen et al. (2001) defined a set of **criteria**, which are sufficient to characterize the "model" research unit. The authors point out that the criteria should be relevant to the DM and that they should emphasize different aspects of research performance in the same spirit as the (abstract) characterization of the "model" research unit did. After several discussion sessions, the Helsinki School of Economics ended up with the following set of criteria:

- Quality of research
- Research activity
- Impact of research
- Activity in educating young scientists (especially doctoral students)
- Activity in the scientific community

It is interesting to note that the abovementioned criteria are rather close to the criteria applied in the Quality Assessment of Academic Research in the Netherlands (Economics 1995; Mathematics and Computer Science 1997): scientific quality, scientific productivity, relevance, and long-term viability.

As Korhonen et al. (2001) point out, the above-listed criteria are suitable for a general discussion, but too abstract for enabling the DM to make a concrete evaluation based on them. That is why it is necessary to introduce concrete indicators (attributes, signals), which can be employed to make the criteria suitable for evaluation. Indicators are concrete in the sense that it is possible to somehow more or less objectively "measure" alternatives with them.

It is important that the indicators contain enough (objective) information about the values of the criteria, but even more important is that the indicators cannot be manipulated without an influence on the performance of the unit in terms of the corresponding criterion.

Korhonen et al. (2001) proposed the use of the following indicators. Note that the same indicator can have relevance for several criteria. The above hierarchy

---

[3] This description was already written in 1988 in the memorandum by Korhonen and Tainio.

provides a basis for a systematic evaluation of research but also for a structured discussion:

(a) Criterion: quality of research

- Articles published in international refereed journals
- Scientific books and chapters in scientific books published by internationally well-known publishers
- Citations

(b) Criterion: research activity

- Publications exceeding a minimum quality standard (articles in refereed journals and scientific books and chapters in books)
- Papers in conference proceedings, domestic reports, reports in nonrefereed national journals, working papers, and other unpublished reports
- Conference presentations

(c) Criterion: impact of research

- Citations by other researchers (in journal articles, books, published conference proceedings, and Ph.D. dissertations)
- Invited and plenary presentations in international conferences
- Number of foreign coauthors in journal articles

(d) Criterion: activity in educating young scientists

- Doctoral degrees produced
- Number of doctoral students supervised

(e) Criterion: activity in scientific community (not currently used)

- Memberships in editorial boards
- Edited books and special issues of journals
- Service as an expert
- Scientific conferences organized, memberships in program committees, etc.

When it is desired to carry out a systematic and quantitative evaluation of research units, it is necessary to introduce the scales for the criteria and locate alternatives using these scales. In case all indicators are quantitative, the problem is to define a function which aggregates the values of the indicators into a criterion scale. If some indicators are qualitative, they first need to be quantified using appropriate tools (see, e.g., Korhonen and Wallenius 1990). One of the simplest ways to aggregate the indicator values is to use weighted sums. This is a commonly used method, but as the MCDM scholars are aware there are many problems in its use. At the Helsinki School of Economics, the decision was to use the weighted sums while trying to take into account the problems associated with their use to the extent possible.

11.2.4 The Data

In total, 18 research units at the Helsinki School of Economics were included in the study. Many of the units represented functional business school areas, such as organization and management, accounting, finance, marketing, logistics, etc. Some of the units were interdisciplinary by nature, such as management science and quantitative methods. Basic research institute was an outlier in the sense that its staff consisted solely of full-time researchers. For reasons of confidentiality, the identity of the research units has been disguised. For the same reason, Korhonen et al. (2001) did not publish the original but the scaled values of the indicators. In the performance evaluation, the authors used four criteria: quality of research, research activity, impact of research, and activity in educating doctoral students. As the authors were not able to obtain reliable information about the indicators comprising the fifth criterion, it was ignored in the analysis. To introduce the scales for the criteria, the indicators mentioned in Sect. 11.2.3 were used.

First, the values of all indicators were scaled into the [0, 1] range, so that the best value corresponded to one. Table 11.1 provides a summary of the data, which was used as the basis of the analysis. The information was collected from different data files. Korhonen et al. (2001) explain the calculation of the scores for the criteria in Table 11.1 as follows:

The nine members of TUTKE (Research Development Group) at the Helsinki School of Economics were asked to evaluate the relative importance of various indicators with regard to each criterion. (They were informed that the best value of each indicator was always the same.) The Analytic Hierarchy Process (AHP) was used (Saaty 1980) for this purpose. The average of the weights of the nine members was taken as the set of final weights. The weighted sum of the indicators was used as a scale for each criterion. In the context, of the study, the weight simply stands for the value to which the best value of each indicator is scaled.

The last column in Table 11.1 is an input measure. It is the estimated monthly cost in Finnish Marks of producing the research output. It can be seen that the size of the units varies considerably.

Korhonen et al. (2001) further point out that when the weighted sums of indicators are used to find the scores for the criteria, it is implicitly assumed that the units are homogeneous enough.

11.2.5 Analysis of Research Performance at the Helsinki School of Economics

The authors performed an efficiency analysis of the 18 research units, using four output measures and one input measure as described in Table 11.1 (cols. C1, C2, C3, C4, and the last column). The data represent actual data from 1996. They first

Table 11.1 Criterion values as the weighted sums of scaled indicators and resources

Years	Ref. art. 1992–1996	Books 1992–1996	Citat 1990–1995	C1	Art +books 1992–1996	Other 1994–1996	ConfPres 1995–1996	C2	Citat 1990–1995	Invit. pres 1995–1996	For. Co-A 1992–1996	C3	Dis. 1992–1996	Sup. 1992–1996	C4	1,000 FIM/month
Weights	0.55	0.27	0.18	Σ=	0.60	0.23	0.17		0.48	0.27	0.25		0.65	0.35		
A	0.70	1.00	0.10	67	1.00	1.00	1.00	100	0.10	1.00	0.67	48	1.00	1.00	100	70
B	0.67	0.03	0.05	38	0.36	0.38	0.33	36	0.05	0.50	0.67	32	0.30	0.15	25	32
C	0.03	0.13	0.00	5	0.10	0.08	0.00	8	0.00	0.00	0.00	0	0.13	0.00	9	34
D	0.30	0.16	0.01	21	0.25	0.26	0.12	23	0.01	0.05	0.00	2	0.52	0.04	35	101
E	0.90	0.13	0.06	54	0.54	0.13	0.08	37	0.06	0.00	0.25	9	0.04	0.08	6	25
F	0.20	0.95	0.38	43	0.71	0.77	0.23	64	0.38	0.23	0.33	33	0.70	0.27	55	64
G	0.50	0.24	0.06	35	0.41	0.50	0.35	42	0.06	0.41	0.17	18	0.83	0.31	65	46
H	0.00	0.05	0.02	2	0.03	0.14	0.00	5	0.02	0.00	0.00	1	0.30	0.08	23	25
I	0.30	0.24	0.24	27	0.31	0.47	0.40	36	0.24	0.14	0.17	19	0.26	0.23	25	28
J	0.47	0.32	0.00	34	0.44	0.41	0.00	36	0.00	0.00	0.00	0	0.17	0.00	11	23
K	0.07	0.13	0.00	7	0.12	0.03	0.00	8	0.00	0.00	0.00	0	0.09	0.04	7	7
L	0.40	0.45	0.42	42	0.49	0.30	0.50	45	0.42	0.41	0.17	35	0.70	0.15	51	68
M	0.00	0.16	0.01	4	0.10	0.02	0.02	7	0.01	0.05	0.00	2	0.00	0.00	0	8
N	0.27	0.05	0.13	18	0.17	0.02	0.23	15	0.13	0.45	0.33	27	0.00	0.08	3	15
O	0.43	0.00	0.08	25	0.22	0.17	0.23	21	0.08	0.45	0.33	25	0.30	0.15	25	37
P	0.90	0.26	0.92	74	0.63	0.18	0.33	47	0.92	0.55	0.92	82	0.00	0.15	5	29
Q	0.13	0.74	0.01	27	0.54	0.37	0.62	51	0.01	0.73	0.00	20	0.00	0.00	0	12
R	1.00	0.11	1.00	76	0.58	0.58	0.44	55	1.00	0.05	1.00	74	0.00	0.08	3	119
				602				636				427			447	

Table 11.2 Value efficiency analysis with an output-oriented model

Depts.	BCC efficiency					BCC value efficiency				
	Efficiency	A	P	Q	R	Efficiency	A	P	Q	R
A	1.00	1.00				1.00	1.00			
B	0.79	0.30	0.39			0.55	0.43	0.73		−0.16
C	0.17	0.49				0.08	1.04	0.38		−0.42
D	0.35	1.00				0.32	1.12			−0.12
E	0.88	0.02	0.81	0.03		0.75	0.05	1.01		−0.07
F	0.68	0.89	0.05	0.06		0.65	1.02	0.32		−0.34
G	0.98	0.66				0.54	1.19	0.16		−0.35
H	0.64	0.35				0.06	3.76	4.73		−7.49
I	0.77	0.32	0.13	0.17		0.41	0.85	0.56		−0.40
J	0.77	0.13	0.37	0.32		0.49	0.53	0.77		−0.30
K	0.86	0.08	0.04			0.11	0.63	0.91		−0.54
L	0.64	0.79	0.21			0.62	0.81	0.50		−0.31
M	0.23	0.00	0.07	0.52		0.07	1.12	0.63		−0.75
N	0.67	0.01	0.48			0.30	0.50	3.61		−3.11
O	0.58	0.42	0.27			0.38	0.64	0.95		−0.59
P	1.00		1.00			1.00		1.00		
Q	1.00			1.00		0.45	1.49	1.06		−1.55
R	1.00				1.00	1.00				1.00

performed a standard output-oriented BCC[4] data envelopment analysis (Banker et al. 1984) (Table 11.2). Four units (A, P, Q, and R) received the highest possible BCC efficiency score = 1. Table 11.2 also describes the reference set for each unit and the corresponding weights.

The authors have also performed a corresponding value efficiency analysis of the units. For the analysis, they used Pareto Race (Korhonen and Wallenius 1988) to freely search the efficient frontier corresponding to the BCC model above. For using Pareto Race, they first formulated a multiple objective linear programming model that characterizes the efficient frontier of the BCC model. The model is simple: maximize all output variables and minimize the input variable. The model is shown in Table 11.3.

Figure 11.1 shows the Pareto Race interface and the final solution at which the search was terminated. This point, which is a convex combination of units A and R, was taken as the MPS for the VEA. The corresponding values of the basic variables are A (0.748) and R (0.252). Both values are positive, and thus the nonnegativity constraints corresponding to these variables are relaxed in the value efficiency analysis. The results of the value efficiency analysis are given in Table 11.2.

Only three of the four previously BCC-efficient units remained value efficient. Commonly not all DEA efficient units remain value efficient. Korhonen et al. (2001) also calculated the reference sets for the inefficient units as they did for the BCC

---

[4] To be precise, the model is a nonincreasing returns to scale one (NIRS).

Table 11.3 A multiple objective linear programming model for finding the MPS

	A	B	C	D	E	F	G	H	I	J	K	L	M	N	O	P	Q	R		
Quality	67	38	5	21	54	43	35	2	27	34	7	42	4	18	25	74	27	76	↑	Max
Activity	100	36	8	23	37	64	42	5	36	36	8	45	7	15	21	47	51	55	↑	Max
Impact	48	32	0	2	9	33	18	1	19	0	0	35	2	27	25	82	20	74	↑	Max
Postgrad	100	25	9	35	6	55	65	23	25	11	7	51	0	3	25	5	0	3	↑	Max
1,000 FIM	70	32	34	101	25	64	46	25	28	23	7	68	8	15	37	29	12	119	VI	Min
	1	1	1	1	1	1	1	1	1	1	1	1	1	1	1	1	1	1		1

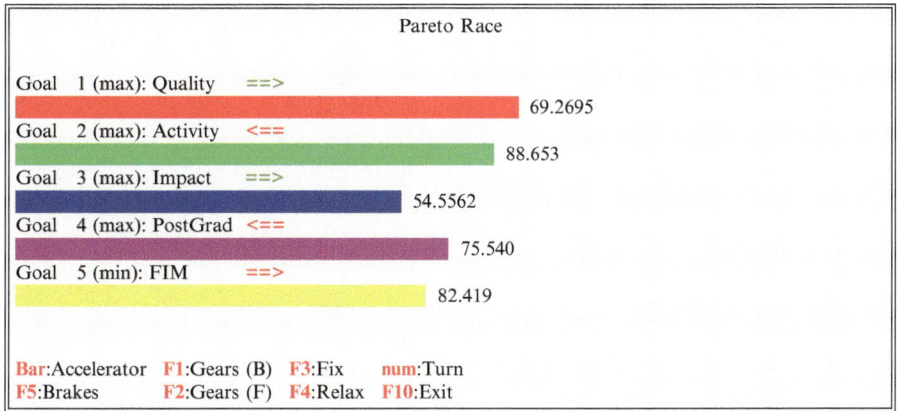

Fig. 11.1 Pareto Race screen

analysis. Note that in VEA weights corresponding to the most preferred solution, unit R, are negative for all other units under evaluation. This is not always the case, but here none of the projections landed on a faced adjacent to unit R. It is also worth noting that all value efficiency scores are the same as or lower than the corresponding scores of standard DEA. This is intuitively understandable because the "value-efficient frontier" in a sense "covers" the standard efficient frontier.

11.2.6 Conclusion

The paper by Korhonen et al. (2001) tackled an important and difficult task of setting a system to evaluate academic research performance, using VEA to incorporate the preference information.

The evaluation of research is today becoming more commonplace, but models can be rather simplistic, often based on impact factors and publications in top journals indicated on various lists. They generally neglect other aspects of research output, as well as the whole input side.

At the Helsinki School of Economics, the decision makers—while expressing their original reservations about the usability of OR models in this context—viewed the results useful.

11.3 Using Value Efficiency Analysis to Benchmark Nonhomogeneous Units

11.3.1 Introduction

The Evangelical Lutheran Church is Finland's largest religious body. By the end of 2013, 75 % of Finns were members of the Church. The Helsinki area is divided into

Finnish-speaking religious parishes on a geographical basis. The parishes offer numerous services and activities to their members. During the period under consideration (1999–2001), the number of Finnish-speaking parishes in Helsinki was 24.[5]

In the late 1990s and early 2000s, big changes took place in the economic administration of the parishes. One of the members of an economic board appointed by the executive committee of the Church was active in the search for approaches that could aid their efforts to control changes in the parishes. This person was very influential and active in the introduction of new economic thinking in the church organization. He was aware of data envelopment analysis and interested in cooperation in order to apply the approach in his context. In our case study he plays the role of the DM. The actual analysis was carried out in 2002–2003

Whereas the previous example on academic research was a rather straightforward application of DEA, here the emphasis is not so much in efficiency scores or degrees of inefficiency, but in the reference set—benchmarks—that the analysis will produce. The DM indicated that there is a great deal of heterogeneity among the parishes and that it is crucial that the benchmarks given to inefficient parishes share the same environmental and demographic key characteristics. It became obvious that the results from standard DEA were unsatisfactory in this sense. Thus Halme and Korhonen (2013) turned to VEA and use the concept of MPU to factor in the heterogeneity. The key idea is that by selecting for each unit an MPU with similar key characteristics, the resulting reference set will yield to more meaningful benchmark information.

11.3.2 Sources of Heterogeneity

As is probably the case in any major city, different areas seem to roughly "cluster" households in such a way that each area attracts similar kinds of households. Thus, it can be said that within an area households are relatively homogeneous, but there can be significant differences across areas: demographics, economic measures, and ways of life.

In the areas where young families live, there is much demand for services for children and families, whereas different kinds of outputs are required in the areas inhabited mostly by more middle-aged and retired people. The degree of migration is also a dividing factor. In some areas the majority of apartments is small and thus only suitable for single people or young couples. It is a challenge for the parish to attract the individuals to church activities during the few years they inhabit the area. The supply of various commercial services is not the same in all areas (shops,

---

[5] For Swedish inhabitants there were six parishes in the Helsinki area, but they were excluded from the analysis as they are dispersed in area and based on the language, not the area as the Finnish-speaking ones.

cinemas, private health services, etc.), and this affects how much time inhabitants spend in the area.

Thus, it is not realistic to assume that all parishes are comparable without taking into account the heterogeneity of the environment. The DM verbally described the features that caused heterogeneity, and he was also quite capable of specifying a set of typical benchmark parishes.

11.3.3   Benchmarks and the DEA

Benchmarking is at the core of even the basic DEA. For each inefficient unit a virtual reference unit is determined by the analysis using efficient existing units. The set of those units is called a reference set. Thus, the DEA also produces benchmarks in the form of the units that belong to the reference unit. Even for an efficient unit, it is possible to find benchmarks using the DEA procedure proposed by Andersen and Petersen (1993).

However, often the benchmarks produced by the DEA turn out to be too different from the unit under analysis to be convincing. Also, the units in the reference set may be very heterogeneous. The difference may originate from environmental circumstances as well as internal structure factors. (See Banker and Morey, 1986, for use of DEA with exogenously fixed environmental factors.)

The approach used in Halme and Korhonen (2013) overcomes this problem. Assume that a DM is able to describe the heterogeneity of the units by nominating (efficient) example units (benchmarks). An example unit may be any efficient existing (or virtual) unit. The benchmark units thus represent different facets/types of goodness of performance. These benchmarks are then used as most preferred solutions in VEA.

As this approach takes into account the DM's preference information in the form of benchmarks that represent the dissimilarities of the units, it does not require the quantification or even identification of the sources of heterogeneity.

If carried out, the identification and quantification of environmental factors causing heterogeneity of the units can be expected to be a task requiring major effort. In the approach by Halme and Korhonen (2013), such factors are not needed as inputs in any phase in the analysis process.

11.3.4   Benchmarking Approach

If a DM is able to name example units (benchmarks) among the DMUs, they are interpreted as the units maximizing the DM's value function in the set of a certain type of units. Thus it is possible to assume that the DM has several value functions depending on the environmental conditions and structure of the units. Because the production possibility set is defined as a polytope and the maxima are reached at its extreme points, this leads to an assumption that the value functions of the DM are linear.

In the original VEA, it was assumed that the functional form of a value function is pseudoconcave. The pseudoconcavity assumption means that the maximum of the value function can be any efficient point—not only an existing one. Yet, a linear value function is a special case of a pseudoconcave function and the LP problem solved is the same.

As discussed in Sect. 10.1, the linearity assumption can be strongly questioned: DMs' observed behavior is often inconsistent with it. Yet we have repeatedly encountered cases where DMs have a preference toward the use of existing units as MPSs or benchmarks. It can be speculated that this is because as existing units they feel more concrete and are "easier to sell" to the organization. In this example the DM expressed a preference for using existing units, and the selection of the MPSs for the analysis was done accordingly.

Hereunder, the approach from Halme and Korhonen (2013) is described step-by-step:

Step 1: Carry out an ordinary data envelopment analysis with proper scale assumption.

Step 2: Ask the DM to evaluate the efficiency scores and the units in the reference set of inefficient units. Does everything appear to be sensible? Are all the inputs and outputs correctly included in the analysis? Is there something missing?

Step 3: If he/she thinks that the units in the reference set are reasonable, stop and use the results from *Step 1*. Otherwise proceed to *Step 4*.

Step 4: If the DM thinks that the solution is not acceptable because some of the units in the reference sets are not reasonable for the reason that the units operate in different environments or that they are different in their structure, ask him/her to name a set of typical (efficient) units that represent different types of good performance. If he/she is not able to do so, or the reason that the solution is not acceptable is something else, stop and try other approaches. Otherwise proceed to *Step 5*.

Step 5: Provide the DM with the possibility to subjectively assign each unit to one of the benchmarks.[6]

Step 6: Calculate the VEA score for each unit across all benchmarks. If the DM chooses k types of environments or structures, i.e., if there are k types of heterogeneity represented by k benchmark DMUs, then the problem is solved $n*k$ times. The result is k VEA scores for each one of the DMUs.

Step 7: Assign each unit to the benchmark that produced the highest value efficiency score. (You may also specify a value δ and assign the unit to all benchmarks having the highest score within the tolerance of δ.)

---

[6] This approach may be feasible only in the case when the number of units is small and the unique assignment is easy.

Step 8: Display the results to the DM. Ask him/her to evaluate the results and especially focus on the following:

- How much lower is the highest VEA score of the benchmarking analysis from the original DEA score? If the VEA scores for some unit are substantially smaller, ask the DM to consider whether the type of that very unit is represented in the set of the benchmark units.
- If he/she subjectively assigned each unit in advance to a specific benchmark in *Step 5*, ask him/her to reconsider such cases where the highest VEA score across the benchmarks recommends the assignment of the unit to a benchmark other than he/she proposed. Is there an explanation for the phenomenon? Could it be justifiable to assign the unit to the benchmark that produced the highest score in the VEA? Was there possibly an error initially in the assignment?
- If a unit under consideration has several almost equally highest VEA scores across the benchmarks, ask the DM if there is any obvious reason for this.

11.3.5   Inputs, Outputs, and Data

The statistics produced annually with regard to the parishes included, at the time of consideration, information on the number of participants of different services and activities. The following set of output variables was used in the analysis: attendants (1) in services, (2) in music and other events, (3) in adults' and senior people's groups, (4) children's and young people's groups, as well as (5) contacts with individuals in social work (see Table 11.4). In the second, third, and fourth output variables, the final figure is a weighted sum over participants or contacts in different activities, and the sum is used to reduce the number of outputs. The weights used were provided by the DM.

As an input Halme and Korhonen (2013) used the budget funds (€) received from the Helsinki parish group, originating from taxes paid by members (Table 11.4, averaged over the years 1999–2001).

11.3.6   Basic Analyses

The variable returns to scale assumption was a natural choice for the DEA model, because the requirements for the constant returns to scale model were not met. The productivity of small parishes was allowed to be lower than that of the bigger ones. Halme and Korhonen (2013) carried out three kinds of basic analyses with the VRS assumption:

(1) *The basic analysis employing the BCC model.*

They first calculated efficiency scores using an output-oriented BCC model. The output orientation was used because in this case much of the heterogeneity leads to

Table 11.4 Helsinki parishes

Parish	Service attendants	Other event attendants	Children and young	Adults and seniors	Social work contacts	Budget 1,000 Euros
Alppila	5,982	10,105	2,288	662	703	755.7
Hakavuori	9,332	3,149	1,770	366	868	832.7
Tuomiokirkko	97,935	170,746	7,372	423	2,960	3,510.7
Herttoniemi	18,295	13,975	1,237	1,008	5,594	1,273.2
Huopalahti	12,429	3,699	3,399	319	473	814.2
Kallio	22,713	29,095	2,057	2,730	2,301	1,396.9
Kannelmäki	21,885	6,111	18,287	374	1,686	1,431.7
Kulosaari	4,865	2,905	2,336	157	994	330.0
Käpylä	10,007	4,067	4,393	269	1,868	670.3
Lauttasaari	13,769	2,902	5,227	269	1,185	1,054.3
Malmi	57,871	26,565	14,655	3,254	10,629	4,547.3
Meilahti	14,973	7,784	2,491	710	2,626	1,188.4
Mellunkylä	23,909	7,953	13,302	316	3,050	1,879.7
Munkkiniemi	8,957	2,785	2,588	312	920	655.0
Munkkivuori	10,214	8,936	1,680	323	437	604.6
Oulunkylä	19,211	6,869	3,083	364	1,839	1,262.9
Paavali	13,602	14,780	5,306	617	1,749	1,062.6
Pakila	15,399	5,999	7,498	302	901	1,128.0
Pitäjänmäki	11,240	2,149	8,753	225	1,290	896.9
Roihuvuori	19,873	12,720	6,165	490	2,407	1,614.4
Taivallahti	24,501	58,885	1,222	109	2,431	869.9
Töölö	11,298	7,116	3,366	292	750	834.1
Vartiokylä	18,219	2,710	12,354	237	1,723	1,132.3
Vuosaari	19,079	12,095	3,504	476	2,297	1,484.5

different strategies to produce the outputs. The BCC scores can be seen in the first column of Table 11.5. With such a small number (24) of units and large number (6) of inputs/outputs, the BCC efficiency scores tend to become large.

(2) *The possible superefficiency scores are computed for efficient units.*

To obtain additional information on the units, the authors next applied the procedure proposed by Andersen and Petersen (1993) and produced superefficiency scores for some BCC-efficient units. As the superefficiency scores can be greater than 1 for efficient units, the approach can be employed for ranking all units. Such a ranking approach has been proposed also by Li and Zhu (2005). The superefficiency analysis explains how much the units with scores exceeding 1 can increase costs and still remain efficient.

(3) *The efficient frontier is supposed to consist of the benchmark units exclusively and the rest of the units are projected radially on that frontier.*

Table 11.5 Some output-oriented DEA scores with VRS

Parish	BCC model	BCC model with superefficiency	BCC model comparison to benchmarks[a]
Alppila	0.70	0.70	2.01
Hakavuori	0.55	0.55	0.93
Tuomiokirkko	1.00	3.20	1.00
Herttoniemi	1.00	1.70	1.74
Huopalahti	0.75	0.75	0.96
Kallio	1.00	2.49	3.32
Kannelmäki	1.00	1.43	2.85
Kulosaari	1.00	–	–
Käpylä	0.97	0.97	1.00
Lauttasaari	0.66	0.66	0.97
Malmi	1.00	2.69	1.00
Meilahti	0.72	0.72	0.93
Mellunkylä	0.87	0.87	1.75
Munkkiniemi	0.72	0.72	–
Munkkivuori	0.80	0.80	–
Oulunkylä	0.67	0.67	0.78
Paavali	0.78	0.78	1.15
Pakila	0.74	0.74	1.34
Pitäjänmäki	0.87	0.87	1.75
Roihuvuori	0.68	0.68	0.91
Taivallahti	1.00	1.88	1.00
Töölö	0.68	0.68	0.81
Vartiokylä	0.99	0.99	2.20
Vuosaari	0.64	0.64	0.74

[a]Efficient frontier is characterized by using exclusively the three benchmarks: Tuomiokirkko, Käpylä, and Malmi
– there is no solution for the problem

Before it is possible to proceed to Step 3, the DM needs to consider the BCC results. It became immediately evident that the basic BCC analysis produced units in the reference sets that seemed to have too different environments compared with the inefficient units for which they should have acted as an example of good performance. The authors asked the DM to identify a set of good performing units to act as benchmarks in such a way that they would represent different facets of good performance. He used the superefficiency scores as an aid together with his subjective judgment to select the benchmarks. The DM was clearly thinking in terms of the different environments when exploring the set of units, and he specified three benchmarks (MPUs for the VEA): Tuomiokirkko, Malmi, and Käpylä (note that Tuomiokirkko and Malmi are undoubtedly efficient). He described the parish types in the following way:

- Tuomiokirkko type: Inhabitants are characterized by the fact that they live in the core center or close to the center of Helsinki and they strongly feel they are part of the area. They have a lot of activities outside their home.
- Malmi type: Inhabitants rather permanently living in the area. The areas were built in the 1960s and 1970s; families with children moved in, and the previously rather rural areas were transformed into a more town-like area.
- Käpylä type: Strong commitment to the area's traditions.

An interesting detail—as discussed already in 10.1—was that the DM identified the Käpylä parish as a benchmark, though it was slightly inefficient in the BCC analysis. In other words he saw that Käpylä represented one type of desirable parish, and despite its slight inefficiency, he found it as the best parish. This indicates that here it would have been justified to use the FDH VEA model described in Chap. 10. Because the approach was not then developed, Halme and Korhonen (2013) projected Käpylä radially onto the efficient frontier and in the sequel called the resulting virtual unit "Käpylä" and continued with VEA with convexity assumption with the virtual unit as MPS. In a case when a unit that is considerably inefficient is chosen as a benchmark, the DM can be provided with the possibility to choose the best virtual unit that dominated the inefficient one.

They next used the information of the benchmarks and calculated the DEA scores for the non-benchmark units with respect to the efficient frontier that is made up by the benchmarks exclusively. Table 11.5 shows that in this data set the approach does not result in practical useful scores because a number of the BCC-inefficient units become superefficient with scores exceeding 1. The reason for this is that the three benchmarks do not very well represent the efficient frontier.

11.3.7 Value Efficiency Analysis with Benchmark Units

The VEA scores with different benchmark units are presented in Table 11.6 (Step 6). For ease of comparison the BCC scores from Table 11.5 are included. Note that the VEA scores are never more optimistic than the BCC scores.

The gray shade in a row indicates that the DM subjectively assigned the parish to the benchmark indicated by the corresponding column. Thus, e.g., for Alppila the benchmark is Tuomiokirkko. For 17 units out of the total of 24, the most optimistic VEA score (employing a tolerance of 0.02) lies in the highlighted column, i.e., where, in the VEA, the MPU was the benchmark assigned to the unit by the DM (Step 7). It can be concluded that these units have directed their operations in the same way as their benchmark and emphasize the same outputs.

However, there are some exceptions. Alppila, Munkkivuori Pakila, Töölö, and Vartiokylä parishes performed better in the VEA with a benchmark other than the one assigned. Thus, the analysis "suggested" another benchmark for consideration (Step 6).

Table 11.6 Output-oriented models: the VEA scores with three different benchmark units: Tuomiokirkko, Malmi, and Käpylä[a]

Parish	VEA scores			BCC
	Benchmark Tuomiokirkko	Benchmark Malmi	Benchmark Käpylä[a]	
Alppila	0.57	0.5	0.63	0.7
Hakavuori	0.54	0.46	0.53	0.55
Tuomiokirkko	1	1	0.81	1
Herttoniemi	1	1	1	1
Huopalahti	0.73	0.54	0.63	0.75
Kallio	1	1	1	1
Kannelmäki	1	1	1	1
Kulosaari	0.86	0.56	1	1
Käpylä	0.83	0.76	0.97	0.97
Lauttasaari	0.66	0.6	0.65	0.66
Malmi	1	1	0.81	1
Meilahti	0.72	0.7	0.72	0.72
Mellunkylä	0.87	0.87	0.79	0.87
Munkkiniemi	0.7	0.55	0.7	0.72
Munkkivuori	0.77	0.5	0.66	0.8
Oulunkylä	0.67	0.64	0.65	0.67
Paavali	0.74	0.73	0.78	0.78
Pakila	0.74	0.65	0.7	0.74
Pitäjänmäki	0.8	0.74	0.86	0.87
Roihuvuori	0.68	0.68	0.64	0.68
Taivallahti	1	1	1	1
Töölö	0.66	0.53	0.62	0.68
Vartiokylä	0.96	0.92	0.98	0.99
Vuosaari	0.64	0.63	0.6	0.64

A shaded cell indicates the DM's subjective assignment. The BCC scores are presented for comparison
[a]Käpylä is inefficient and an efficient projection is used instead

Halme and Korhonen (2013) report the authors' discussion on the results with the DM as indicated in Step 7:

First, there did not seem to be any units, the VEA score of which would have been substantially smaller than the BCC score, and thus all environment types seemed to be represented. In the cases where the analysis "suggested" a benchmark that was different from the one assigned by the DM he reconsidered the assignment. With regard to all the mentioned units, with one exception he said he could see good reasons (e.g. member base) to reassign the unit to that "suggested" benchmark. In the case of Töölö he even changed his mind and saw the original assignment to be a mistake. However, no immediate straightforward explanation was found with regard to why Huopalahti has the highest score with benchmark Tuomiokirkko.

The Pakila unit seemed to have a very similar score in comparison with any of the benchmarks. In this regard, an interesting view was provided by the DM: the parish is very heterogeneous containing several types of sub-areas with different inhabitant bases and there was at least one sub-area that resembled each of the three benchmarks. This was obviously reflected in its VEA scores.

Thus using the VEA with the benchmarks chosen by the DM we were able to produce a score for the parishes that was more accurate than the DEA score. With the benchmarks included it could be guaranteed that the reference unit truly makes sense. Moreover, in some cases the approach could provide additional information. When the VEA with the "obvious" benchmark did not produce the highest score of the benchmarks we had a closer look at the reasons for this. In many of our example cases the DM could use his subjective information that could explain the "suggested" benchmark, the one for which the VEA produced the highest score. The DM may even make a re-assignment of a unit. The valuable feedback from the DM was that with the interactive process he got new insights not only into the parish performance comparisons but also into how the parishes are different from each other in general.

11.3.8   Conclusions

The approach in Halme and Korhonen (2013) does not require analyses with additional variables outside inputs and outputs, not even to list the environmental variables and their quantification. Rather, it requires the DM to identify benchmark units which are then used to solve a new LP problem for each of the units in order to achieve new never more optimistic scores for the units.

The DM used the information provided by the analysis in the discussions within the church. The authors reviewed the results with this DM in 2010, and he reported that the analysis and the results were dealt with in many conversations with his colleagues. The discussions on how to make the parishes function more efficiently and whether productivity measures should be used in resource allocations expanded in the 2000s. In the words of the DM, "the numbers opened the eyes of many church stakeholders to see among other things that some of the parishes were getting more funds per outputs than others."

As mentioned, one of the benchmarks, Käpylä, was convex dominated and thus inefficient. The fact that regardless of this the DM chose it as a benchmark suggests that the use of a non-convex approach would have been justified and there is a need for the FDH VEA approach described in Chap. 10 in practical applications.

11.4 Analyzing the Efficiency of Bank Branches

11.4.1 Introduction

Helsinki OP is a retail bank operating in the Helsinki metropolitan area. It belongs to OP-Pohjola Group, a leading financial service group in Finland. The bank provides financing, investment, daily banking, and insurance services to private customers and small businesses, and the branch network is an important channel for the sale of its financial services. The management was seeking opportunities to improve the sales performance of the branches. Especially, the management wished to identify the units giving a poor performance even under the most optimistic assumptions and thus needed the most urgent attention.

An investigation by Halme et al. (2014) into the sales efficiency of the branches of Helsinki OP Bank, which was carried out in collaboration with the bank, is among the few studies that specifically analyze branch sales (see also Athanassopoulos 1998; Cook and Hababou 2001; Portela and Thanassoulis 2007). Like Cook et al. (2004), they used existing units as benchmarks.

The cross-sectional analysis reported in Halme et al. (2014), based on aggregated data from the years 2007–2010, covered all 25 branches of the network. The sales performance of a branch was defined as the value of sales generated in it by its sales force.

As the management had a preference over the output structure and was able to articulate it by identifying the best performers among the branches, VEA was used in the analysis. Furthermore, the bank wished to identify the units that without doubt and with no excuses were showing poor performance. To achieve this, the FDH version of VEA was chosen, as the FDH assumptions restrict the comparisons to existing units. These units identified as inefficient by the FDH VEA would form the set of units that most urgently needed to improve.

11.4.2 Inputs, Outputs, and Data

The outputs of the investigation represent the transactional sales volumes of the branches. Sales were given in two categories covering: (1) financing services and (2) investment services. The bank considers these two categories the primary ones and they were used as outputs in the model. Daily banking services including cashier services were considered a consequence of the sales of these primary services and were thus excluded from the analysis. Some of the insurance services were included in investment services and others in financial services. However, nonlife insurances intermediated by the bank were excluded. The management defined the task as output maximization. The branches are assumed to increase their sales by actively approaching their existing and potential customer bases. The authors applied weights provided by the bank's management in aggregating outputs from the sales of individual products.

Only one input was employed in the analysis: the work of the sales force. The management decided to omit other operational costs because they considered them less significant and mostly nondiscretionary to the branch. The input quantity used is the overall use of work time in sales activity as a full-time equivalent. This defined the orientation as the amount of output (sales) could not be considered given.

11.4.3   Analysis of the Branches

Halme et al. (2014) calculated the output-oriented FDH efficiency scores (Table 11.7) to identify the set of units as objects for the most urgent measures. The authors explained to the management that they are scores when the units are compared with each other without any assumptions or preference information. They found that 12 units of the 25 were FDH efficient. Next the sales network management identified B12, B13, and B15 as the best performing branches (MPUs). The resulting FDH value efficiency analysis was thus based on the information that branches B12, B13, and B15 were the MPUs, preferred to all the others. The introduction of value judgments lowered the scores of six units.

Note that with constant or variable returns to scale, the selected MPU B13 is not efficient; it is convex dominated—thus a non-convex production possibility set used in the investigation could be considered justified. Halme et al. (2014) used four-point cones in which all the other (efficient) units except those three were the vertices. Units B12, B13, and B15 were thus used to define the cones in which the vertices varied. In theory they could also have constructed three additional cones consisting of these three best units, each of them being a vertex of one cone. However, in this case the managers meant that the three units belonged in the "top" category and were undoubtedly performing better than the other units. As discussed in Sect. 10.3, several MPSs in the model simultaneously may lead to conflicting information and unbounded solution, and thus the additional cones were not employed.

The authors solved model (10.5) for each cone and each unit. Two FDH-efficient units turned out to be inefficient when preference information was included, i.e., dominated by at least one cone. The total score of the six units changed when the preference information was added to the analysis and the FDH value efficiency scores were calculated. Note that unit B3, for example, was almost FDH efficient

Table 11.7   The FDH efficiency scores and the FDH value efficiency scores

Units	Sales of financing services	Sales of investment services	Work of sales force	FDH efficiency scores	FDH value efficiency scores
B1	1,090	497	26.0	0.924	0.924
B2	2,633	1,111	47.7	1	0.917
B3	3,320	1,477	60.7	0.987	0.887
B4	1,147	353	25.2	0.972	0.972
B5	1,180	540	21.6	1	1
B6	3,821	1,769	75.5	0.870	0.852
B7	1,574	716	36.4	1	1
B8	1,171	1,004	29.1	1	1
B9	1,174	449	22.5	0.995	0.995
B10	1,203	568	27.2	1	1
B11	928	384	22.0	0.786	0.786
B12 (MPU)	4,393	2,210	65.9	1	1
B13 (MPU)	2,642	931	38.8	1	1
B14	3,362	1,505	53.1	1	1
B15 (MPU)	2,263	541	26.9	1	1
B16	3,619	1,541	70.3	0.824	0.824
B17	4,163	1,594	73.6	0.948	0.947
B18	3,075	805	46.7	1	1
B19	5,757	2,601	93.0	1	1
B20	1,763	496	29.0	0.917	0.917
B21	3,825	1,961	83.1	0.887	0.786
B22	2,354	792	42.4	0.891	0.891
B23	5,289	3,160	104.0	1	0.892
B24	1,108	332	24.2	0.939	0.939
B25	743	354	22.4	0.656	0.656

even if it was identified as clearly inefficient in the FDH value efficiency analysis: this kind of information is considered valuable.

11.4.4   Conclusion

The bank branch management group had some previous experience of DEA. Halme et al. (2014) report that in the course of their conversations with the managers, the managers indicated that they liked the idea of first identifying the units that were inefficient from even the most optimistic perspective. They found the process of providing preference information easy and its use justified. The bank ranks growth highly in its strategy and believes that the benchmarks could play an important role in boosting efficiency in the branches. The management planned to review the inefficient units in two phases. First they would consider units that were inefficient in FDH, in which the improvement needs were most urgent. Second, they would look at the units that were FDH efficient, but not equally efficient when management preference was taken into consideration: they needed improvement in order to approach the benchmark performance.

Having looked closely at the data and the results, the management made the following remarks:

• Comparison of the other branches to B5 seems unfair given that its efficiency is based on one super-salesperson who is responsible for most of the branch's sales. That outlier needs to be removed.
• Branch B25 should also be removed due to its young age and the fact that it had started from scratch.
• It is hard to confirm the efficiency of unit B10: it has the same size as unit B15 and produces about the same amount of investment services but almost 50 % less of financial services.

The management view was that in the hands of a knowledgeable DM who was familiar with the branch network, the analysis tool would work well in terms of efficiency assessment.

References

Andersen P, Petersen NC (1993) A procedure for ranking efficient units in data envelopment analysis. Manage Sci 39(10):1261–1264

Athanassopoulos AD (1998) Nonparametric frontier models for assessing the market and cost efficiency of large-scale bank branch networks. J Money Credit Bank 30(2):172–192

Banker RD, Charnes A, Cooper WW (1984) Some models for estimating technical and scale inefficiencies in data envelopment analysis. Manage Sci 30:1078–1092

Banker RD, Morey RC (1986) Efficiency analysis for exogenously fixed inputs and outputs. Oper Res 34:513–521

Cook WD, Hababou M (2001) Sales performance measurement in bank branches. Omega 29 (4):299–307

Cook WD, Seiford LM, Zhu J (2004) Models for performance benchmarking: measuring the effect of e-business activities on banking performance. Omega 32(4):313–322

Halme M, Korhonen P (2013) Using value efficiency analysis to benchmark non-homogeneous units. Int J Inform Technol Decision Making

Halme M, Korhonen P, Eskelinen J (2014) Non-convex value efficiency analysis and its application to bank branch sales evaluation. Omega 48:10–18

Korhonen P, Tainio R, Wallenius J (2001) Value efficiency analysis of academic research. Eur J Oper Res 130(1):121–132

Korhonen P, Wallenius J (1988) A Pareto race. Naval Res Log 35:615–623

Korhonen P, Wallenius J (1990) Using qualitative data in multiple objective linear programming. Eur J Oper Res 48:81–87

Li H, Zhu J (2005) Ranking the efficiency performance within a set of decision making units by Data Envelopment Analysis. Int J Inform Technol Decision Making 4:345–357

Portela MCAS, Thanassoulis E (2007) Comparative efficiency analysis of Portuguese bank branches. Eur J Oper Res 177(2):1275–1288

Quality Assessment of Research, Economics (1995) Association of the Universities in the Netherlands, Leidseveer 35, PO Box 19270, 3501 DG Utrecht

Quality Assessment of Research, Mathematics and Computer Science (1997) Association of the Universities in the Netherlands, Leidseveer 35, PO Box 19270, 3501 DG Utrecht.

Saaty T (1980) The analytic hierarchy process. McGraw Hill, New York

Chapter 12
Conclusion

Incorporating Preferences in DEA: Value Efficiency Analysis

This book presents the theory, extensions, and some applications of value efficiency analysis. Value efficiency analysis is based on sound theory and aims at behavioral realism: we seek to provide the decision maker with an approach and interface that makes it as easy and straightforward as possible to express his/her preferences and thus guarantee reliable results. The applications included in the book showcase the suitability of the model in real-world decision making.

Most approaches used to incorporate preference information in data envelopment analysis are based on restricting the weights in the multiplier model. The real word interpretation of this is that whereas DEA allows free pricing, now some limits are imposed. This approach works when the inputs and outputs involved in the analysis are something we can put a price tag on. However, this is not always the case. When we are faced with outputs or inputs that are of more complex, abstract, and intangible in nature, thinking in terms of prices can be difficult for decision makers. For example, it is extremely complicated, both practically and politically, to compare and price different outputs of, say, hospitals or universities.

Unlike the existing approaches, the ones presented in this study do not require the decision maker to think in terms of prices. Instead, he/she elicits his/her preferences either in the form of a preferred existing or hypothetical unit.

Although mathematically also this approach leads to the identification of implicit restrictions to weights, or prices, there is a fundamental difference in these approaches, emerging from the way in which the preference information is gathered.

Value efficiency analysis produces (in)efficiency scores that reflect not only technical efficiency but also decision maker's preferences and values. The models presented are computationally easy and immediately applicable in practice.

© Springer Science+Business Media New York 2015
T. Joro, P.J. Korhonen, *Extension of Data Envelopment Analysis with Preference Information*, International Series in Operations Research & Management Science 218, DOI 10.1007/978-1-4899-7528-7_12

Acknowledgments

We would like to express our appreciation to all those people who have helped us to finish this book. First, we would like to thank our co-authors of the articles dealing with DEA: (in alphabetic order) Juha Eskelinen (Aalto University School of Business), Merja Halme (Aalto University School of Business), Petri Hilli (Helsinki School of Economics), Matti Koivu (Helsinki School of Economics), Mikulas Luptacik (Vienna University of Economics and Business Administration), Paul Na (J.P.Morgan), Seppo Salo (Helsinki School of Economics), Aapo Siljamäki (NumPlan Ltd.), Margareta Soismaa (Aalto University School of Business), Mikko Syrjänen (Helsinki School of Economics), Sari Stenfors (Helsinki School of Economics), Risto Tainio (Aalto University School of Business), Esa-Jussi Viitala (Finnish Forest Research Institute), and Jyrki Wallenius (Aalto University School of Business).

At last we would like to thank all those persons who deserve our thanks, but we have forgotten to thank!

© Springer Science+Business Media New York 2015   187
T. Joro, P.J. Korhonen, *Extension of Data Envelopment Analysis with Preference Information*, International Series in Operations Research & Management Science 218, DOI 10.1007/978-1-4899-7528-7

Index

© Springer Science+Business Media New York 2015
T. Joro, P.J. Korhonen, *Extension of Data Envelopment Analysis with Preference
Information*, International Series in Operations Research & Management
Science 218, DOI 10.1007/978-1-4899-7528-7